INTERNATIONAL INDUSTRY
AND BUSINESS

INTERNATIONAL INDUSTRY AND BUSINESS

Structural Change, Industrial Policy and Industry Strategies

Robert H. Ballance

United Nations Industrial Development Organization

London
ALLEN & UNWIN
Boston Sydney Wellington

Allen & Unwin, the academic imprint of
Unwin Hyman Ltd
PO Box 18, Park Lane, Hemel Hempstead, Herts HP2 4TE, UK
40 Museum Street, London WC1A 1LU, UK
37/39 Queen Elizabeth Street, London SE1 2QB, UK

Allen & Unwin Inc.,
8 Winchester Place, Winchester, Mass. 01890, USA

Allen & Unwin (Australia) Ltd,
8 Napier Street, North Sydney, NSW 2060, Australia

Allen & Unwin (New Zealand) Ltd in association with
the Port Nicholson Press Ltd,
60 Cambridge Terrace, Wellington, New Zealand

First published in 1987

British Library Cataloguing in Publication Data

Ballance, Robert H.
    International industry and business :
    Structural change, industrial policy and
    industry strategies.
1. Industry
I. Title
338   HD2328
ISBN 0–04–339037–4
ISBN 0–04–339038–2 Pbk

Library of Congress Cataloging in Publication Data

Ballance, Robert H.
    International industry and business.
    Bibliography: p.
Includes indexes.
1. Economic history – 1945 –   2. Industry –
History.   3. Competition, International.   4. Strategic
planning.   5. International economic relations.
I. Title.
HC59.B3537   1987   338'.09'04048   86–28793
ISBN 0–04–339037–4 (alk. paper)
ISBN 0–04–339038–2 (pbk. : alk. paper)

Typeset in 10 on 12 point Palatino by Columns of Reading
and printed in Great Britain by Billings and Sons Ltd, London and
Worcester

Contents

CONTENTS

List of Tables

xi

List of Abbreviations

ACP	African, Caribbean and Pacific Countries
AISI	American Iron and Steel Institute
ASEAN	Association of South East Asian Nations
ATT	American Telephone and Telegraph
BMW	Bavarian Motor Works
CAD	computer-aided design
CAM	computer-aided manufacture
CAP	Common Agricultural Policy
CKD	completely knocked down kits
Darpa	Defence Advanced Research Projects Agency
EC	European Community
ECE	Economic Commission for Europe
ECIL	Electronics Corporation of India Limited
EFTA	European Free Trade Association
ERSO	Electronics Research Service Organization
ESCAP	Economic and Social Commission for Asia and the Pacific
ESPRIT	European Strategic Programme for Research and Development in Information Technology
FBI	Federal Bureau of Investigation
GATT	General Agreement on Tariffs and Trade
GDP	gross domestic product
GM	General Motors
IBM	International Business Machines
ICL	International Computers Limited
ICOT	Institute for New Generation Computer Technology
IDE	Institute of Developing Economies
IISI	International Iron and Steel Institute
ILO	International Labour Organization
IMF	International Monetary Fund

ISIC	International Standard Industrial Classification
JECC	Japan Electronic Computer Company
KD	knocked down kits
KIET	Korean Institute of Electronics
LDC	less developed country
LTA	Long Term Arrangement for International Trade in Cotton Textiles
MAP	manufacturing automation protocol
MCC	Microelectronics and Computer Technology Company
MCT	Microelectronics and Computer Technology Corporation
MFA	Multifibre Arrangement
MFN	most-favoured-nation
MITI	Ministry of International Trade and Industry
MVA	manufacturing value added
NEC	Nippon Electronics Corporation
NTB	non-tariff barrier
NTT	Nippon Telegraph and Telephone
OECD	Organization for Economic Cooperation and Development
OMA	orderly marketing agreement
OPEC	Organization of Petroleum Exporting Countries
R and D	research and development
SIA	Semiconductor Industry Association
SITC	Standard International Trade Classification
TPM	trigger price mechanism
UAW	United Auto Workers
UNCTAD	United Nations Conference on Trade and Development
UNCTC	United Nations Centre for Transnational Corporations
UNIDO	United Nations Industrial Development Organization
VER	voluntary export restraint
VTR	video-tape recorder

To JC, REB and
other intrapreneurs

Preface

For almost two centuries manufacturers and industries operated in a spatial context which was predominantly local. The search for inputs, materials and revenues seldom extended to regional markets and it was rarer still that these activities were nationwide. This characteristic was swept aside during the years following the Second World War. Whatever their country of origin, modern firms tend to function in an environment which is international, if not global, in scope.

It was some time before the consequences of this transformation were fully appreciated. Although the importance of industrial matters was readily acknowledged by policy-makers and analysts, most continued to regard industry as a sphere of economics having limited international significance. Those concerned with international relations saw a world in which politics was predominant. Even specialists in international economics tended to accept a framework which tacitly acknowledged that matters of industrial economics were either secondary or totally unrelated to politics. On the other hand, practitioners who focused on aspects which were essentially 'domestic' in scope found a greater affinity between industrial economics and politics. But the latter had comparatively little to say about the impact which changes in the international environment would have on the domestic scene.

The inappropriateness of these assumptions became evident as the post-war period wore on. The need for a reassessment was partly prompted by significant changes in the world's industrial map. Once the international standing of leading industrialized countries began to be eroded, governments looked for explanations in their national policies and domestic circumstances. At the domestic level, the need for a more integrated approach was equally apparent as foreign products, workers and firms began to over-run national boundaries. Changes in domestic and international circumstances had dramatic repercussions for consumers, workers and industrialists alike. The most obvious consequences, however, were in the realm of public policy. Governments became increasingly willing to seek *dirigiste* solutions to their industrial problems, regardless of whether these might be attributed to 'domestic' or 'foreign' causes. These simple facts cannot convey the full extent of the post-war transformation of industry. They do, however, indicate the need for contemporary analysis to encompass not only the international dimension but also to fuse the role of economics with that of the politics of industry.

Practitioners and analysts alike have responded to the need to incorporate new dimensions into their work. However, no widely accepted body of ideas or methods of analysis yet exists for this purpose. In the present intellectual environment, fashions rather than paradigms are apt to flourish. There may be advantages in this approach. For instance, the designer alone does not create new fashions. He also anticipates or interprets the mood of policy-makers, industrialists or others with the power to influence major industries. But there are risks as well. Without a paradigm to challenge, the costs of designing and marketing each year's fashions may be negligible. Many will go on sale but not all are subject to the quality controls which a fully developed body of theory would impose.

No new paradigms are developed in the following chapters. At the same time, the book draws freely on the work of business analysts and industry specialists, as well as economists. To guard against the dangers of embracing fleeting fashions, the development of world industry is seen in a long-term context and use is made of various elements of economic theory. However, extensive use of economic models and simplifying assumptions would complicate the presentation and restrict the scope of discussion. The book is a work of application, not theory, and the relevant material is examined (and described) from the viewpoint of the empiricist rather than the theoretician.

In conclusion, the book is intended to complement, rather than be a substitute for, a core text. It is written for students who have previously studied economics at the first-year university level or its equivalent and is relevant for use in courses on international business, industrial economics or economic development. The material should also be of interest to others concerned with the problems and policies of industry and trade in all countries, either developing or developed. The general purpose is to help the reader obtain a better understanding of how each of the foregoing elements – international and domestic, economic and political – interrelate and ultimately shape the development of the manufacturing sector and the industries which make up that sector. A more specific objective is to convey some of the richness and diversity in the political and economic landscape of modern industries and to provide a real-world background for the study of economic and business theory in a more pristine form.

At the time when this book was being written, the author was employed by the United Nations Industrial Development Organization (UNIDO) and the views expressed here are those of the author and do not necessarily represent those of UNIDO.

CHAPTER ONE

The Internationalization of Industry

This book is concerned with the period after the Second World War and particularly the years since 1970. However, some historical perspective is still helpful. Less than three hundred years ago the production of manufactures in Southern Asia is thought to have exceeded that of all Europe, while in America the manufacturing sector consisted of a few households in a sparsely settled sub-continent. Several of the dominant features of this era provide a marked contrast with present circumstances and serve as a point of departure for the study.

Throughout most of the previous two centuries industrial development was largely a local affair, often carried out in a spatial context which was not even nationwide (Pollard, 1981, pp. 3–4). In contrast, many of today's industries are international, if not global, in scope. A majority of modern industries are composed primarily of small firms serving local markets. But each industry's economic health and vitality is usually determined by the performance of a few large and dominant firms. Today, these firms find themselves increasingly vulnerable to circumstances in foreign economies. They may depend on foreign suppliers for raw materials, intermediate inputs, capital equipment or technology. Foreign labour or management skills may be essential or overseas buyers are particularly important. Foreign competitors can suddenly intrude to threaten complacent firms in their home or export markets. Prolonged imbalances in exchange rates

1

can undermine the international competitive ability of firms and eventually force a contraction of the industry concerned.

These are but a few examples of the circumstances and uncertainties which will shape an industry once it has achieved international status. Despite their rather obvious nature, some of the consequences of internationalization are not always fully appreciated. One of the themes of this book is that industries and industrial policies cannot be examined, much less evaluated, purely within a national, or even supra-regional, context. Whatever their particular objectives, businessmen, policy-makers and economists cannot afford to adopt a parochial attitude to industrial matters.

Another fundamental distinction between the previous two centuries and the post-war period concerns the extent of government involvement in the manufacturing sector. During the time when the foundations for the industrial transformation of society were being laid, governments were irrelevant and frequently played a negative role (Pollard, 1981, p. 7). The industrialization process drew its primary impetus from outside the political and governmental sphere. Even in some of the more recently developed countries 'such as Germany, Italy or Russia, it is difficult to argue that industrialization followed a deliberate course mapped out by the state' (Kemp, 1978, p. 90). By the 1970s, however, the scope and diversity of government intervention in most countries was significant. This attribute can be observed even in countries where there is a well-known preference for market principles and non-intervention. And it also applies to economies as disparate as Austria and Brazil or Singapore and the USA.

An obvious way to gauge the extent of government involvement is in terms of public ownership or control over assets. Paradoxically, the continuing spread of government influence has occurred alongside well-publicized programmes to relinquish control over state-run operations. Two facts should be immediately noted here. First, in some Western countries the issue of privatization is more philosophical than real since the governments concerned own few businesses. Even in countries where state ownership is widespread the efforts to dispose of publicly-owned enterprises have been modest. Most Western governments, for instance, prefer to sell only minority shares in the industries they own. Such moves would rarely jeopardize government control, which anyway can be achieved through other means discussed later in this book. In the less developing countries (LDCs), the extent of government ownership is proportionately greater than in the West and the task of privatization is more complicated. Major Latin American governments hope to dispose of hundreds of companies in the next ten years, but this would be a small portion of the number they operate. The Mexican government, for example, owns more than 500 companies, producing every-thing from tortillas to basic petrochemicals and newsprint. Likewise, the public sector in Argentina employs roughly one-quarter of the total working population and the state-owned sector in Brazil is huge. Even the extent of public ownership is unclear in some LDCs, owing to accounting procedures and budgetary practices which are inadequate, incomplete or intentionally misleading.

Second, the reasons for the previously expanding role of government involvement in industry are different from those now fuelling the debate on privatization and state ownership. In reality, many of today's state-owned firms trace their lineage to the 1930s and 1940s. The original motives for state acquisition are no longer relevant, while the costs of operating a burgeoning network of public enterprises have risen as a result of post-1970 recessions. As a consequence, the current justification for privatization is most often the promise of greater efficiency.

Modern forms of government involvement typically stop short of public control or state ownership. No claims are made regarding the need to achieve control over industry's 'commanding heights'. Government intervention is primarily intended to bolster a faltering industry or to foster the growth of embryonic industries which are thought to be crucial to the country's economic future. These motives have given rise to a whole new range of public policies which are industry-specific in scope and are intended to meet the needs (or desires) of a particular group of firms. The purposes of such policies are discussed in more detail in later chapters, but it is clear that they differ from the governments' responsibilities with regard to inflation, investment, unemployment or the balance of trade.

The growing involvement of the state has had profound repercussions for industry, giving rise to another characteristic which distinguishes the post-war era from earlier periods. Extensive intervention has created greater scope for influencing a government's decisions; there are simply more decisions to influence. Increasingly, the formulation of industrial policy has become the product of protracted negotiation and bargaining between public officials and 'industry representatives', where the latter include major corporations, trade unions, representatives of industry associations and even foreign competitors. The existence of such pressure groups is not unique to the post-war era. Pressure group activities are age-old practices. Moreover, the ability of these groups to wield significant policy-making powers should not be exaggerated. With these provisos, however, there are reasons to believe that today's policy-makers – in LDCs as well as Western countries – operate in an environment which is subject to considerable pressure from special interest groups. Although governments as a whole are impervious to outside control, their separate parts are uniquely susceptible to pressures from the types of groups noted here.

Despite the considerable influence which such unofficial groups appear to wield, they have been the subject of comparatively little scrutiny. Among the earliest contributors to the field was Olson (1965) who pointed out that the growth of such lobbying activities could lead to substantial, although virtually unquantifiable, welfare losses for the economy. The basis for his argument is that the members of associations or coalitions formed to alter patterns of resource allocation may gain very little from efforts to make their societies more efficient. However, they 'do gain from obtaining a larger share of the social output for their members, even if the social loss from the redistribution is a substantial multiple of the amount distributed to them' (Olson, 1982a, p. 145). In using their ability to influence public policy, industry representatives of all types have added a political dimension to the normal range of economic

4

and corporate issues that are traditionally regarded as part of a firm's normal decision-making responsibilities. Post-war experience in industries such as autos, steel, electronics, and others shows that, for analytical purposes, industrial policy cannot be divorced from issues involving the rise and decline of specific industries.

Another useful distinction between modern industry and its pre-war predecessor concerns the role of technology, in particular the pace of development and the widening impact of consequent changes on both national and international markets. By today's standards, technological advances in the pre-war period occurred at only a moderate pace and filtered through the international economy in a leisurely manner. For modern industries, such features do not necessarily apply. In fields where technological advancement is most rapid the lifetime of a typical product has shrunk dramatically. Heretofore, the developers of new products could expect to have several years in which to recover their investments, but now this period may be as little as one to two years. Simultaneously, technological advances are demolishing traditional industrial boundaries. Even in relatively staid industries, such as automobiles, shipbuilding or textiles, firms have found they must automate their production processes in order to survive. A corollary of the technological anarchy which now prevails is that national boundaries are of less importance to industry than ever before. When products have only a brief lifespan, development costs cannot be recovered in local, or even national, markets. Technological change has spurred on the internationalization of industries, with associated consequences for related fields such as trade and foreign investment.

Aside from qualitative distinctions such as these, the starkest contrast between the historical and current period is a quantitative one. The extent and rapidity of change in the world industrial map was probably of a magnitude not previously experienced by the international community. From a vantage point of 1950, few could have envisaged the industrial and economic strides which later occurred in Western Europe, Japan, and even in some LDCs. During the period 1950–70, the combined gross domestic product (GDP) of major Western countries nearly tripled, while the corresponding figure for manufacturing value added (MVA) was quadrupled.

There are certainly other important distinctions to be made between the two periods. Two of the more obvious ones are the exceptional growth of post-war trade in manufactures and the expanded flow of capital across national boundaries. These and other aspects are of fundamental importance for the evolution of industry, and some of their repercussions will be considered in later chapters. However, the foregoing list deserves to be singled out: the consequences of their occurrence have been gradual and sometimes diffuse but of fundamental importance for world industry.

One aspect which is largely absent from the following discussion should also be mentioned here. In contrast to the pre-war period, the impetus for the rapid internationalization of manufacturing since 1950 probably owes as much to political motives as it does to economic forces. In many LDCs the goal of industrialization had assumed considerable importance by the 1960s. With successive waves of decolonization, the governments of these countries embarked on a drive for economic independence and saw the development of the manufacturing sector as the *sine qua non* for this goal. The links between political objectives and industrial progress were equally important, but less obvious, in Western countries. With the legacy of two world wars, and the prospect of a prolonged Cold War, the leaders of these countries were preoccupied with the need to construct an international economic system which would serve their political objectives. Although political motives for the internationalization of industry were probably just as important as economic motives, they cannot be treated fully in a book such as this and are only briefly sketched in Chapter 2.

Industry and Interdependence

In the introductory section of this chapter several contrasts between industries in the 1950s and today were noted. In addition to these features, a more broadly-based phenomenon – in today's parlance, an extended degree of interdependence – took hold during the post-war period. Despite the acknowledged importance of the concept, interdependence is an ambiguous term and is employed in a variety of contexts. The word is often used when referring to 'North–South' relations. Interdependence referred to in this context provides the most striking examples of mutual dependence which involve issues such as debt, finance, the evolution of trade relationships or energy balances. However, a viewpoint which focuses exclusively on North–South issues yields an incomplete impression of interdependence.

For those who are particularly interested in the economic aspects of interdependence, the extent to which markets are integrated across national boundaries is one essential ingredient. But market integration, however complete, is not synonymous with interdependence. Cooper (1985, p. 1198) suggests that the degree of influence any one economy exerts on other members of its peer group constitutes a more accurate measure of interdependence. Economic events in one country will have significant repercussions for the economies of other countries. And in a truly interdependent system the objectives of economic policy in one country will be at least partially circumscribed by the policies and goals of other countries. The degree of policy interdependence can sometimes be so great that a preferred course of action in one country depends decisively on the decisions of policy-makers elsewhere, with the relationship working in both directions. Clearly, economic and political forces become intermingled in any discussion of the concept. Because much of the following discussion takes place against a background of market integration, it would be accurate to say that the contents of this book are concerned not so much with the concept of interdependence as with the simpler notion of 'mutual economic dependence' between countries. In some instances, however, the issues raised extend beyond the role of market integration and have implications of a truly interdependent nature.

Most observers would agree that the foundation for interdependence was laid during the era of rapid world growth between 1950 and the early 1970s. Industrial progress was a widespread phenomenon which accentuated the importance of overseas markets, suppliers, investors and innovators at the expense of their domestic counterparts in each country. Rapid growth did much to foster the economic links which today typify the nature of industrial interdependence. Simultaneously, greater market integration contributed to an improved pattern of resource allocation within countries, increased product specialization, the realization of larger economies of scale and similar advances which would boost efficiency and overall productivity.

While these are some of the positive benefits of interdependence there are also other, less beneficial, side effects. Interdependence has led to a change in the way industrial policies are formulated and in the objectives they are intended to serve. This is particularly true for Western countries. The accentuated importance of overseas competitors has reduced the efficacy of domestic policies and has forced policy-makers to operate in the face of greater uncertainty. To note only a few examples, policy-makers often lack familiarity with foreign markets or suppliers and have limited means to influence these firms through domestic policies. They can only idly watch the emergence of large tracts of competitive capacity in foreign countries – even in industries where significant surplus capacity already exists in their own country and elsewhere. Interdependence has also made domestic firms vulnerable to the whims of foreign suppliers and governments who may arbitrarily cut deliveries, raise prices or enforce embargoes. Excessive reliance on imported capital goods can relegate domestic users to inferior technologies and reduce their ability to influence the nature of technological advances.

Governments throughout the world are compelled to consider difficult questions such as these when reaching decisions on industrial policy. But the bulk of the world's manufacturing activities, whether measured in terms of production, trade, foreign investment or technological capabilities, is largely concentrated among Western countries. The extent and nature of these interrelationships between Western countries is the single dimension which really gives significance to the notion of interdependence. This does not mean that other elements (North–South or, for that matter, East–West) do not exist, or that they can be ignored without loss. It does mean, however, that any policy response to problems of an international nature is largely determined by the attitudes and actions of governments and industries in Western countries. Even when other parts of world industry have an intimate interest in a particular issue – whether textiles or technology transfer – the preponderance of Western industry usually means that responses are shaped accordingly.

If the locus for interdependence is to be found in the Western world, economic conditions in these countries are doubly relevant to the following discussion of industrial structure and policy. Table 1.1 provides evidence which vividly demonstrates a series of dramatic changes in the growth patterns of Western countries. The early post-war years were clearly a unique period in the economic history of these countries. The rates of growth recorded for GDP and MVA during the period 1950–70 were exceptional. The fact that after 1970 there was a general slump in world economic activity is probably well known by all readers of this book and is also evident from the figures. The pace of economic progress slowed noticeably after 1973. Another significant feature of the data concerns the relationship between the rates of growth for GDP and MVA. Prior to the 1970s, manufacturing output expanded at a pace which consistently surpassed the corresponding performance of GDP. In recent years, however, the two growth rates have converged and in many instances the growth of MVA has even lagged behind GDP.

By pre-war standards, growth in the 1970s was impressive but a number of observers (e.g. Maddison, 1979, p. 415; Giersch and Wolter, 1983, p. 50), doubt that the robust performance recorded by Western industries in the 1950s and 1960s can be resumed. Slow growth did not necessarily weaken the existing interdependent framework between Western countries. Patterns of investment, trade, demand, technological development and other fundamental determinants of world industry were all predicated on the basis of continued economic interdependence. Businesses responded

Table 1.1 Growth of GDP and MVA in Selected Western Countries, 1913–1984

	Annual average compound rates of growth at constant prices									
	1913–50		1950–70		1970–79		1973–79		1979–84	
	GDP	MVA	GDP	MVA	GDP	MVA	GDP	MVA	GDP	MVA
Belgium	1.0	1.4	4.0	5.2	3.4	3.4	2.4	1.9	1.0	1.0
Canada	2.9	3.9	4.9	4.5	4.4	3.9	3.3	2.5	1.7	0.2
France	1.0	0.8	5.0	5.9	3.8	3.9	2.9	3.1	1.1	0.2
Germany	1.3	...	6.3	8.1	2.8	2.2	2.3	2.0	0.9	0.1
Italy	1.4	1.9	5.6	8.3	2.8	3.7	2.3	2.9	1.1	0.6
Japan	1.8	2.7	9.8	16.0	5.3	6.2	4.0	5.7	4.0	8.6
Netherlands	2.4	3.2	4.9	6.4	3.1	3.3	2.5	1.8	0.3	0.6
Sweden	2.8	3.5	4.0	4.4	1.6	1.1	1.6	−0.5	1.5	1.8
UK	1.3	2.2	2.8	3.2	1.9	0.6	0.8	−0.5	0.6	4.3
USA	2.8	3.7	3.5	3.5	3.1	3.4	2.3	2.7	2.0	1.5
Arithmetic average	1.9	2.6	5.1	6.6	3.2	3.2	2.4	2.2	1.4	1.0

Sources: Figures for GDP were taken from Maddison, 1980, p. 283 and OECD, 1986. For MVA, data for 1913–50 were taken from Maizels, 1970, p. 297. Data for later years were obtained from United Nations, *Yearbook of National Accounts Statistics* (various issues) whenever possible. If not reported, growth rates for MVA were estimated using the index of industrial production as provided in United Nations (1963a) and United Nations, *Yearbook of Industrial Statistics*, Vol. 1 (various issues) and United Nations, *Monthly Bulletin of Statistics*, January, 1986.

to the slowdown by intensifying their search for new markets, products and production processes and by extending it to new areas of the globe. In doing so, they have had the active support of their governments. Despite stagnating growth, 'the level of interdependence between countries may never have increased faster and the underlying structure of power changed more deeply' (Bressand, 1983, p. 745).

The two phases of post-war development had significant repercussions for the relationships between Western countries and the nature of their interdependence. Exceptionally rapid growth during the first period led to a new configuration of the industrial map, with a realignment in the industrial hierarchy of the Western countries. Up until then, the USA had been the pre-eminent Western industrial power. After two decades of growth, however, there was a more equal distribution of industrial influence and capabilities in the West. A polycentric system of industrial relations emerged (and is discussed more fully in Chapter 2) which consists of several major industrial powers such as the European Community (EC) and Japan, as well as the USA. The rearrangement of industrial capabilities profoundly changed the way industrial policies were formulated. The ability of Western governments to co-ordinate their policies and to agree on means to address international problems has become more difficult. Without an international leader these decisions require a broad consensus among participants of relatively equal status and divergent interests.

By the late 1970s the cumulative effects of these trends had altered the way in which governments viewed their position in international hierarchies of different types – including their standing in various industries. Countries had previously seen the policies of their international rivals as little more than an attempt to catch up, or to close the gap, with American leadership in important industries. Under the new circumstances the same policies, when adopted by near equals, contain an implied threat to change international hierarchies in several industries. Governments now find themselves operating in an environment where interdependence has assumed an element of 'competitive coexistence'.

Nations, as well as industries and companies, are seen as competing in world markets, and industrial expansion in one country holds the threat of a contraction in the same industry elsewhere.

In conclusion, this brief survey of the world's changing industrial landscape suggests that the post-war period might be regarded as consisting of several phases. The initial phase was preceded by more than a century of steady industrial progress, carried out in a narrow spatial context and without extensive government intervention. Following the Second World War manufacturing activities took on broader international dimensions. The legitimacy of state intervention in manufacturing came to be widely accepted and the new era was marked by rapid growth and greater interdependence. More recently, world industry may have entered another phase characterized by slower growth, a more competitive form of interdependence and a much closer relationship between policy-makers and pressure groups representing the interests of various industries.

Economic Structure and Structural Change

Like other fields of study, industrial economics is rife with jargon. While an effort is made to minimize the use of terminology, not all terms can be supressed. Because the following chapters make frequent reference to economic structure and the process of structural change, some explanation of their meaning is needed. Briefly stated, a country's economic structure can usefully be described in terms of the underlying composition of different economic aggregates. An economy-wide picture could focus on the sectoral breakdown of GDP into manufacturing, agriculture, services, construction, exports, imports, and so on. The actual structure of GDP would be represented by the sectoral distribution of the shares of value added or, alternatively, employment. In a similar fashion, analysts concerned with the manufacturing sector are interested in examining the composition of activities which comprise that sector. Here, the most convenient framework for international comparisons is offered by the International Standard Industrial Classification (ISIC) which enables the investigator to describe the sector's structure in terms of twenty-eight constituent branches or industries. These two levels of structural analysis are used throughout this book. For certain topics an economy-wide perspective (derived from national accounts data) is appropriate. In other instances the scope of discussion is narrower and lends itself to a description of manufacturing in terms of its various industries.

If the notion of structure were merely a synonym referring to the composition of economic aggregates, however, it would add little to the analysis. The term carries other implications. First, some degree of constancy in the economic structure is presumed; changes in structure are seldom abrupt. And such changes are permanent alterations rather than temporary or cyclical fluctuations. Second, structural changes are the consequence of shifts in more fundamental but obscure economic determinants involving the pattern of resource allocation, the nature of technological advancement and other features which are lasting (not transient) shifts in market conditions. Thus, the pace and direction of structural change can provide useful clues about these underlying economic determinants and their interrelationships with industrial policies.

Although the concept of structural change may appear to draw upon esoteric elements of economics and statistics, the reader who assumes that the subject is relevant only to the specialist is badly mistaken. To cite one example, politicians in many Western countries have noted with trepidation the tendency for the manufacturing sector's share in total employment and/or GDP to decline. Often, the decline is relative, meaning that the sector's rate of growth was less than that of agriculture or services. But in other cases the decline entails an actual fall in manufacturing output or employment. Whatever the nature or underlying reasons, the prospect of a prolonged contraction of manufacturing has sparked fears of 'de-industrialization', and has led to calls for programmes to 're-industrialize' and appeals for a new set of industrial policies. The implications of these slogans are clear. Recent patterns of structural change appear to be unfavourable; they threaten to undermine the country's economic future and should be reversed.

Neither policy-makers nor politicians are immune to these fears. They have responded in a variety of ways, searching for means to bolster performance in troubled industries while simultaneously devising methods to foster the development of new industries. In many countries a whole new set of policies and other forms of assistance have been spawned. A distinguishing feature of these new measures is that they are industry-specific, being tailor-made to suit the needs of an industry or even an individual firm.

Thus the concepts of structure and structural change find ready application in the analysis of economic conditions in individual countries. This book, however, is about world industry. Industrial growth and structural change are best seen in an international context. For instance, the fact that the share of the USA in both world MVA and in the aggregate MVA of Western countries has declined steadily since 1960 cannot be ignored. The downtrend led Western governments to alter their approaches to both domestic and international policy matters. Inter-country comparisons of the structure and pace of structural change provide one means of judging the international implications of domestic change. A more direct approach, the examination of the changing international distribution of MVA, can also be employed and will help to shed light on the policy positions and approaches of individual countries or groups of countries.

Similar approaches apply when the scope of investigation is narrowed to specific industries. For instance, the recent development of significant petrochemical capacity in Saudi Arabia casts a shadow over European competitors and is reshaping the plans and policies of governments and producers in the EC. The rapid emergence of Japanese leadership in steel and automobiles, or the comparatively abrupt transfer of the consumer electronic industry from North America to the Asian Basin, created shock waves affecting all established producers in these industries while aspirants in other countries and industries see such developments as models for their own success. Just as the examination of changes in the composition of MVA in individual countries provides a convenient framework for analysis, so, too, the study of international structural change – relative shifts in the geographical composition of productive capacity and output – is useful in today's interdependent world.

The interrelationship between structural change and industrial policy is an essential ingredient for a discussion of world industry. Economists are particularly interested in the direction of causation between all kinds of variables. In the present case, it is appropriate to ask whether structural changes give rise to new policies or, alternatively, whether governments can alter the economic structure according to the policies they choose to employ. One interpretation would maintain that a major purpose of a given country's industrial policies is to create the type of economic structure desired by the government concerned. Certainly, policy-makers or planners would like to believe that the direction of causation works in this way. And to some extent they are correct. Public policies intended to foster the expansion of high technology industries are examples of attempts to 'guide' the pattern of structural change. But the opposite line of causation can also be observed. For instance, the gradual decline of the American steel industry spawned a whole range of policies intended to deter (or even reverse) the prevailing direction of structural change. In this respect it is worth noting that policy-makers sometimes find themselves subject to considerable pressure from groups with a vested interest in a particular industry. It seems, then, that the issue of causation may be a two-way street. Governments sometimes take the initiative and attempt to influence the composition of manufacturing activities while, in other instances, policy formulation is a response to impending changes that are regarded by some as undesirable.

In conclusion, the concept of structural change offers a useful framework for analysis of world industry and associated policy. However, by definition, the concept is not a static one. Also, much of the impetus for structural change is to be found at the level of individual industries or even

15

firms. At this level of specificity, generalizations about the behaviour of the various actors (domestic firms, workers or overseas competitors) are difficult. One notion which does enjoy fairly widespread acceptance (albeit subject to different interpretations) is that industries and firms undergo a 'maturing process'. Certainly, the objectives and constraints of participants in a given industry will change over time and these changes can be pictured as evolving in a systematic fashion. Several alternative interpretations are outlined in the following section.

Views of Industrial Maturity

Do industries experience a maturing or aging process over time? Opinions vary but many, including some politicians and goverment officials, have come to accept the age of an industry as an indicator of future performance and international competitive ability. Journalists and politicians may advocate the creation, and/or encouragement, of new or 'sunrise' industries as a way to rejuvenate a country's ailing manufacturing sector. Traditional fields of manufacturing are often thought to be less deserving of favour, being depicted as mature or 'smokestack' industries. This interpretation makes no assessment of the subsequent evolution of sunrise industries and whether they will eventually take on the characteristics of maturity. It merely serves as a basis for distinguishing between different industries at a particular point in time. Nevertheless, the opinions clearly imply certain value judgements; the distinction between sunrise and smokestack industries has been adopted by some as a guide in the formulation of industrial policy.

There are several reasons why this dichotomy is too simplistic to serve as a reliable basis for making industrial policy. First, acceptance entails the presumption that technological inputs are always high or predominate in sunrise industries but are of little importance in mature industries. Second, sunrise industries are seen as being responsive to competitive threats and sudden market changes, although more mature industries are not viewed in this way. Finally, these new industries are pictured as a breeding ground for dynamic entrepreneurs and seedling companies, while mature industries are seen to offer a much less fertile atmosphere for entrepreneurial initiatives.

Behind each of these statements is a contrast which is overdrawn. For instance, the automobile industry in Western countries is certainly 'mature'. But a modern automobile plant is also an intensive user of automated machinery, or robots, and will rely heavily on computer aids in both the design and manufacturing processes. Similarly, mature industries cannot ignore mounting competitive pressures. Producers of steel, automobiles, bulk chemicals, machine tools and other such products have all responded to contracting markets and foreign competition in conventional ways by reducing capacity, shedding employees and generally cutting production costs. These measures were sometimes reluctantly adopted, or were pursued simultaneously with more obstructionist tactics, but they were nevertheless common to established firms in the USA, Western Europe and Japan. Also, the entrepreneurial successes associated with sunrise industries can be exaggerated. A vast majority of the companies created to exploit new products were started by individuals with long experience as managers in well-established firms. More important, evidence of successful entrepreneurship is abundant in older, mature industries – even in steel where mini-mills and medium-sized producers of special steels have demonstrated their ability to innovate and to identify market niches.

The distinction between sunrise and mature industries is little more than a caricature. However, more useful expositions can be constructed. An industry on the road to maturity is, by definition, a growing one. Growth is accompanied by the emergence of several characteristics which can serve as benchmarks for a description of the process of maturity. One such is an increase in the size of the said industry's leading firms. An enlarged scale of operations has a number of implications that distinguish between the new industry and the maturing one. For example, larger firms are often better able to substitute capital for labour, to introduce production processes which allow for greater economies of scale and to establish far-flung distribution channels and service organization. Second, the nature of demand will change significantly during the process of maturity. Product specialization and product differentiation become prominent features of a maturing industry. Large firms may develop a diversified range of products or may evolve into highly integrated operations which are concerned with all phases of the transformation from raw materials to finished products. Also, the nature of technological advancement will change as firms and industries mature. At early stages in the maturing process the pace of technological progress is rapid. It may include the development of new products, improvements in existing products or modifications in production processes (usually making these processes more capital intensive, increasing the economies of scale and facilitating vertical integration). But with the onset of maturity new technological breakthroughs become more expensive and problematic. Similarly, the existence of a pool of experienced, repeat buyers and a more slowly growing market for the industry's products will mean that the research programmes of firms must give greater emphasis to cost reductions and to service-related considerations.

Numerous versions of the 'maturity' thesis or life cycle experienced by industries and firms can be found in the literature on economics and business policy, and several are discussed in later chapters.

Among the characteristics of maturity highlighted in this book, the three mentioned above – changes in the size of firms, a sequential evolution of demand and systematic changes in the nature and rapidity of technological development – figure prominently. On the basis of these three aspects several informal interpretations are offered below. The first of these is based on the work of industry specialists and might be described as representing a 'managerial' point of view. The second is more closely identified with the viewpoint of economists, while the third looks at maturing industries from the standpoint of the policy-maker. The three views are not necessarily competing but overlap, and all may be useful when examining a particular industry. The chapter concludes with a look at the process of maturity from the standpoint of the LDC.

A Managerial View

Not surprisingly, a managerial interpretation of the industry life cycle is predominantly microeconomic. Such an orientation is logical as the main concern of managerial consultants and corporate specialists is to analyze the operations of firms and to advise on ways to improve their competitive position.

Throughout much of the 1950s and 1960s, the strategies of many firms were dominated by two lines of thought. First, those who advised management stressed the need for companies to enlarge their own market share. As sales rose, unit costs were expected to fall owing to greater economies of scale and improvements in labour productivity. This opinion found support in several influential books (Galbraith, 1967; Servan-Schreiber, 1969) which strongly suggested that the industries of the future would be dominated by very large corporations. For Europeans, the appeal of larger firms was their supposed ability to compete with US giants. With the creation of the EC, a sufficiently large internal market would permit large firms to enjoy the economies of scale which were presumed to exist (Geroski and Jacquemin, 1985, p. 171). In the USA, it was argued that the market mechanism was being supplanted by a process of planning carried out by corporations. The most obvious requirement for effective planning of this type was said to be a large size (Galbraith, 1967, p. 74). This recurrent theme was conveniently suited to the economic conditions which prevailed in the 1960s. The creation of large, dominant firms proceeds best when growth in demand is buoyant and markets are expanding.

A second common feature of many managerial strategies was the importance given to the task of marketing. As plant size increased and demand grew, the major responsibility of managers was to market the output which their factories effortlessly provided. Improvements in production skills and production techniques generally received less attention (Abernathy, Clark and Kantrow, 1983, p. 7). So long as the domestic markets of Western countries were a comparatively safe haven for their industries, such complacency was not a serious problem.

Modern markets, however, are marked by a degree of turbulence and uncertainty not known in the 1950s and 1960s. As the nature of markets changed, the typical characteristics of a mature firm (a large scale of operations, a diversified range of products, or a production process which is highly integrated from raw material to finished product) were found to have less desirable attributes. The volatility of today's markets can take many forms. For instance, industries may experience rapid changes in the number and composition of domestic and foreign competitors. Instability will undermine long-standing agreements (whether tacit or explicit) between industry leaders regarding pricing behaviour or the distribution of market shares. Capricious shifts in consumer demand or in the composition of imports can render a large firm's product mix poorly suited to meet demand. And the quickening pace of technical change can upset the position of industry leaders or prove their recent investments to be ill-timed. Large firms may perform poorly under these conditions.

Such changes in the business environment have shifted the focus of study for managerial analysts and corporate strategists. Troubled firms have become the primary subject of analysis, and the search for ways to 'catch up' with foreign competitors or to prevent a further decline in market shares are also subjects of major interest. Drawing on international comparisons of productivity levels and product quality in individual firms or industries, analysts have often singled out technological innovation as the ingredient which is either absent or non-disruptive in maturing industries and lagging firms. With the onset of maturity a firm's ability (or willingness) to cultivate innovation and adapt to techno-logical change may wane. Analysts distinguish between an 'invention', which refers only to an idea, and an 'innovation' which connotes realization of the idea as a new product or production process. According to the managerial view, it is essential to hasten the conversion of new ideas into genuine innovations. By their very nature, large firms are not adept at methods which would foster such an 'intrapreneurial' spirit, that is, the willingness to start new businesses inside existing companies (see Pinchot, 1984).

A variety of organizational tactics have been proposed for mature firms in order to restore the pace of technological innovation and put them on an equal footing with their more aggressive (and sometimes smaller) competitors. Examples include: the deliberate creation of satellite firms or spin-offs staffed by former employees with promising ideas; the development of a 'business venture' division to support new in-house ideas; and the establishment of a venture capital fund within the given corporation. Concern with technological development has added another characteristic, perhaps belatedly, to the picture of mature firms. Such firms tend to complacency and may lack the technological dynamism possessed by younger and more agile foreign competitors.

A systematic description of the technological aspects of maturity is provided by van Duijn (1980). His schema, expressed in terms of the evolution of individual products, is based on the assumption of an 'innovation life cycle' composed of up to four successive phases. In the introductory phase there is a large number of product innovations and firms know very little about the nature of demand. In the second phase buyers are familiar with the product. More standardized production technologies allow for the introduction of measures to cut costs but there are fewer innovations in the product. In the third phase maturity, the growth of demand and output decelerates and product differentiation becomes the vehicle of competition. In the final stage sales fall, and firms which wish to remain committed to the industry face another series of options. They may replace the original product with a new one or endeavour to extend the life of the existing product through minor changes in design. Alternatively, the firm can attempt to reduce production costs, and thus prices, through improvements in production technology.

For mature firms in internationally competitive markets, the most popular (and perhaps easiest) ways to ward off maturity are product modification or replacement. These tactics, sometimes described as 'finding the market niche', can be motivated by the need to further differentiate an aging firm's product from that of its more efficient competitors, as well as attempting to boost sagging demand. Thus, textile producers in Western countries sought to develop new products in order to move out of those product lines where price competition was prevalent and suppliers in LDCs were more efficient. Some of these efforts were of relatively minor importance (the upgrading of key materials or improvements in the appearance of garments) but others have been more significant. They include: specialization in one or two high-technology fibres used in producing synthetics, production of lightweight fibres used in the inner pannels of aircraft, more durable nylon to replace plastics and the use of heat-resistant fibres (Ballance, Ansari and Singer, 1982, pp. 196–205).

When moving from description to prescription, today's analysts are careful to stress that the negative aspects of maturity should not be regarded as irreversible. This opinion is clearly stated by Abernathy, Clark and Kantrow (1983, p. 29) who maintain that 'the possibilities of a restored technology-based competition . . . can turn the threat of maturity into an attractive program for industry renewal'. But the views of managerial specialists suffer from one inherent weakness, that is, that the single-minded concern with the individual firm limits the generality of their remedies and runs the risk of methodological inconsistencies. One such problem is the inappropriateness of arguing from the particular to the general, encapsulated in the economist's notion of the 'fallacy of composition'. For instance, the identification of market niches can afford a mature firm some respite from their more efficient overseas competitors. But if a number of firms opt for the same strategy its attractiveness will be seriously diminished.

The tendency to focus on the individual firm runs the risk of a second, and related, methodological difficulty. In an open economic system, where countries trade more or less freely, the economist's law of comparative advantage reigns supreme. The law, which will be examined in more detail in subsequent chapters, stipulates that international competitiveness is determined by *relative* costs and not by absolute costs. And, if relative costs are the true determinants of international competitiveness, it follows that no country can expect to be internationally competitive in *every* product or industry. Even if a floundering American steel industry were to embrace all the latest technologies and organizational innovations, it is unlikely it would regain competitive leadership in world steel markets (to reclaim a relative cost advantage). Most industries could not realistically expect to readapt to such an extent. Some companies will survive or even flourish, while the industries of which they are a part contract or otherwise adapt to the changing realities of international competition. These methodological difficulties underline the need to consider the life cycle not only from the perspective of the firm but from that of the industry as well. Here, the views of the economist are particularly useful and are sketched in the following section.

An Economist's View

In describing an economist's view of the industry life cycle, a difficult task is to specify what is meant by the term 'industry'. In fact, no one definition is possible. Microeconomic theorists clearly have one conceptual framework, while industrial specialists working in the steel or textiles industries have another. In turn, these perceptions differ from those used in studies on international trade or antitrust. Moreover, the availability of data may impose a definition upon the user which does not necessarily suit conceptual requirements.

In applied studies the criterion for assigning firms to a particular 'industry' must be subjective, depending on the researcher's judgement of the extent to which products serve as substitutes for each other. An unambiguous definition would be possible only if the products involved are fairly homogeneous and have a high degree of substitutability. But when the products supplied by a cluster of firms are differentiated (as they almost always are), a precise delimitation of the industry can not be found. In reality, industries consist of shifting groups of competitors which are clustered around particular products or processes. The boundaries of an industry may be more evident for some products than for others, but the pattern is always changing. A corollary is that it can be misleading to speak of the maturity of industries such as steel or textiles. Firms producing speciality steels or running mini-mills would hardly meet any criteria for maturity.

Despite the necessarily vague usage of the term, at least three characteristics can be cited to develop a stylized picture of a maturing industry. First, like managerial specialists, many economists stress the fact that average plant size tends to increase as a new industry evolves into a mature one. Wide variations may exist, even among competitors in the same country, but there is a general drive to realize greater economies of scale. Second, changes in demand characteristics can be associated with the transition of a new to a maturing industry. Demand for the industry's products usually experiences an initial phase of rapid growth. This is followed by a subsequent period of continued growth but at a slackening pace, due to the effects of market saturation and (possibly) a slowdown in the development of new products. Third, the nature of firms' resource requirements may change systematically as the industry matures. Firms in a new industry frequently devote a disproportionate amount of funds to research and development (R and D) as their products and production processes are new and not optimal. Technological advances are often easiest during the earlier phases of a country's evolution and this, too, will justify proportionately higher outlays on R and D.

Turning to the first of these characteristics, the growth of average plant size stems from the development and diffusion of technological improvements and the influx of additional capital as profits attract new entrants. In newly emerging industries plant size is small. Entry is relatively easy and the investment outlays required of new competitors are not onerous. But pressure for greater standardization (needed in order to realize economies of scale) mounts as maturity approaches. Increasing plant size has a number of implications for the industry. For instance, it may allow larger firms to substitute capital for labour, to establish captive distribution channels and to utilize national advertising. Eventually, the structure of firms also becomes more 'concentrated', meaning that a very few producers will account for much of the industry's total output. At this point, investment outlays required of new competitors will have become large enough to constitute a deterrent to the entry of new firms.

The semiconductor industry provides a recent and dramatic example of how these requirements can change. Two of today's largest producers, National Semiconductor and Intel, entered business in the 1960s with only $1–3 million in capital (UNIDO, 1981c, p. 102). But the cost of initial investment soared as the need to realize greater economies of scale became important. By 1980, a capital outlay of $50 million was required of potential entrants in order to erect a basic chip-making facility. The evidence is even more telling in the case of a long established industry such as steel where the first moves to enlarge plant size began around the turn of this century. Annual capacity in integrated iron and steel units was then between 100,000–200,000 tonnes but, by 1920, a typical rolling mill had an annual capacity of 600,000 tonnes. More recently, with the advent of huge open-pit mines, deep-water ports and new technologies, integrated units with capacities of 3–10 million tonnes have become common (Ballance, 1985, pp. 8–9).

The growth pattern in demand for the industry's products provides another important basis for distinguishing between new and mature industries. The possibility of market saturation is a real one, as the producers of many products – ranging from tennis equipment to snowmobiles – have found. Product improvements and the design of new products can mean that the effects of saturation are not seriously debilitating, but a mature industry that does not encounter these limits would be a rare one indeed. Furthermore, the existence of experienced, repeat buyers and a possible slowdown in the pace of technological advance in maturing industries will often force firms to change their tactics as they become more conscious of cost and service implications. Slower growth will also give rise to new forms of competition for market share.

25

Here, the chemical industry provides a telling example. Prior to the advent of petrochemicals (around 1920 in the USA), producers were mainly suppliers of intermediate inputs used by other industries. While this function still persists, the emergence of petrochemicals led to all sorts of new product lines based on synthetics – tyres, textiles, paint, clothing, etc. Chemical firms outgrew their 'supplier role' and entered a second 'product' phase dominated by items intended mainly for the final consumer rather than other industries. More recently, the effects of market saturation and over-capacity have taken their toll. These problems, compounded by rising energy costs and environmental concerns, have converted chemicals into a mature industry with a service-oriented mode of operation. The tactics which predominate in the present phase include efforts to focus technologies on the development of new chemicals to meet specific uses and/or the needs of specific markets. The reorientation requires much more attention to customer service. A parallel trend has involved attempts to increase the proportion of value added in total production to compensate for declining growth in the volume of sales. And, like firms in other maturing industries, chemical producers have become increasingly willing to sell their know-how. These features provide a marked contrast to the mass production approach which marked earlier phases in the chemical industry's development.

A third benchmark for gauging industrial maturity is the notion of a product life cycle. An industry's products are pictured as passing through several phases or stages – introduction, growth, maturity and decline. New industries and products are distinguished by their comparatively large requirements for skilled labour and expenditures on R and D. Initially, the new producers enjoy excess profits. As the technologies are transferred abroad and production processes are standardized, however, the location of production sites will move to countries where costs are lower (Vernon, 1970; Krugman, 1982). Relocation will be associated with a change in the industry's input requirements; expenditures on R and D will fall relative to the share of funds expended on semi-skilled and unskilled labour.

The product cycle highlights changes in the cost structure of typical firms as the industry matures. Because the stylized approach singles out expenditures in R and D and skilled labour it has implications for the pace of technological innovation in the industry. But the hypothesis has also attracted legitimate criticism. The duration of each stage varies widely from industry to industry and a logical progression from one stage to the next is not always followed. These weaknesses not only limit the usefulness of the concept but also suggest that the relationship between technological innovation and industrial maturity is more complex than the representation sketched here.

Small firms clearly play an important role in the development of technologies in new industries. There are few, if any, large firms to begin with. But the composition of firms in the industry is highly unstable. Industry leaders and other innovators may be required to take substantial risks, with little ability to prevent imitation. This means that some firms – even the innovator – may fail. As the industry matures, the prospect that an aggressive imitator might grab a commanding technological lead will diminish. The volume of funds for R and D will increase, along with the firm's scale of operations, and permit it to assume the role of a 'fast imitator' once a competitor brings a new innovation to the market. At this point, generalizations about the relationship between firm size and the propensity to innovate become more difficult. Previously, it was thought that research efforts would tend to diminish as firm size increased (Scherer, 1965; Hamberg, 1966). More recent studies (Soete, 1979; Freeman, Clark and Soete, 1982, Chapter 2) have served to qualify this interpretation by showing that large firms in several maturing industries have tended to be major sources of innovation.

The debate with regard to the association between firm size and research effort will continue in the future. And, if large firms are successful in decentralizing their research programmes and stimulating in-house entrepreneurship, any possible link between firm size and research effort will be further blurred. However, one assertion which can be made with confidence is that the research efforts of large firms are a crucial, if indirect, ingredient for technological progress in mature industries. Large firms have always invested heavily in research and have also attempted to retain unorthodox ideas and their originators, in the hope that both would one day prove useful. But in today's turbulent and competitive markets, this tactic is the first step in the creation of a new competitor. The source of small, new competitors is very rarely from outside the industry. Instead, new competitors are more likely to be spin-offs. And they are only as good as the best parts of the firms which spawn them. Without the heavy spending on research which large firms provide, there would be far fewer innovations – whether originating within large firms or serving as the catalyst for spin-offs. The research efforts of large firms must be seen to be crucial for the industry's technological progress as they provide an essential 'research base' for so many innovations.

A Policy-Maker's View

Those charged with making policy tend to take a broader view of maturity than industry specialists but one which is more pragmatic than that of economists. Today, a major concern is to craft a set of industrial policies which respond to the pressures of structural change and/or channel these forces of change along desired paths. The interests of policy-makers are twofold. One is to find ways to accommodate a contraction in a major industry and, perhaps, to rejuvenate that industry by restoring some measures of international competitiveness. A second objective – to hasten the development of new industries around which the country's industrial future may be built – has emerged in the prevailing international atmosphere of competitive coexistence.

Like the other groups surveyed here, the policy-maker's view of maturing industries has also been modified during the post-war era. With regard to the criterion of enlarged plant size and its corollaries (greater firm concentration and heightened entry barriers), anti-trust policy was traditionally one of the major policy tools in Western countries. The behaviour of large firms in mature industries was subjected to particular scrutiny. Producers of steel or automobiles were known to operate in an oligopolistic manner, often attempting to set prices, to deter new entrants and to reduce the level of domestic competition. Fairly stringent anti-trust regulations were imposed in most Western countries (particularly in the USA). However, the gradual internationalization of industries has forced a change in the application of anti-trust legislation. Companies may now have a dominant share of their domestic market and still encounter intense foreign competition. Thus, policies governing outright merger or inter-firm collaboration in specific fields such as R and D have become more lenient. With the emergence of worldwide markets for many manufacturers, efficiency as well as market share has come to be a criterion for acceptance of oligopolistic behaviour.

Policy-makers and governments in some countries had previously subscribed to the opinion that the enlargement of firm size was essential if firms in maturing industries were to improve their efficiency. The consequences are vividly illustrated by the experience of the state-owned British Steel Corporation where, in 1971, the government endorsed plans to expand production capacity to almost 40 million tonnes by 1980. Ironically, 1980 was marked by a tripartite dispute between government, industry and labour regarding a production level of 15–16 million tonnes (Ballance and Sinclair, 1983, p. 117). The recent tendency among several Western governments to relinquish control over state-run firms and industries is evidence that this view, too, has lost favour with changes in the international business environment.

With regard to the manipulation of demand, the policy-maker's distinction between new and maturing industries is clearcut. Government support for new industries can take many forms. Two of the most common methods are: government funding of R and D and government purchases to provide the new industry with an assured market. Until well into the twentieth century, government funding of R and D was rare. A fundamental scientific discovery required no more investment than a serendipitous flash of insight by a brilliant person. Today, however, governments spend large amounts on R and D and new industries are major recipients of these funds. Government purchases can be of even more immediate benefit to new industries where demand has yet to reach sufficient levels. For instance, in the 1950s the US government was the only major purchaser of computers. Ten years later, American producers of integrated circuits were entirely dependent on the military for their market. The Minuteman missile was the largest single user of those components, accounting for 20 per cent of all sales by the US semiconductor industry (Grunwald and Flamm, 1985, p. 41). The Japanese government supported new industries in other ways. For example, a leasing scheme was introduced in the early 1980s to bolster domestic demand for industrial robots. The scheme, which was modelled on a previous version intended to help fledgling computer firms, provided robots to users at subsidized rates (*Far Eastern Economic Review*, 4 December 1981). These are only a few ways by which governments attempt to spur on the growth of favoured industries. A variety of other government policies and practices, all with a similar aim, will be examined in later chapters.

At the other end of the spectrum, policy-makers' efforts to influence demand in mature industries are mainly attempts to preserve a sufficient share of the domestic market for their home industries. This objective is usually achieved through trade restrictions. But the adoption of such an objective has also entailed a profound shift in the policy goals which trade restrictions (for example, tariffs and quotas) were intended to serve. Previously, such restrictions were commonly regarded as macroeconomic tools which could be used to influence the balance of payments or to alleviate problems of unemployment. Today, however, trade restrictions are employed as part of the arsenal of measures to influence the structure of the manufacturing sector and are therefore industry-specific.

The series of tariff-reducing negotiations held in the post-war period – the Dillon, Kennedy and Tokyo Rounds – progressively restricted the ability of governments to impose new tariffs. At the same time, however, success in this regard has probably contributed to the wider use of non-tariff barriers. Two of the most common forms of non-tariff barriers are the voluntary export restraint (VER) and the orderly marketing agreement (OMA). In the first case major overseas suppliers of a product 'agree' – usually under threat of potentially more restrictive unilateral forms of protection – to reduce the exports into a country to specified levels. The procedures are similar for an OMA as the exporting country restricts shipments to specified levels which, if exceeded, are enforced by the importing country through an explicit import quota. A third form of non-tariff barrier is domestic content regulation. The scheme requires that a given percentage of domestic value added or domestic components be included in a final product. Grossman (1981, p. 583–4) notes the widespread use of this trade restraint in Australia (applying to automobile parts, petrochemicals, various foods, industrial machinery and tractors), in the USA (shipbuilding) and in various LDCs. More recently, American auto-workers, in alliance with some producers, launched a highly publicized campaign for domestic content regulations. The proposal, which never became law, stipulated that the domestic content of American automobiles must reach 90 per cent for firms selling over 900,000 vehicles. These, and other forms of non-tariff barriers, are disguised means of protection – employed to avert some of the domestic and international opposition that additional tariffs might evoke. They are all less transparent than tariffs or quotas and are often imposed by executive organs, while the more traditional forms of trade restraint have been the responsibility of legislative bodies.

There is one aspect of maturity which is unique to the field of industrial policy and should be noted here. The growing industrial involvement of the state in the manufacturing sphere has already been mentioned. But the growth of state intervention has rarely been accompanied by institutional arrangements required to co-ordinate the government's expanded role. As a larger role for government has come to be accepted, special interest groups in various industries have found the traditional dispersion of authority much to their liking.

With certain qualifications, mature industries can wield

greater political influence than newer ones. Murrell (1982, p. 990), for instance, suggests that the policy-making influence of special interest groups is greatest in capital-intensive industries which have high concentration ratios and are widely unionized. These characteristics, in turn, would suit the notion of industrial maturity as outlined here. The economic health of cities, or entire regions, are often heavily dependent on mature industries. Dependency can even be nationwide owing to the geographical dispersion of productive units, all supported by an elaborate network of suppliers, subcontractors and distributors. Newer industries can seldom claim such large constituencies and, therefore, may command less attention from policy-makers. The distinction, however, is only a relative one. The desire of many governments to foster the development of selected new industries has meant that these, too, can influence policy. In addition to traditional industries like textiles, steel or automobiles, others such as computers, electronic components or aerospace have developed fairly elaborate networks to co-ordinate the given industry's efforts to influence industrial policy.

The LDCs' View of Industrial Maturity

A great deal of the foregoing discussion would seem far removed from the realities faced by the industrialist or policy-maker in an LDC. Contrary to the picture of ruthless competitive ability often drawn by industry representatives in Western countries, the vast proportion of manufacturing activities in LDCs are conducted on a modest scale and cater to small or fragmented markets. The contrast between industries in LDCs and Western countries is found in each of the three broad features which have been used to describe maturity.

Industries in LDCs have not experienced the evolutionary development known in Western countries. There was no history of gradual technological advance during which plant size was enlarged and a given industry's structure was transposed from one predominantly composed of small firms into another comprising a number of large firms.

Often, it was only after technologies became relatively standardized, and industries in Western countries had matured, that investors turned to locations in LDCs as an alternative to high-wage conditions elsewhere. Many large firms operating in LDCs are either affiliates of multinationals or, alternatively, state-owned. In either case, the dominant firms in many LDCs did not emerge through any process of maturity but were implanted on top of a modest and fragmented industrial base.

Contrary to the picture which has been drawn of manufacturing in Western countries, the structure of an industry in an LDC typically consists of three groups:

(1) A cluster of large firms, using comparatively modern technologies and located mainly in urban areas where infrastructure, manpower and skills are most readily available;
(2) A number of small to medium-sized firms, employing various intermediate levels of technology, located primarily in urban areas but also in some rural areas;
(3) A larger number of small industrial enterprises and artisan workshops, using traditional or intermediate technologies, located in both rural and urban areas.

The importance of each group will vary depending upon the industry. Some, such as petrochemicals or steel, will consist predominantly of firms in group (1). The necessary production technologies in such industries are widely available, having been transferred by multinationals or purchased by governments of LDCs. In other cases – for example, food processing, textiles, clothing, plastics, glass or building materials – firms of all sizes may be represented or, alternatively, the industry may consist of some combination of the three groups. The markets they serve are often very fragmented or small, competition from overseas is restricted by government policy and the pace of technological advancement can be slow.

With regard to the pattern of domestic demand in LDCs, the possibility of market saturation is again somewhat different from the experience of Western industries. Saturation may still occur, as in the case of the South Korean market for televisions or Singapore's home market for various types of consumer electronics. In a majority of LDCs, however, the levels of per capita income are extremely low and the distribution of income can be highly inequitable. Both characteristics mean that 'effective' demand for manufactures is limited. Thus, the growth of domestic markets for manufactures is more likely to be hampered by a lack of purchasing power or income than by the effects of saturation.

In the field of technological development most LDCs are regarded as being technologically dependent, meaning that the major source of their technology comes from abroad (Stewart, 1977, p. 116). Firms rely heavily on imitative tactics. Technologies may be acquired through foreign investment by a multinational or through outright purchase, usually by the government. In any case, the technologies obtained are almost always mature, standardized ones. The absence of innovation or genuine technological advancement is not an issue. Instead, attention is focused on the problem of identifying those technologies (if they exist) which provide a 'suitable' match with the LDC's resource endowments. Desirable technologies would make optimum use of those inputs – for example, unskilled labour and raw materials – which are locally abundant and would minimize the use of other inputs such as capital and skilled labour which are scarce. This desire can, however, conflict with other objectives. For instance, when LDCs aspire to compete in international markets, the technologies necessary to accomplish this feat are unlikely to meet selection criteria based on domestic endowments. For an LDC, the issues relating to industrial technology are difficult and complex and they are also different from those confronted by policymakers in Western industries.

Despite the lack of a clearly defined industrial life cycle in LDCs, the notion of industrial maturity is nevertheless relevant. For those LDCs that aspire to enter international markets, industries which are already mature in Western countries can be a logical place to start. It is no accident that the industries in which LDCs are comparatively important producers and exporters include textiles, clothing, footwear, consumer electronics, certain non-ferrous metals or crudely refined petroleum products. The input requirements of such industries are usually fairly labour-intensive or are dependent on natural resources which are abundant and of good quality. The issue of industrial maturity is, therefore, seen to be pertinent as it has definite implications for the structure of manufacturing and the pattern of structural change.

An Outline of the Book

The foregoing description cannot indicate the true extent to which today's industries differ from their predecessors in the early post-war period. Because the transformation has been both fundamental and complex, the impressions obtained from any review of that process will, to some extent, depend on methods of analysis and the perspectives adopted. With this in mind, it may be helpful to provide the reader with an idea of the way in which this book is organized. The foregoing discussion has introduced some of the concepts which are repeatedly used throughout later chapters. These concepts are neither defined nor employed in any rigorous way but serve, instead, to provide a loose framework for discussion of the issues and trends which motivate governments, industrialists and pressure groups.

The material in subsequent chapters can best be understood in terms of three broad areas of discussion. As the spatial boundaries of industrial enterprises have expanded, the need to fuse the international and domestic aspects of industrial change and policy formulation has grown. Chapters 2, 3 and 4 describe the post-war transformation of industry from several different points of view. Chapter 2 looks at these developments in terms of their international implications. It examines the network of policies and institutions created after the Second World War and considers some of the consequences of the subsequent realignment of industry. The realignment can also be illustrated in terms of its domestic repercussions. In that case the development of the manufacturing sector and its constituent industries are of major interest and are examined in Chapter 3, providing the basis for a comparison of post-war trends in Western countries and LDCs. The growing tendency to focus on issues and problems which are narrowly defined in terms of particular industries and firms has already been noted. This fact, coupled with the increasing involvement of government in industry, led to a range of confrontations and disputes which have divided Western countries and pitted them against the LDCs. Chapter 4 contains an industry-specific description of post-war trends which serves as a basis for judging some of the consequences of these events.

The extent and rapidity of the post-war transformation inevitably raised issues involving international differences in competitive abilities. The second section of the book, comprising Chapters 5 to 8, is concerned with this subject. Again, a conceptual framework is needed, and in this instance elements drawn from theories of international trade offer a useful point of departure. Chapter 5 begins the section by examining the intuitive content of several of these theories. The purpose of the discussion is not to evaluate alternative theories but to consider how analysts have used them in order to gain some impression of international differences in competitive ability.

Most conventional theories of comparative advantage imply that international differences in competitive ability result from the interaction between three sets of variables. These include the patterns of factor usage (or relative factor intensities) associated with specific industries, the resource endowments which are available in each country and trade performance of the country's industries. Drawing together evidence from several industries and markets, Chapters 6, 7 and 8 consider each of these elements in turn. The primary emphasis of all these chapters is on the empirical issues and policy implications which can be derived from the available evidence.

Ultimately, the story of this book concerns industries rather than the manufacturing sector in its entirety. The final section develops the idea of 'industry strategies'. An underlying assumption is that a certain measure of commonality can often be found among some of the major firms in a given industry. The strategies described in Chapters 9, 10 and 11 are a mixture of public policies and corporate tactics. Using evidence compiled from a number of industries, the discussion is designed to illustrate the changing nature of interrelationships between various groups of decision makers concerned with corporate and public policy. In some instances public officials may play a dominant role, but in other cases the strategies adopted are the outcome of protracted bargaining between 'industry representatives', public officials and even foreign competitors. The discussion, however, is not intended to provide a comprehensive catalogue. Moreover, the choice of any one particular strategy does not mean that others have to be excluded. The alternatives described are neither mutually exclusive nor contradictory and several might be advantageously pursued at the same time.

The suggestion that industrial policies can actually constitute a part of an industry's response to its circumstances is based on the fact that special interest groups frequently wield considerable policy-making powers. By using their growing ability to influence public policy these groups have added another dimension to the normal range of economic and corporate issues that make up a firm's decision-making responsibilities. One result is that some industrial policies are no longer devised solely by public officials. Nor are the tactics of major firms the exclusive domain of corporate officials. The overlap between government policy and corporate tactics is at its greatest in those industries which have outgrown their national boundaries.

Above all, the book is an exercise in applied economics and relies heavily on a range of international data sources. The quality of industrial statistics, however, varies widely. Countries use different statistical systems, employ various definitions and do not always use identical procedures for collecting data. The Statistical Appendix to the book reviews some of these limitations and serves to alert the reader to the major limitations of these data.

Supplementary Reading

Among the literature on interdependence, one of the most frequently cited sources is Keohane and Nye (1977). Kindleberger (1973) was influential in suggesting that the present system of interdependence requires a 'national leader' at its centre in order to function in an orderly and productive way. A different view is taken by Keohane (1984) who argues that the declining efficiency of the post-war system is not necessarily attributable to an erosion of American power. Strange (1985), too, suggests that international trade and other forms of economic exchange are dependent on much more than the enforcement of any set of international rules. A broad survey of various forms of economic interdependence can be found in Frey and Schneider (1984). Cooper (1985) conducts a systematic analysis of the relationship between interdependence and economic policy. Other contributions which stress a belated awareness of interdependence, at least among American analysts, are Hoffman (1977) and Strange (1982).

An introduction to the concepts of economic structure and structural change could begin with Machlup's views on the appropriate meaning and usage of these terms (Machlup, 1958). Flammang (1979) provides an interesting discussion which relates these concepts to the experiences of both industrialized countries and LDCs, while Arndt (1985) traces the origins of the structuralist interpretation back to the early 1930s.

Interpretations of industrial maturity are many. Norton (1986), in his survey of industrial policy, summarizes several views and traces their origin back to the 1930s. During the latest period of slow economic growth, the value of the maturity hypothesis has been reaffirmed by van Duijn (1983) who also suggests possible variations in the industry's post-maturity patterns of growth. The relationship between the maturity hypothesis and the role of special interest groups in the policy-making process is argued by Olson (1982a, 1982b, and 1983). Among the burgeoning literature on business strategies, one of the most influential books is that of Ohmae (1985). Kotler, Fahey and Jatusripitak (1985) offer a different approach on the role of international competition in industry. Porter (1985) combines the tools of the business strategist with those of the economist. An example of the contrasting views on the distinction between emerging and maturing industries can be found in Reich (1983) and Melman (1983). Both authors see the original basis for American industrial superiority in the simplification of tasks and the high-volume production of standardized products. Reich's arguments suggest the existence of an industry dichotomy based on production volume and flexibility, while Melman disputes the existence of a distinction between sunrise and sunset industries.

CHAPTER TWO

The Development of Manufacturing – a Global Setting

The end of the Second World War marked a watershed in the evolution of world industry but many of the forces that would shape the post-war institutional and policy environment had emerged long before.

Throughout much of the previous century the world had followed British leadership on economic and policy issues. Inspired by Kindleberger (1973), many economists came to view the 1920s and 1930s as years of uncertainty brought on by the declining ability of the UK to provide continued leadership. By that time, the USA had surpassed the UK as the world's predominant economic and industrial power, although American governments still hesitated to use their new-found influence. Chaos was added to uncertainty by the Great Depression which disrupted long-term patterns of growth and led to drastic changes in macroeconomic policy. Further complications included the break-up of industrialized countries into three political groups – Western democracies, national socialist regimes and communist governments. All these events meant that the years between 1920 and 1945 were marked by considerable economic and political instability. The culmination of the Second World War began a process of international realignment. In the industrialized countries a bi-polar form of leadership, provided by the USA and the USSR, supplanted the ternary division of the 1930s. But the experiences of the earlier period lived on. Governments, policy-makers and economists everywhere were acutely concerned with the political implications of international economic circumstances and these concerns were reflected in the post-war system of policies and institutions which they created.

Most economists' interpretations of international relations during this period stress the importance of hegemonic leadership. That view is questioned by others (for instance, Rangarajan, 1984; Strange, 1985) who tend to see international relations in a broader context. But the degree to which hegemonic domination is essential to an international system is not the primary issue in the following discussion. More important is the need to see the formulation of post-war policies against a background of sweeping changes which involved not just manufacturing but all fields of economic activity. The significance of the economic transformation is suggested by the fact that during the past thirty-five years, world GDP (at constant prices) has quadrupled. Rapid economic growth was accompanied by the emergence of major new centres of economic activity in Japan, socialist countries and Western Europe, while per capita incomes rose briskly throughout the world. The phenomenal increase in the volume of trade, investment and technology moving across international borders is indicative of the extent to which the world economy has been transformed since 1950. In most countries the manufacturing sector provided a major impetus for growth and the internationalization of economic activities was readily applied in the industrial sphere.

The Changing Map of World Industry

The post-war evolution of world industry is sketched in Table 2.1. The figures show a gradual fall in the share of Western countries – from 77 per cent of world MVA in 1963 to 64 per cent by 1984. The decline was primarily a result of the rapid expansion of manufacturing in socialist countries. At the other end of the spectrum, the achievements of the

Table 2.1 Global Distribution of MVA and Rates of Growth, 1963–85[a]

Year	Western countries	Socialist countries	Total LDCs	LDCs of which: Africa	LDCs of which: Asia	LDCs of which: Latin America
			Share of world MVA			
1963	77.0	15.2	7.8	0.8	2.6	4.4
1964	77.3	14.8	7.9	0.8	2.5	4.6
1965	76.8	15.4	7.8	0.8	2.5	4.5
1966	76.7	15.5	7.8	0.8	2.5	4.5
1967	75.6	16.6	7.8	0.8	2.5	4.5
1968	75.1	17.0	7.9	0.8	2.6	4.5
1969	74.5	17.5	8.0	0.8	2.6	4.6
1970	73.3	18.3	8.4	0.8	2.7	4.8
1971	72.4	19.0	8.6	0.8	2.8	5.0
1972	72.1	19.2	8.7	0.8	2.8	5.1
1973	72.1	19.1	8.8	0.8	2.8	5.1
1974	70.2	20.7	9.1	0.8	2.9	5.3
1975	67.9	22.5	9.6	0.9	3.2	5.5
1976	67.9	22.4	9.7	0.9	3.3	5.5

1977	67.5	22.7	9.8	0.9	3.4	5.4
1978	67.1	22.9	10.0	0.9	3.6	5.5
1979	66.8	23.0	10.2	0.9	3.6	5.6
1980	65.5	23.8	10.7	1.0	3.8	5.9
1981	65.2	24.2	10.6	1.0	3.9	5.7
1982	63.5	25.8	10.7	1.0	4.0	5.7
1983(b)	63.2	26.1	10.7	1.0	4.4	5.3
1984(b)	63.5	25.7	10.8	1.0	4.6	5.2
1985(c)	63.9	24.8	11.3	1.0	4.8	5.3

Average annual rates of growth

1963–73	4.6	8.6	5.1	4.5	5.0	5.1
1973–84	0.9	4.2	2.9	2.1	4.9	1.3

Sources: UNIDO, 1985a, p. 5–7, UNIDO, 1986a, p. 5–6.

[a] Figures for country groups may not add up to the corresponding totals owing to rounding up errors. All estimates were derived from national accounts data expressed in constant dollars. For further discussion see the statistical annex.
[b] Preliminary figures.
[c] Estimate.

LDCs were painfully modest. Although the years between 1950 and 1974 were a period of exceptionally rapid growth in world industry, many LDCs were onlookers rather than active participants. Traditionally, Latin America has had the most extensive manufacturing base but, owing to rapid progress in several Asian countries, the latter region may soon assume industrial leadership among the LDCs. In contrast, the manufacturing base in Africa is miniscule and its relative position has changed very little in the post-war period.

During much of this period the international economic system functioned smoothly by adjusting to the new configuration of world industry. The relative gains of the socialist countries were significant and were accommodated without the eruption of major economic or political problems. More recently, the industrial strides made by LDCs have attracted considerable attention although, ironically, their present share of world MVA is much less than that attributed to socialist countries in 1963. There is no reason to suppose that the industrial growth of certain LDCs presents fundamentally new problems for the world economy. Rather, as Turner and McMullen (1982, p. 269) have argued, they may simply have emerged at the wrong time, that is, at a time of slow growth and high unemployment, when there is obvious scepticism about the workings of the economic adjustment process.

The slowdown after 1973 is also evident from the growth rates shown in Table 2.1. Western countries were hardest hit; rates of growth plummeted and levels of manufacturing output actually contracted in several years between 1973 and 1984 (UNIDO, 1985a, p. 7). In the more insular group of socialist countries, growth rates were halved but were still significantly higher than those in other parts of the world. The resilience of Asian manufacturing is illustrated by the fact that the post–1973 pace of industrialization in that region was maintained, while growth in other developing regions slowed abruptly.

The foregoing data are adequate to provide a general impression but they obscure several important aspects of world industry, one of which is the excessive concentration of industrial capabilities among a very few Western countries. Chenery (1977, p. 472), for instance, notes that in 1950 fifteen Western countries accounted for as much as 72 per cent of world MVA. More detailed information on this aspect is given in Table 2.2. The industrial predominance of the USA during the years before 1960 is readily apparent. The country's contribution to the combined MVA of all Western countries was several times that of the UK, its nearest rival, and far greater than the corresponding measure for any other Western country. American dominance during the early post-war years was equally impressive in other economic spheres: it accounted for more than one-half the gross product of all non-socialist countries and held nearly two-thirds of the world's monetary gold (Vernon, 1981, p. 18).

Given the pre-eminence of the USA, it was that country's policies which constituted one of the key elements in the post-war system. Two initiatives were especially noteworthy. The first, known as the Marshall Plan, was intended 'to force the European countries to view their separate economies as part of an integrated European whole and to cooperate in the formulation of economic policies' (Krause, 1968, p. 25). Begun in 1948, the Plan was originally intended to span a period of four years and to provide war-torn Europe with the financial resources necessary to restore its industrial capacity. Economic assistance was subsequently provided for only two years and then discontinued in favour of military assistance following the outbreak of the Korean War. Because of its premature curtailment the results of the programme are somewhat difficult to evaluate, but most economists regarded the Marshall Plan as having a positive impact on European economies. Even more important was the political implication that the USA saw the reconstruction of Europe as a vital and integral part of its international strategy.

The second US policy initiative was known as the Reciprocal Trade Agreements Act and had a longer life. Established as a means of overcoming the consequences of the Great Depression, the Act was periodically renewed and eventually became a cornerstone of American trade policy.

Table 2.2 Distribution of MVA among Major Western Countries[a] (as a percentage of world MVA)

Year	France	West Germany	Japan	Italy	UK	USA
1948	4.8	3.9	1.2	2.6	10.6	61.1
1953	4.3	7.7	2.6	3.0	9.4	58.8
1958	5.7	10.3	4.0	3.6	9.6	51.0
1963	5.8‖7.3	9.7 ‖ 11.0	6.3‖ 6.9	4.0‖3.9	8.1‖8.1	50.4‖49.1
1970	7.3	12.6	12.0	4.4	6.5	42.2
1975	9.2	14.3	13.6	5.0	6.0	33.3
1980	9.5	15.0	15.5	5.9	6.4	30.6

Source: UNIDO, 1983, pp. 27 and 30.

[a] Figures were derived from national accounts data for MVA. Because information for 1948-63 was stated in current prices while that for 1963-80 was at 1975 prices, the two series are not comparable. Data were not available for New Zealand and Switzerland.

The approach was based on fundamental propositions of trade theory. It endorsed the principle that more trade was preferable to less trade and that a trading system relatively unencumbered by restraints and barriers would stimulate more trade. Furthermore, the Act stipulated that all trading partners should be treated on an equal, or reciprocal, basis. Accordingly, any tariff reduction granted by the USA should be matched by an equivalent concession from its trading partners. The line of reasoning later served as a model in the negotiations which led to the creation of the post-war trading system.

Because political influence stemmed from economic leadership, American representatives were established as the primary architects of the international system to be created after the Second World War. Many of the premises that guided US officials were based on their perception of the international political scene at the time. Foreign policy considerations overshadowed all other issues; the presumed Soviet threat was the overriding concern to American officials. The officials sought a system which would foster closer economic integration of Western Europe. In particular, closer ties between France and West Germany were thought to lessen the chances of another conflict. The objectives were somewhat different in the case of Japan. Rather than attempting to reintegrate that country with the economies of its Asian neighbours, the intention was to link the Japanese economy more closely with other Western countries. The American approach was to provide unilateral trade concessions to Japanese exporters of textiles and, later, steel, television sets, cameras, ships and other items. With economic assistance, and behind a military shield provided by the USA, the Japanese economy was to be integrated with that of other Western nations.

While the objectives of the new system were a product of the *realpolitik* of the 1950s, the economic mechanisms by which it was to function were largely shaped by the experiences of the 1920s and 1930s. The economic failures of the pre-war period were still fresh in the minds of many. There was speculation that the German 'economic problem' might persist into the 1960s (Hoover, 1946, p. 649). Many observers even feared that the Western world would be plunged into another great depression. The preoccupation of the system's architects is noted by Pollard (1981, p. 310) who observed that all the institutions established during this period 'strongly bore that mark of being designed to overcome one or other of the pre-war problems'.

Foremost among the economic concerns was the desire to avoid another collapse of the international trading system similar to that in the 1930s. Negotiators sought to establish a new trading system more durable than its predecessor. Discussion focused on two subject areas. The first was a code of conduct for trade policy which would apply to all trading partners and which would embrace the principle of non-discrimination. The second concerned a means to bring about a gradual reduction in trade barriers. With only minor concessions, these objectives were accepted in 1947 when the draft charter of the General Agreement on Tariffs and Trade (GATT) – drawn up largely at the behest of the USA – was signed by twenty-three countries. The corner-stone of the Agreement was the most-favoured-nation (MFN) principle which stipulated that any tariff reduction negotiated between two countries must be applied to the trade of all GATT members.

The trading system was buttressed by the Bretton Woods Agreement in 1944 which provided for a new international monetary system. The arrangements which emerged from the Agreement were based on the 'near-universal assumption of the impregnability' of the US economy (Vernon, 1981, p. 19). Governments were expected to buy and sell their own currencies to the extent necessary to maintain an unchanged rate of exchange with the dollar. The USA, on the other hand, would make its vast gold supply available to those foreign governments that had surplus dollars and were quixotic enough to surrender some of these for gold. In addition to establishing a monetary system, the Agreement also provided for the creation of the International Monetary Fund (IMF) and the International Bank for Reconstruction and Development (now the World Bank).

Significantly, many of the economists' proposals at Bretton Woods were not implemented. Keynes himself argued for the creation of an international trade organization to stabilize commodity prices, for the establishment of a world central bank and for a big world development authority. The first of these, the International Trade Organization, was not constituted owing to disagreement on the extent of regulatory powers. In fact, even the USA failed to ratify the organization's charter. As for the other institutions, the role of the IMF is still somewhat less than envisaged in the second case and the World Bank has a smaller mandate than was originally proposed. The reluctance to conclude multilateral agreements on many of these matters was due as much to the political concerns involved as to differences of opinion based on economic grounds.

Despite political differences, the formation of GATT and the Bretton Woods Agreement can now be seen as part of a broad approach to foreign policy. There was a general consensus that the political benefits to be derived from expanded trade relations probably outweighed the economic gains, although the importance of the latter were clearly recognized. The post-war framework tacitly accepted the principle that national actions which influenced trade were matters of mutual concern. This amounted to a departure from earlier beliefs; prior to the Second World War national actions were regarded as purely of domestic concern. However, the principle proved to have only a one-way application. American negotiators were unsuccessful in convincing their allies to accept the principle of non-discriminatory market access in its entirety. The US position reflected the country's overriding concern with security issues. It strongly supported the objective that Europe should play a leading role in the international economic system. Therefore the Americans permitted their European allies to use trade policies in a discriminatory fashion, so long as domestic free trade interests prevailed over trade protectionist sentiments. Prior to the Second World War, trade barriers had been a widely accepted form of government policy in Europe and war-torn industries pressed their governments for additional protection from US competitors. In addition, European countries extended special tariff concessions (or preferences) to many of their ex-colonies and in return were accorded reverse preferences from these countries. Both practices violated the MFN principle and worked against competitors in the USA and Latin America.

One American response was to increase direct investment in Western Europe, thus moving behind the tariff wall and reducing the discriminatory impact of European policy. But European resistance to American control of key industries mounted and the flow of foreign investment was eventually slowed. Organized labour in the USA also began to work aggressively to limit American foreign investment, arguing that the trend was tantamount to a practice of 'exporting American jobs'. In the early 1960s, the US government responded by enacting the Foreign Direct Investment Program to limit the amount for foreign investment.

The American focus on Europe also influenced economic policy in other fields. The contrasting attitudes of the US government to the formation of the EC and the European Free Trade Association (EFTA) suggest the extent to which economic policy served political goals. The former effort at integration was warmly supported by the USA But the latter, which originally included the UK and neutral countries such as Austria, Sweden and Switzerland, received little or no American support. As one former State Department official noted at the time, the American attitude toward EFTA 'was explainable by the overriding political importance of the Common Market as a stage in the development of the political unity of the Six, where the Free Trade Area was viewed as a purely commercial arrangement' (Frank, 1961, p. 127–8).

From 1947 until the late 1960s, most parts of the post-war system functioned well. Success was most apparent in the field of trade where international exchanges between Western countries thrived without frequent disputes involving market access, supplies of raw materials, trade wars or the re-emergence of international cartels. The trading environment was decidedly more liberal than during the inter-war years when, for example, roughly 42 per cent of world trade was cartelized or subject to similar arrangements and almost all of this involved manufactures (Balassa, 1978a, p. 429).

However, gradual changes in the international economic

landscape hampered the smooth functioning of the new system and posed new problems that it was ill-equipped to handle. The declining share of Western countries in world MVA was not the only fundamental change attributable to economic growth. Table 2.2 on p. 46 shows that an extensive realignment in the relative industrial capabilities of Western countries also occurred in the post-war period. The over-riding feature of the realignment was the precipitous decline in the USA share of MVA. Between 1948 and 1980, the American share in MVA of all Western countries was reduced by roughly one-half – from over 60 per cent to 30 per cent. West Germany and, more recently, Japan were the major beneficiaries but the relative position of other countries (including several not shown in the table) also improved. The realignment altered many fundamental relationships between Western countries and the burden of adjustment fell heavily on the USA.

Experience suggests that proper functioning of a liberal system for international trade, investment and finance may be facilitated by the existence of a powerful leader or regulator. In other words, the internationalization of economic relations will proceed most effectively when one nation has virtually complete responsibility for the system's functioning (Interfutures, 1979, pp. 77). Because of its economic and political position, such a country can act as a leader in absorbing shocks to the system and in cajoling other nations into co-operative efforts (Aho and Bayard, 1982, p. 399). Until the mid–1970s, this role was performed by the USA. But with the erosion of American pre-eminence, a polycentric form of leadership has evolved. Japan, the EC or even its larger member states may now negotiate or debate issues of international economic significance as near-equals with the USA. In these circumstances, the achievement of the necessary political consensus for fundamental policy reform becomes more difficult. One result has been a growing number of industry-specific disputes which pit the USA against Japan, the EC or its individual member countries.

The effects of industrial realignment were reinforced by another, more specific, form of convergence. Throughout the 1950s and 1960s, growth in many Western countries was largely a process of 'catching up' with the industrial leaders. The capital stock in war-devastated countries was steadily built up, while educational and training institutions turned out an increasing number of skilled workers and scientists. Gradually, the relative endowments of capital, skilled labour and technologies in Western countries began to converge. The US share in total world capital is estimated to have fallen from 42 per cent in 1963 to 33 per cent in 1975, while Japan's share rose from 7 to 15 per cent in the same period. Similar trends were found in the ratio of capital to labour in many Western countries: Belgium, France, Italy, Japan, Netherlands and West Germany all closed the gap with the USA (Bowen, 1983, pp. 403–5). For a wide range of products, the relative abundance of most inputs and factors of production have become very similar across Western countries and, perhaps, some LDCs (Aho and Bayard, 1982, p. 383; Cline, 1982, p. 39).

The tendency for factor endowments to converge meant that cost components of individual industries varied less widely between Western countries than had been the case in the 1950s and 1960s. For industries where the range of products produced in different countries was largely similar, small changes in cost conditions could result in large shifts in international competitive ability, in trade balances, production and employment. Consequently, industrial policies that were traditionally regarded as being purely 'domestic' in scope (for example, anti-trust legislation, programmes to assist depressed regions within a country, industry subsidies, and so on) might bring about significant changes in an industry's cost structure relative to its overseas competitors. In this sense, many 'domestic' policies in Western countries now have international consequences. The convergence in factor proportions has increased the likelihood that international comparative advantages may be malleable through industrial policy; where this is the case, special interest groups in particular industries will redouble their efforts to sway the decisions of policy-makers. Under such conditions Western governments gradually found it possible – or deemed it necessary – to adopt more *dirigiste* approaches to industrial issues.

The LDCs in World Industry

Although the framework of post-war policy and the associated development of world industry were dominated by events in Western countries, the global spread of manufacturing activity should also be seen in terms of its impact on LDCs. Table 2.3 shows levels of MVA per capita in various country groupings and at selected points in time. With regard to the growth of per capita MVA, the achievements of socialist countries were not matched by the LDCs or by Western economies. Per capita MVA in the socialist countries trebled between 1963 and 1981 and in the latter year was 77 per cent of the level attained in Western countries. The corresponding figures for LDCs show only a doubling in per capita MVA and levels of manufacturing production which were miniscule in comparison with other countries.

Significant differences between levels of per capita MVA in the LDCs and the industrialized countries are to be expected. More striking comparisons are found among the figures for the LDCs themselves. For the United Nations category known as the 'least developed countries', per capita MVA in 1981 was only $13 or 3 per cent of the Latin American figure. Regional averages for Africa and Asia suggest that both groups of countries lag far behind Latin America. This fact, too, is somewhat surprising, as Asian industrial performance is much more impressive when judged in terms of the growth in manufacturing output or the region's share of world MVA. Nevertheless, in 1981 the per capita MVA of Asia was only one-half the average for all LDCs and less than one-sixth of the level in Latin America.

Because the manufacturing performance of the LDCs is so diverse it is helpful to look at the experience of these countries in more detail. Table 2.4 shows the distribution of MVA when LDCs are grouped according to the level of per capita income. The poor growth performance of manufacturing is most evident for countries at the lower end of the income spectrum and seems to have persisted throughout the post-war period. Together, low income and lower

Table 2.3 MVA per capita in Selected Country Groupings (in 1975 dollars)

Year	Socialist countries	Western countries	Total LDCs	LDCs, of which:				
				Africa	Middle East	Asia	Latin America	Least developed LDCs
1963	407	996	48	24	83	22	172	9
1973	897	1623	81	38	153	34	289	14
1981	1333	1729	101	46	175	51	332	13

Source: UNIDO, 1985b, p. 24.

middle-income countries accounted for little more than 20 per cent of total MVA attributed to all LDCs in 1982. This fact is ominous as almost 70 per cent of the population of LDCs is found in these countries. Development of manufacturing has proceeded most rapidly in countries at intermediate and upper-middle levels of income. However, these countries are comparatively small, accounting for just over one-quarter of the total population in the LDCs. Although the share of the richest LDCs also shows a decline in recent years, the figures may be somewhat misleading as many of these countries are oil exporters and undertook a rapid expansion of the energy sector in the 1970s.

The poor industrial performance in low-income countries is matched by an excessive concentration of manufacturing capacity in a very few of the larger and more advanced LDCs. The latter fact is vividly illustrated in Table 2.5 which shows the ten largest producers of manufactures in selected years. Throughout the 1960s and 1970s as much as 70 per cent of the MVA attributed to all LDCs (which number more than 120) was accounted for by this select group. Moreover, the list of major manufacturers changed very little, being dominated by Brazil, Mexico, India and Argentina. Together, the four countries accounted for 53 per cent of total MVA for all LDCs in 1963 and, despite the emergence of South Korea and Hong Kong as industrial centres, the same four countries still claimed 50 per cent of the corresponding total in 1981.

The figures presented in these tables naturally conceal wide differences in individual LDCs. But they do suggest several features of the post-war period shared by most of these countries. First, performance of manufacturing in LDCs is most impressive when stated in terms of growth rates but much less so when judged by the sector's contribution to income or basic needs. Second, industrial progress has done very little to reduce relative differences in the level of MVA per capita among the LDCs. This result contrasts with the experiences of Western and socialist countries where differences in levels of per capita MVA have been reduced markedly since 1963. Finally, the development of manufacturing capabilities has been highly concentrated

Table 2.4 Distribution and Growth of MVA[a] in LDCs by Level of Income (percentage)

Income level[b]	1963	1973	1980	1981	1982	Growth rate of MVA 1963–1982	Share in population of LDCs, 1982
Low	18.5	13.3	11.8	12.4	12.5	4.4	50.7
Lower-middle	10.0	9.4	10.5	11.2	11.5	7.5	17.9
Intermediate	17.2	19.0	19.9	20.8	21.1	8.1	15.9
Upper-middle	36.0	40.2	42.1	40.6	39.7	8.0	12.2
High	18.3	18.1	15.7	15.0	15.2	5.3	3.3
LDCs	100.0	100.0	100.0	100.0	100.0	6.9	100.0

Sources: UNIDO, 1986a, Table 4.

a Based on data at constant prices.

b Income levels are defined in terms of the 1978 values of GDP per capita in each country as follows: low income are those below $295; lower-middle income, $295 to $600; intermediate income, $600 to $1,320; upper-middle income, $1,320 to $2,415; and high income $2,415.

Table 2.5 Ten LDCs with the Largest Share of the MVA[a] of that Country Grouping[b] (percentage)

Country	1963 Share of MVA	Country	1973 Share of MVA	Country	1981 Share of MVA
Brazil	19.64	Brazil	22.74	Brazil	22.71
India	13.48	Mexico	12.36	Mexico	13.88
Mexico	10.71	India	9.06	India	8.61
Argentina	9.02	Argentina	8.40	South Korea	4.86
Venezuela	3.81	Turkey	4.21	Argentina	4.85
Turkey	3.43	Venezuela	3.08	Turkey	3.69
Philippines	2.82	South Korea	2.85	Indonesia	2.77
Peru	2.76	Philippines	2.48	Philippines	2.62
Chile	2.40	Peru	2.30	Venezuela	2.46
Egypt	2.10	Iran	2.06	Hong Kong	2.27
Total	70.17	Total	69.54	Total	68.72

Sources: UNIDO, 1985b, p. 21.
[a] At constant (1975) prices.
[b] Data were available for ninety-seven LDCs.

among a very few LDCs. Many have yet to establish a manufacturing base which is sufficient to allow active participation in world industry.

The LDCs and the Post-War System

Like their Western counterparts, the governments of LDCs entered the post-war period with some degree of consensus. In political terms the position of many LDCs was largely determined by their relationships with Western countries. The rejection of colonialism and the wish for independence contributed to the solidarity of LDCs on certain issues. The desire to remain free from Cold War entanglements added further impetus to what became a non-aligned group. Originally composed of 77 countries (now more then 120), the non-aligned movement came to serve as the political body through which the LDCs attempted to push for economic changes of the post-war system.

The approach rested on the assumption that there was sufficient overlapping interests among the LDCs to enable them to arrive at a common set of objectives which could then be pursued in international negotiations. The fragmented manufacturing base which existed in these countries following the Second World War gave validity to this assumption. In 1953, the combined MVA of all LDCs was only 5 per cent of the world total (Ballance and Sinclair, 1983, p. 14) and this disparity was not lost on government officials in newly independent countries. Economists and government planners maintained that rapid industrialization was a sufficient condition for self-sustaining economic growth. Advocates offered a variety of economic and theoretical arguments to support their preference for manufacturing but many of the reasons were pragmatic as well. First, the manifest post-war concentration of manufacturing capacity in Western countries was probably the overwhelming factor in focusing the ambitions of the LDCs on that sector. They associated a large manufacturing base with economic and political power, with control over natural resources and access to international capital markets. Second, domestic considerations favoured a preference for manufacturing over agriculture. Rapid growth of income was needed to alleviate the situation of the poverty-stricken majority in many LDCs. Because the general impression was that the manufacturing sector promised the most dynamic growth opportunities, many planners opted for a goal of redistributing income through industrial growth. Finally, the experience of many LDCs during the first half of the twentieth century was relevant. There was a sense of pessimism in the LDCs regarding their ability to participate competitively in international markets. This pessimism led planners to favour the development of economies that was internally self-sufficient and fairly comprehensive manufacturing bases were therefore required.

From the viewpoint of the LDCs, the emphasis on trade as the key economic element in the post-war system left much to be desired. The American response to appeals for increased aid came to be encapsulated in the slogan 'trade, not aid', taken from a foreign policy study which argued that with tariff reductions and increased trade the costly burden of US foreign aid could be reduced. Hindsight suggests two reasons why the emphasis on trade rather than aid was unsatisfactory for LDCs. First, political objectives were the major concern of Western countries. During the Cold War, the desire to create a strong and unified Europe undercut economic goals – including the hopes of LDCs for expanded trade or aid. Second, because the Western approach to freer trade was based on the MFN and the principle of reciprocity, it tended to favour intra-Western trade over other suppliers. By definition, the tariff cuts that were implemented were the result of concessions by one or more governments to producers in yet another country. In the bargaining process, however, only Western countries had the potential to make use of improved access to foreign markets. They had little interest in obtaining greater access to the small and fragmented markets in many LDCs. In other words, tariff negotiations served to stimulate trade between those Western countries that already possessed a broad manufacturing base and reinforced a pattern of world trade which partially excluded the LDCs.

Much of the ensuing debate was shaped by views of the

future opportunities for and benefits of international trade. Several of the original arguments can be traced back to the nineteenth century and were restated by Prebisch (1950) with particular reference to Latin America. At the risk of oversimplifying these arguments, supporters of industrialization contended that LDCs rely heavily on the export of primary commodities and that the prices of these products are determined in world markets which operate under competitive conditions. Western countries, however, tend to export manufactures which are sold in international markets that are largely monopolistic. During the normal trade cycle the prices of primary products will rise and fall but will exhibit little upward trend over time. In contrast, the prices of manufactures will rise in periods of expanding world demand but will not fall when the demand is slack. This means that there is a long-run tendency for the export prices of LDCs to decline relative to the price of manufactures (that is, a deterioration in the terms of trade of the LDCs).

Subsequent developments led to a new optimism on the part of the LDCs with regard to their prospects for manufactured exports. With the rapid growth in post-war incomes and demand, world trade expanded at an unprecedented pace. Several LDCs eventually succeeded in establishing modest manufacturing bases and afterwards began to export simple, labour-intensive manufactures. The virtues of an export-oriented approach for LDCs were extolled by international institutions and private economists alike and the focus of attention in some of these countries shifted away from import substitution. The LDCs pleaded for improvements in their access to Western markets through the relaxation of restraints on trade, including manufactures.

Following the striking successes of the Organization of Petroleum Exporting Countries (OPEC) in the early 1970s, negotiations between LDCs and Western countries assumed a more confrontational tone. Under the rubric of a 'new international economic order', governments of LDCs called for a new framework to control the operations of multinationals, to ensure national sovereignty over natural resources and to provide improved access to new technologies at lower prices. The demands of the LDCs had gradually turned from purely trade-related issues to a broader focus on accelerated development of the manufacturing sector, with explicit implications for investment and technology as well as trade.

Nevertheless, as in the case of Western countries, economic growth and political change has led to the partial disintegration of the negotiating body created by the LDCs. First, several of the originally cohesive forces are now less significant. The goals of decolonization and independence have been largely realized and the desire to avoid the East-West conflict through non-alignment has been undercut by the emergence of socialist regimes in a number of LDCs. Second, these countries no longer share a clearly defined set of priorities and are forced to take contradictory positions on important issues. Oil exporters, for instance, strive to maintain high oil prices but oil importers seek to reduce these prices. Leading exporters of manufactures among the LDCs wish to restrain the prices of internationally traded commodities while major producers of tin, copper, rubber and other commodities attempt to stabilize prices. Ex-colonies endeavour to extend preferential trading and financial arrangements with Western countries, although other LDCs regard such relationships as discriminatory. Indeed, as Killick (1980, p. 368) has noted, 'outside the diplomatic conveniences of international agencies and other aid donors, there is a real sense in which the Third World no longer exists'.

In retrospect much of the international framework which emerged after the Second World War was founded on the *realpolitik* of the 1950s and the presumption that the economic base of the USA would continue to be unchallenged. The subsequent realignment of the world economy not only hampered the smooth functioning of that system but posed new problems which it was ill-equipped to handle. The financial mechanisms established by the Bretton Woods accord were largely discarded after the US government cut the link between the dollar and gold in 1971. In the field of trade relations the principle of non-discrimination was steadily eroded, sometimes by formal agreement, sometimes by exception and sometimes by violation. By the beginning of the 1980s, political and economic trends in both

Western countries and the LDCs led to a fragmentation of each group's position on a wide range of issues with international significance. In the field of manufacturing the repercussions were dramatic. Industrial issues were eventually thrust closer to the centre of the international policy arena.

Supplementary Reading

Structural change and economic policy in Western countries during the present era of slow growth are surveyed by Leveson and Wheeler (1980). Mueller (1983) looks at the growth-related aspects of political economy in Western countries. The same aspect is considered by Plessz (1981) who focuses on Western European countries. For a more specific focus on industrial policy in Western countries the reader may consult Pinder, Hosomi and Diebold (1979) or Driscoll and Behrman (1984). Destler's (1980) examination of selected policy decisions reached by successive US governments highlights the predominance of domestic interests over foreign policy concerns.

In the LDCs much of the post-war experience of industrialization has been evaluated and debated in the context of import substitution and export promotion. Opposing views on this subject have been summarized by many authors and are widely available in the literature on economic development. Hirschman's (1968) interpretation of the political economy of import substitution is useful and offers a good starting point for the discussion of industry strategies in later chapters of this book. Schmitz (1984), in re-examining these issues, stresses some of the dynamic, as well as the static, considerations involved. Morawetz (1977) assesses the growth performance of LDCs in relation to their overall development objectives. Killick's studies of development planning in LDCs (1976, 1983) emphasize the relationships between the policy recommendations of economists and political realities faced by these countries.

CHAPTER THREE

Sectoral Patterns of Structural Change

Quite often, descriptions of industrial progress in individual countries, as well as the evaluation of their industrial problems, are conducted in terms of the manufacturing sector in its entirety. This chapter begins with a survey of research on patterns of structural change. The stylized picture of structural change, which emerges from an examination of the approaches, assumptions and results, highlights the role of manufacturing in the overall process of development and growth. In the second section post-war trends in world industry are considered in relation to this stylized picture. In the final section several of the issues which have arisen from experiences during the post–1973 era are evaluated.

The Analysis of Structural Change

The search for similarities in patterns of structural change dates back to the work of Fisher (1939) and Clark (1940). Attention was originally focused on the interrelationships between agriculture, manufacturing and, to a lesser extent, services. The progressive movement of labour from agriculture to manufacturing was a prominent feature of Western industrialization during the nineteenth and early twentieth centuries. Kuznets (1965 and 1966) was among the first to note sectoral similarities in the pattern of structural

63

change in different countries as per capita incomes rose. When these changes were measured in terms of the contribution of each sector to total output, a steady decline in the share of agriculture was observed. A corresponding increase in the share of manufacturing occurred, while no clear trend was observed for the service sector. When a country's economic structure was expressed in terms of the sectoral distribution of its labour force, a fall in the share of agriculture was again evident. Although the share of manufacturing in total employment rose, gains were less pronounced than in the case of output but the share of employment in the service and transport sectors showed a consistent increase (Kirkpatrick, Lee and Nixon, 1984, p. 26).

The subsequent proliferation of data led others (Chenery, 1960; Chenery and Taylor, 1968; UNCTAD, 1976; UNIDO, 1979a) to extend the scope of the investigation to LDCs. At the same time, analysts made increasing use of evidence from other fields relating to patterns of consumption, savings behaviour and the formulation of industrial policy. A primary objective of these studies was to provide a basis for generalization about structural changes, particularly with regard to the share of manufacturing in GDP. A basic premise was that, as per capita income rose, the industrialization of different countries would proceed with a certain degree of uniformity owing to underlying similarities in patterns of resource allocation, factor usage and related phenomena. Chenery and Syrquin (1975, p. 5) cited several 'universal factors' which contributed to a uniform pattern of structural change. These included:

(1) similarities in the evolution of demand patterns, mainly due to a decline in the proportion of total expenditures for basic necessities, coupled with a rise in spending on manufactures;
(2) an increase in the available capital and labour skills, usually at a rate exceeding the growth of the labour force;
(3) access of all countries to similar technologies, international trade and capital markets.

Analysts recognized that other factors – cultural, economic, political and social – could all serve to render the process of structural change unique to each country. These characteristics were referred to as 'group factors' (to be distinguished from the universal factors noted above). For some countries group factors were expected to exert an important influence on the economic structure. In order to deal with these departures from uniformity, countries were arranged in several homogeneous subgroups reflecting a greater degree of commonality. Patterns of structural change were then estimated for each subgroup. A variety of group factors were proposed. Three of the more prominent ones – the size of the domestic market, the level of resource endowment and the stage of development – are considered below.

The size of a country's domestic market is thought to affect the pattern of structural change in several ways. First, the timing of structural changes can be influenced by this factor. Amongst the poorest countries the share of manufacturing in GDP tends to increase most rapidly in those with large domestic markets. Accelerated growth of the manufacturing sector, however, is often delayed in these countries until somewhat higher levels of per capita income are attained. Second, for countries at comparable levels of income the volume of trade is of greater importance in small economies than for those with large domestic markets. Finally, the size of the domestic market can influence the nature of some policy decisions (Chenery and Syrquin, 1975, p. 74). At early stages of development, the observed pattern of imports provides a useful guide for identification of new manufacturing opportunities. A 'natural' process of import replacement or substitution will occur in any country – large or small – as new industries are developed to supply domestic needs previously met through imports. The substitution of domestic production for imports is mainly attributed to changes in the relative costs of factors of production as incomes rise and to a reorganization of industries which leads to mass production and away from handicraft methods and service-related manufacturing (Chenery, 1960, p. 644). Governments have frequently made a concerted effort to accelerate this process. Through the use of tariffs, quotas, import licences and other forms of import restriction they may attempt to insulate domestic manufacturers from foreign competitors. 'Protection' of domestic industries allows producers to begin operation, despite relatively high costs. The hope is that costs will eventually fall as the scale of production rises and the quality of the labour force improves. Such tactics are common in countries with domestic markets large enough to provide a wide range of opportunities to protect domestic firms and able to absorb additional output as the scale of production is increased. Brazil, Germany, India, Pakistan and the USA have – at various times in their history – opted for a set of industrial policies giving preference to producers geared to serve the home market, usually in competition with importers.

A second acknowledged group factor is the level of a country's resource endowments. The availability and composition of natural resources will have both a direct and an indirect effect on the sectoral composition of economic activity. A direct effect may be observed in the extent to which the availability of resources either limits or facilitates the growth of major sectors such as mining, manufacturing and agriculture. The availability of precious resources, for example, oil or certain metals, can mean that the relative size of the manufacturing sector is unexpectedly small, while another sector (agriculture or mining) is comparatively large. In contrast, an abundance of the more ubiquitous resources (raw materials for making bricks, cement or certain synthetics) is of little consequence for the country's economic structure. A comparison of structural changes in countries with ample resource endowments and those with only limited resources shows that in the former countries the share of manufacturing in GDP tends both to be smaller and to increase at a slower pace as per capita income rises (UNIDO, 1979a, pp. 49–50).

Resource endowment exerts an indirect effect on economic structure by circumscribing a country's choice of industrial and trade policies. Virtually all countries with ample resources have used them as an export base. For countries which are poor in resources but which have relatively abundant supplies of labour, the link between resource endowment and structural change is perhaps not so strong, although the tendency to specialize in the production of labour-intensive manufactures is common. In exceptional cases, where there is an abundant natural resource base (Australia, Saudi Arabia or Zaire), or a total lack thereof (Hong Kong), endowment can dictate the choice of policies to a large extent.

The 'stage of development' is another group factor to be accounted for in the study of structural change. As per capita income rises, the composition of demand and supply will change, sometimes significantly. In attempting to generalize about the nature of changes in demand patterns, analysts (Chenery and Syrquin, 1975, p. 60) drew attention to Engel's law. The law specifies that the proportion of income spent on food will decline as incomes rise. A corresponding rise in non-food consumption – particularly in manufactures – used to be expected. More recent and precise formulations of Engel's law have cast doubt on this supposition, however. Pasinetti (1981, p. 70), for example, has argued that 'the proportion of income spent on any type of good changes as per capita increases'. Furthermore, shifts in patterns of consumption may depend on some vague order of priority of consumers' needs. Although products will eventually be developed corresponding to new consumer wants, the empiricists' original supposition that the evolution of consumer wants will be similar in different countries now seems questionable.

On the supply side, investigators offered more extensive reasons to expect some degree of uniformity in patterns of structural change. A country's available stock of capital was observed to increase with economic growth and rise in income levels. The share of savings in national income was expected to rise due to rapid growth in the modern, capitalist sector which has a high potential for saving. With greater affluence, investments in education and training would expand, leading to an increase in the proportion of the work force which is skilled or semi-skilled. All these trends should help to boost labour productivity, since a growing number of skilled workers would be provided with additional capital equipment.

Once per capita incomes have reached levels common in most Western countries, the predominant features of demand and supply characteristics change. Further additions to income are likely to be spent on social services, entertainment and recreation. The age structure of the population in Western countries is also considerably older than that in LDCs, resulting in heavy demands for specialized services such as medical treatment and welfare programmes. On the supply side, a rising proportion of investment funds may be required for pollution abatement or for the extraction of increasingly scarce raw materials and energy. Both requirements reduce manufacturing output per unit of investment, making industrial growth more expensive. Finally, certain trends in the job market – an increasing demand for leisure and part-time employment or a decline in geographical mobility, for example – will mean that manufacturing offers a less attractive source of employment than in the past.

Based on such lines of reasoning, empirical studies of structural patterns have served several useful purposes. First, they have provided a yardstick for classification and a framework for analysis. Second, the evidence which has accumulated has led economists to reconsider the traditional notion of a dichotomy between developed countries and LDCs and to replace it with the more accurate concept of a transition from one structure to another. Third, studies of structural change have broadened the search for the causes of industrial growth. Contrary to the usual presumption that shifts in the composition of demand were the main cause of growth, the studies have also stressed the importance of changes in supply conditions (for example, shifts in relative factor costs or the substitution of domestic production for imports). Finally, such studies have raised important issues relating to the nature and consequence of structural change and have permitted a more informed discussion of those issues (Kirkpatrick, Lee and Nixson, 1984, p. 39).

Despite these benefits, structural analysis has not escaped criticism. One danger is that the results are interpreted in a normative sense, meaning that they are regarded as indications of a 'desirable' pattern of structural change which, in turn, can yield inferences for policy formulation and planning in LDCs. Some critics have cautioned that structural analysis can merely provide an indication of typical patterns which are neither necessary nor desirable (Sutcliffe, 1971, p. 62). Others have gone further to suggest that the significance of a universal set of structural determinants is exaggerated. Attempts to identify structural patterns having general applicability will be frustrated by the diverse number of structural determinants, all of which are particular to the individual country. In practice, the number of criteria involved would be so numerous as to make the exercise futile (Batchelor, Major and Morgan, 1980, pp. 55–56).

An alternative line of criticism concerns the statistics used to derive uniform patterns of structural change. Owing to the lack of sufficient information, investigators have relied upon inter-country (or cross-section) data. Structural patterns are based on figures for a number of countries at different levels of income. However, they incorporate very little data regarding long-run or secular trends in individual countries. Based on this fact, critics of the structuralist approach, notably Kuznets (1971, p. 197) and Jameson (1982, p. 444), have concluded that the results of cross-sectional studies will underestimate long-run trends in individual countries.

In conclusion, most analysts would seem to agree that there is some degree of constancy in the economic structure. Furthermore changes in economic structure can be regarded as permanent, rather than transient shifts which occur as a result of adjustments in underlying economic and/or political determinants. While these characteristics are essentially faithful to the structuralist's viewpoint, the interpretation adopted here differs in certain respects from the larger body of empirical work on the subject. The latter research has been dominated by an inductive approach which seeks to establish laws of growth. The results are then offered as a guide to policy-makers and planners working at both national and international levels. The present volume stops short of this claim. Instead, the lines of causation between structure and policy are thought to operate in both directions. In some instances governments will take the initiative and attempt to alter the structure of the manufacturing sector according to their own objectives. In other instances the formulation of policies is seen as a reaction to agitation and pressure by groups outside the government. This 'concession' to the critics of structural analysis strips the concept of its claim to serve as a basis for policy-makers to chart their actions. The notion of structural change nevertheless provides a coherent framework for the discussion of issues which motivate governments, industrialists and pressure groups alike. Based on this line of reasoning, sector-wide patterns of structural change are surveyed in the following section.

Structural Change in the Post-War Era

The stylized picture of structural change that emerges from the studies described above highlights the role of the manufacturing sector. At relatively low levels of income the share of manufacturing in GDP is small. But the pace of structural change accelerates once intermediate levels of income are attained and the share of the manufacturing sector expands disproportionately. As economic progress continues, and higher levels of income are realized, the manufacturing sector's share in GDP continues to grow, albeit at a slower pace, after the country reaches a 'mature' stage of development.

This impression of the 'typical' pattern of structural change can be examined in terms of post-war trends. Table 3.1 shows growth performance in several sectors in 1960–75, the period of most rapid expansion in the world economy. On average, manufacturing grew more rapidly than other economic sectors, particularly in socialist countries and LDCs. The growth performance of the manufacturing sector in Western countries was not so impressive. Nevertheless, along with transport and communications and wholesale and retail trade, the sector was still among the most rapidly expanding.

The relationship between the size of the manufacturing sector and the level of per capita income becomes clearer from an examination of Table 3.2. The data refer to weighted

Table 3.1 Growth Rates[a] of Selected Sectors, by Economic Grouping, 1960–75 (percentage)

Sector	Western countries	Socialist countries	LDCs	World
Agriculture	1.8	0.8	2.8	1.8
Manufacturing	5.2	8.7	7.4	6.1
Construction	3.6	6.7	6.6	4.6
Wholesale and retail trade	5.1	6.8	6.1	5.4
Transport and communications	5.3	7.4	6.4	5.7
Other[b]	4.1	7.0	6.2	4.3

Sources: UNIDO, 1979a, p. 43
[a] Calculated at constant prices.
[b] Including mining and quarrying, electricity, gas and water, financing, insurance and real estate, community, social and personal services.

Table 3.2 Share of Manufacturing in GDP, by Economic Grouping and Income Level (percentage)

Economic grouping	1960	1965	1970	1975	1980	1981	1982
LDCs by income group[a]							
Low	11.2	13.6	13.8	14.1	15.0	15.2	15.0
Lower-middle	11.0	12.3	13.5	14.6	16.4	16.5	16.6
Intermediate	10.6	12.6	14.4	16.0	17.1	17.6	17.6
Upper-middle	19.4	19.5	21.6	22.0	24.1	23.8	23.3
High	17.2	16.4	16.2	17.0	17.2	17.0	17.9
All LDCs	14.2	15.4	16.6	17.7	19.0	19.0	19.0
Western countries	25.6	27.5	28.3	27.6	27.9	27.6	27.1
Socialist countries[b]	32.0	37.4	42.4	47.3	50.5	50.8	50.8

Sources: UNIDO, 1986a, Table 5.
[a] Income groups are defined in terms of the 1978 levels of gross domestic product per capita as follows: low income <$295; lower-middle income, $295 to $600; intermediate income, $600 to $1,320; upper-middle income, $1,320 to $2,415; and high income, >$2,415.
[b] Figures refer to the share of MVA (estimated) in net material product.

71

averages for the share of MVA in GDP in various groups of countries. The share of manufacturing tended to rise in countries at all levels of income throughout the 1960s and early 1970s. In later years, however, the upward trend in manufacturing has applied to only the poorer countries. Among the richer LDCs (those with a per capita income greater than $1,320 in 1978), the average share of MVA has fluctuated erratically while it has stagnated in the socialist bloc and declined in Western countries. The relative decline in the LDCs was not necessarily due to a slowdown in growth of manufacturing; rather, it resulted from the rapid expansion of petroleum production in OPEC countries. In industrialized countries, however, the fall in the manufacturing sector's share must be due to other causes.

Table 3.3 provides more detail on trends in several Western countries, showing the manufacturing sector's share of GDP and total employment throughout most of the post-war period. With only two exceptions (Italy and Japan), the share of MVA in 1982 was below levels reported for 1955. The contractions were most pronounced when stated in current prices. This result has been attributed to the fact that the prices of manufactures have generally tended to fall relative to non-manufactures (Brown and Sheriff, 1978, pp. 239–240). The relative decline (stated in current prices) was especially sharp in Canada, Netherlands, Norway and the UK, a feature discussed in more detail later in this chapter. Employment figures show a more gradual downward trend. In general, however, the relative contraction of manufacturing is a widespread phenomenon in Western countries and has continued for more than a decade.

Similar figures for several LDCs are given in Table 3.4. The countries concerned are a fairly diverse group in terms of market size, level of development and resource endowment. Wide variations in the figures for different countries underline the difficulties encountered in fitting national trends into a general structural framework. In fact, only one trend is clearly apparent from Table 3.4: the share of manufacturing in total employment has generally risen over time. Data for MVA reveal no similar evidence. A comparison of figures for the first and last years (figures expressed at

Table 3.3 Share of Manufacturing in GDP and Total Employment in Selected Western Countries (percentage)

Country	Share of MVA in GDP at current prices				Share of MVA in GDP at constant prices			Share of manufacturing in total employment			
	1955	1965	1975	1982	1965	1975	1982	1955	1965	1975	1982
Belgium	29	30	27	24	33	27	27	34	35	30	24
Canada	28	23	19	16	28	19	17	26	24	20	18
France	36	35	27	25[a]	36	29	28	27	28	28	25
Italy	26	29	30	28	25	29	31	23	29	33	26
Japan	22	32	30	31	...	30	40	18	24	26	24
Netherlands	31	32	27	18[b]	...	...	...	30[c]	28	24	21
Norway	27	25	22	14	26	20	15	25	26	24	20
Sweden	32	26	26	20	34	23	20	34[d]	32	28	22
West Germany	41	40	34	32	44	34	33	34[e]	38	36	33
UK	37	30	26	21	...	...	...	40	35	31	25
USA	30	29	23	21	27	23	23	26	25	23	20

Sources: UNIDO (1981a), Table I.9; United Nations, *Yearbook of National Accounts* (various issues); OECD, *Labour Force Statistics* (various issues); and ILO, *ILO Yearbook* (various issues).

[a] 1957.
[b] 1981.
[c] 1980.
[d] 1956.
[e] 1961.

Table 3.4 Share of Manufacturing in GDP and Total Employment in Selected LDCs (percentage)

LDC	Share of MVA in GDP							Share of manufacturing in total employment		
	at current prices				at constant prices					
	1960	1965	1975	1981	1965	1975	1981	1965	1975	1981
Argentina	28	31	32	25	31	25	20	...	...	...
Bolivia	13	14	13	17	17	15	16	...	9	10
Chile	...	26	20	22	24	21	21	...	17	16
Columbia	18	20	23	21	19	23	21	...	24	26
Cyprus	10	10	14	17	10	13	16	14	18	21
Egypt	19	20	18	12[b]	19[c]	17	16[d]	11[c]	14	16
Haiti	...	...	...	...	10	14	17	...	6	7
India	14	15	16	15	16	13	14	...	26	26
Jamaica	15	17	16	16	15	18	15	11	11	11
Kenya	8	10	12	11	10	8	12	9	12	14
Korea, South	14	18	27	29	11	26	33	9	19	20
Mexico	19[a]	21[a]	23	22	21[a]	24	25	...	18	18[d]
Panama	13	15	15	10	16	11	10	9	9	10[f]

Country										
Peru	...	...	25	28	22	26	25	...	16	15
Philippines	22	21	25	25	15	24	25	...	11	8
Sierra Leone	6	6	8	7[b]	6	10	9	...	10	13
Singapore	12	15	24	29	15	21	24	14[e]	26	30
Sri Lanka	...	8	25	17	8	25	20	...	19	17[b]
Syria	15	15	10	10	15	7	3	11	12	16[d]
Thailand	13	14	18	20	16	18	21	...	7	8[b]
Trinidad and Tobago	14	17	14	8	...	16	15	19[c]	20[c]	17[c]
Tunisia	9	9	10	12	7	9	12	...	17	22
Venezuela	...	...	16	15	13	16	18	...	15	16
Zambia	...	7	16	18	7	11	11	10	11	12
Zimbabwe	16	17	22	23	...	20	19	...	15	17

Sources: UNIDO (1981a), Table I.9; United Nations, *Yearbook of National Accounts* (various issues); OECD, *Labour Force Statistics* (various issues); ILO, *ILO Yearbook* (various issues).

[a] Excludes basic petroleum manufacturing.
[b] 1980.
[c] Includes mining.
[d] 1979.
[e] 1957.
[f] 1982.

both current and constant prices) show an increase in the sector's share of GDP for a majority of countries. Quite often, however, this was not the result of a consistent upward trend as in several instances a significant fall was reported for interim years.

A more general impression which emerges from Table 3.4 is that the economic structure in many LDCs is probably less stable than in Western countries. Economic and political events can bring about significant shifts in a country's structure in only a few years. In Argentina, for instance, the recent decline in the manufacturing sector's share of GDP can be attributed to the general economic and political malaise experienced in that country. The contraction of manufacturing in Panama, however, is due to a different set of circumstances. Until recently, over 40 per cent of Panamanian manufacturing was concentrated in chemicals (Weeks, 1985, p. 145), a field particularly hard hit by the rise in energy prices in the late 1970s. The country's situation was complicated by the fact that its manufacturers were heavily dependent on export markets and suffered as a result of the slow growth in world markets. Again, other reasons explain the fall in the share of manufacturing in Syria. Mineral extraction (largely petroleum) expanded rapidly during the 1970s and, alongside a modest manufacturing base, led to a relative contraction in that sector (UNIDO, 1981a, p. 49). To some extent, the fragility of the economic structure in LDCs runs counter to the description in Chapter 1 which characterized structural change as representing a gradual but permanent process rather than an abrupt or cyclical phenomena. Certainly, caution must be used in interpreting long-run patterns of change in individual LDCs and a knowledge of the political and social framework is required.

Although the stylized impression of structural change appears to provide a synopsis of post-war trends during years of rapid growth, it is not clear that the same formulation is equally relevant to the experience of many countries after the early 1970s – a period of considerably slower growth in world industry. A more systematic examination is required to gain a clear picture of structural trends in the 'slow growth' era. Table 3.5 provides extensive information for the period 1973–82, which suggests that the presumed relationship between growth of MVA and per capita GDP was much weaker than in earlier years. First, in a significant number of countries the manufacturing sector experienced a relative contraction after 1973. When estimates are in current prices, this was the case for the majority (seventy) of the countries. Even when the sector's share is compared to 'commodity' GDP (defined as GDP excluding services) a contraction was not uncommon. The manufacturing sector lost ground not only relative to services but relative to other sectors as well. Second, a fall in the share of MVA is observed in countries at all levels of development. A levelling off or contraction in the share of manufacturing is not necessarily a surprising result in Western countries, which are widely presumed to have reached a mature stage of industrial development. However, a downward trend occurred not only in the majority of Western countries but in more than one-third of the LDCs, including some of the poorer ones. Moreover, the fall was apparent whether measured at current or at constant prices. This suggests that a general deterioration in the prices of manufactures relative to those of non-manufactures was not the only explanation. Third, most analysts had previously assumed that the direction of change in GDP per capita and the share of manufacturing would coincide – at least for LDCs. After 1973, however, the two measures moved in a contrary fashion in almost one-half the countries considered in Table 3.5. In other words, many countries recording an increase (decrease) in per capita GDP also experienced a decline (increase) in the manufacturing sector's share of GDP.

Together, these results provide some grounds to suspect that the dynamic role commonly attributed to manufacturing in economic growth has waned since the mid–1970s. If such a shift is a lasting feature of world industry, the eventual consequences for trade, investment and other fields will be significant. These trends have more immediate implications for industrial policy, however. Any indication of widespread contraction (even a relative one) within manufacturing has

Table 3.5 Growth and Structural Relationships between MVA and GDP,[a] 1973–82 (number of occurrences)

Country grouping	Countries	Decline in the share of MVA in GDP	Decline in the share of MVA in GDP (less services)	Divergent direction of change between the share of MVA in GDP and the growth of GDP per capita
Western countries	26 (27)	21 (16)	13 (7)	21 (16)
LDCs of which:	95 (98)	49 (41)	43 (32)	37 (34)
Low income	48 (51)	25 (25)	21 (22)	16 (15)
Middle income	24 (24)	10 (9)	10 (6)	9 (10)
High income	23 (23)	14 (7)	12 (4)	12 (9)
Total	121 (125)	70 (57)	56 (39)	58 (50)

Source: UNIDO, 1985b, p. 26.

[a] Figures in brackets are calculated from constant prices data. Other figures are from current prices data.

roused the concern of Western governments, as well as participants in contracting industries and the general public. And in an era already dominated by an atmosphere of competitive competition, this has led to widespread fears of de-industrialization, coupled with calls for re-industrialization and appeals for 'new industrial policies'. Such reactions have been most obvious in the USA, but they are also common in Western Europe. The policies which have been fashioned in response to these concerns are considered in later chapters, while the following section provides a closer look at the actual process of de-industrialization.

De-Industrialization

The prospect of de-industrialization is widely regarded as being undesirable, but there is little agreement on the precise meaning of the term. Blackaby (1978, p. 1) appropriately describes the term as having 'gatecrashed the literature, thereby avoiding the entrance fee of a definition, and also avoiding critical scrutiny at the door'. Some economists (and many politicians) choose to regard the process as another aspect of structural change. According to this interpretation, a relative decline in the manufacturing sector's share of total output or employment is tantamount to de-industrialization. When defined in this manner, however, there are good reasons to expect that de-industrialization is an inevitable result of growth and change. First, labour productivity in manufacturing tends to grow faster than in agriculture or services. A country's overall pattern of employment will eventually change as a result of sectoral differences in rates of productivity growth and it is likely that the share of manufacturing in total employment will decline. Second, in rich countries normal shifts in demand patterns complement the effects of differential rates of growth in productivity. The income elasticity of demand for services usually exceeds that for manufactures. As income rises, the growth in aggregate demand will favour producers of services and mean that a greater proportion of national resources will gradually be channelled into that sector. The implications of this approach pose difficult problems for policy-makers. They are faced with the unenviable task of attempting to formulate policies that will effectively reverse the most fundamental and basic trends associated with long-term patterns of growth in productivity and demand.

But when de-industrialization is pictured in this way, even the measurement of the process raises certain problems. A slowdown in the growth of manufacturing may eventually result in a relatively lower growth rate of GDP. In part, this result is merely a statistical one; manufacturing presently accounts for 25–40 per cent of GDP in Western countries and poor performance in that sector will depress overall economic growth. In addition, manufacturing is an important supplier of capital goods and crucial inputs to agriculture, construction, transport and services. Any deterioration in the performance of domestic manufacturers is likely to have a depressing impact on other sectors – even in open economies which depend heavily on imports. Thus, international variations in the ratio of MVA to GDP may simply reflect national differences in the rapidity with which the effects of a slowdown in manufacturing are transmitted to other parts of the economy.

The use of employment statistics to measure de-industrialization poses other problems. The manufacturing sector's share in total employment is usually expressed according to the number of workers or, alternatively, the number of man-years. But a rise in part-time employment is common in all Western countries and has been concentrated in services. This trend would exaggerate the fall in the share of manufacturing employment. More important is the fact that employment shifts out of manufacturing, if associated with dramatic improvements in that sector's labour productivity, would be a desirable feature. For such reasons, a particular target, or range for the share of manufacturing, in total employment may have little meaning.

Many commentators would prefer a narrower definition of de-industrialization than that sketched above. Some argue that the process can be set in motion by a dramatic improvement in a country's balance of trade – usually the discovery and export of a scarce natural resource. The development of oil or gas exports can undermine the country's manufacturing sector by virtue of the stronger exchange rate which would result from an improvement in the balance of payments. A substantial rise in the rate of exchange would depress the prices of imports and would make exporting more difficult, as prices (when expressed in foreign currency) would be higher. Because trade in manufactures often accounts for such a large portion of the total, the burden of exchange rate adjustments would be borne by that sector.

According to this interpretation, de-industrialization can be described as 'a progressive failure to achieve a sufficient surplus of exports over imports of manufactures to keep the economy in external balance' (Blackaby, 1978, p. 263). Support for this view is found in the experience of the Dutch economy following the discovery of natural gas in the 1960s. But there is also evidence that similar phenomena, in various guises, have occurred in much earlier times. For example, Forsyth and Nicholas (1983) have examined the consequences of the inflow of American treasure into Spanish industry in the sixteenth century, while Maddock and McLean (1984) have considered the effects of Australian gold discoveries on that country's industry in the 1850s. More recently, the 'Dutch disease' was thought to have spread to Norway and the UK when those countries became net exporters of oil. In discussing the recent evidence Corden (1984, p. 359) suggests that the real problem may not be the adverse effects on manufacturing of an appreciation in the exchange rate but rather that the revenues generated by the export boom are expended for purposes which eventually prove to be unsustainable (in the Dutch case, an increase in social services).

In the longer run, one of the symptoms of the Dutch disease is that the domestic prices of non-traded goods tend to rise relative to those of traded goods. A structural problem can emerge as resources are siphoned away from the latter producers which, again, are likely to be manufacturers. This result could be seen to be an ominous one – particularly for those who choose to stress the basic importance of technological progress. Generally, technological progress is thought to proceed fastest in fields such as manufacturing where trade (both imports and exports) is an important feature. Furthermore, technological progress is not necessarily an autonomous process which occurs with the passage of time but, rather, is the result of the accumulated experience of the country's producers (van Wijnbergen, 1984, p. 41). Because manufacturing is a sector where technological progress is particularly important, an absolute (not a relative) contraction may permanently lower per capita income in comparison with what might otherwise have been attained. This possibility could equally apply to LDCs such as Mexico or Venezuela, as well as to the Netherlands, Norway or the UK. And if the manufacturing sector can be aptly regarded as the 'engine room of growth', the consequences of such a contraction may well be serious enough to justify the use of stringent government efforts to prevent decline.

Given the difficulties in defining de-industrialization, it is not surprising there is little agreement as to the causes. Some economists (for example, Bacon and Eltis, 1976) and politicians have attributed de-industrialization to an expansion of the public sector; the government's claim on employment and investment may have 'crowded out' competing demands of private industry. Others have suggested that the fundamental problem may be due to managerial inadequacy or to rigidities in labour markets (Kilpatrick and Lawson, 1980). Still another hypothesis is that the income elasticity of demand for the country's exports may be significantly smaller than the country's income elasticity of demand for imports; again, in the long run, a decline is inevitable.

The difficulties in assessing the extent and consequences of de-industrialization are complicated by the fact that manufacturing activities in most Western countries have gradually taken on a greater 'service orientation'. Quite probably, many functions now being performed by manufacturing firms could more accurately be attributed to the service sector. Although this opinion is widely held, supporting evidence is scarce. In part the problem is a statistical one. National accounting practices in most countries treat services as consisting of all output which does not originate in goods-producing sectors (agriculture, mining, manufacturing and construction). Wholesale and retail trade, producer services, transport, entertainment, finance and many other activities are all included in the service sector, which makes it a residual category consisting of a large number of unrelated operations. Despite the heterogeneous nature, most working definitions include two common characteristics: the fact that services cannot be stockpiled or stored and the stipulation that service transactions usually occur between separate economic units or firms (Hill, 1977). Conventional statistical practices, however, are not sufficiently detailed to permit an identification of the extent to which service activities are carried out in other sectors.

De-industrialization is only partly a statistical artefact, however. At a more fundamental level it reflects the maturing process in various industries and accompanying changes in the organizational structure of firms. Although empirical evidence is not available, there are several reasons for believing that many industries are gradually assuming a greater service orientation in their day-to-day operations which is not accurately reflected in the national data. As has already been noted, there is a tendency for firms in maturing industries to turn away from price competition and to emphasize product differentiation and production special-ization. Such practices necessarily entail a close relationship between producers and consumers. As these relationships evolve, firms must naturally assume various service-related responsibilities. The case of chemicals was offered as one example of the way mature industries endeavour to develop new products to meet the needs of specific users, or to satisfy the characteristics of a specific market. The emergence of service-related functions is even more apparent in indus-tries supplying sophisticated, high-technology products. For instance, the growing range of product applications for computers, microprocessors and electronic components such as integrated circuits has forced producers to augment their original engineering skills. To meet the diverse needs of new buyers it was necessary that such firms undertake additional, service-related tasks, including the design of products to suit specialized needs, the development of software for new applications and assistance in the installation and maintenance of the equipment. Even in staid industries like food processing, however, the proliferation of specialized products (for example, high-protein, low-fat, or vegetarian items) has meant that major firms have gradually expanded service-related functions in fields such as distribution, retailing, packaging, R and D and similar activities.

More generally, there is a synergistic relationship binding the two sectors whereby 'services will splinter off from goods and goods which, in turn, splinter off from services' (Bhagwati, 1984, pp. 136–137). In the first instance, as firms became larger the degree of internal specialization becomes considerably extended. To facilitate such specialization large firms impose a decentralized operating structure by building up the groups responsible for various service functions such as R and D, marketing, advertising, employee relations and government relations. Similarly, manufacturers of high-price consumer items such as automobiles, refrigerators or televisions recognize that they stand to gain almost as much by extending credit (a service function) as by marking up their products. Accordingly, they create new divisions to tap this market. But because the compilation of data on national accounts concerns only exchanges between separate economic units, these intra-unit transactions are recorded as part of the firm's manufacturing operations – not as services. Eventually, however, the economies of scale which originally prompted specialization may be moved out of the firm and become part of inter-firm transactions. Thus transport, accounting, repair and maintenance, the supply of parts and components, or any number of other responsibilities, will be subcontracted to outside firms. This pattern of specialization merely reflects another type of inter-industry relationship. It is independent of any demand influence although, statistically, the result is a fall in manufacturing output and a rise in services.

The reverse sequence – the possibility that new goods emerge from service activities – is illustrated by the development of the gramophone and, more recently, the video recorder. The latter are goods and the technological advances upon which they were based gave rise to new manufactured products. This disembodiment of goods from services has various implications for any assessment of technical progress or trade performance in the two sectors (Bhagwati, 1984, p. 137). The point of immediate concern, however, is that the appeal of these new products or disembodied services – in fact their existence – is dependent on the performance of related services. And the rapid development of new services, coupled with improvements in their quality, can only spur additional spin-offs for manufacturers. The significance of this chain of events for a given country is open to conjecture but the proliferation of service-dependent products is obvious. Ironically, current government responses to de-industrialization are typically attempts to reverse the prevailing directions of structural change and, as a result, could stifle the development of those services with a potential to stimulate the development of new goods.

Given the complexity of the issues involved, coupled with data limitations and the fact that we have less than complete knowledge of the interrelationships between manufacturing and services, the general debate on de-industrialization in Western countries will continue in various forms. Certainly, fears of de-industrialization have captured the attention of governments and their constituencies alike. The consequences are often described in apocalyptic terms, arousing wide sentiment for the appeals of special interest groups in contracting industries. The 're-industrialization' of Western economies has become a popular, if vaguely defined, goal. But such a goal for countries which are steadily becoming more dominated by services (perhaps to a greater extent than we actually know) may be futile.

The following chapter looks at recent patterns of structural change in more detail, examining trends in individual industries within the manufacturing sector.

Supplementary Reading

Arguments for the use of structural analysis as a guide for national and international policy are given in Chenery

(1979). Ranis (1984) compares the methods and lines of emphasis followed by Chenery and his associates with those of other 'structuralists'. A thorough discussion of the statistical considerations involved in estimating sector-wide patterns of structural change is found in Chenery and Syrquin (1975, pp. 141–77). These methods have been applied in the estimation of growth paths for manufacturing by UNIDO (1979a, pp. 331–64). With regard to the empirical evidence on this subject, UNIDO produces the *Industrial Development Survey*, *a biennial review* which examines structural change on a global scale. Similar studies on structural change in Europe are published by the United Nations Economic Commission for Europe (ECE).

An introduction to the issue of de-industrialization is provided by Blackaby (1978). For a more formal analysis of the subject see Corden (1984) and the references cited there. Bluestone and Harrison (1982), in their analysis of American de-industrialization, focus on the total number of jobs lost. Lawrence (1984), who also confines his discussion to the USA, suggests a number of other factors which have led to a contraction of that country's industrial base. Alternative explanations for de-industrialization, with particular reference to the UK, are found in Kaldor (1966), Bacon and Eltis (1976) and Kilpatrick and Lawson (1980).

CHAPTER FOUR

Structural Change within the Manufacturing Sector

A distinctive style of investigation was developed in the course of empirical research on structural change – one which was dominated by an inductive approach which sought to identify similarities in sectoral patterns of growth. The gradually widening industrial base in many countries, along with the greater availability of data, led economists to carry their approach to a more specific level of analysis which focused on groups of industries within manufacturing.

Chapter 4 begins with a review of alternative interpretations of structural change, examining each in terms of recent trends in the composition of MVA. The discussion is confined to a 'domestic' picture of the industrial structure, in that changes in the composition of MVA are gauged in relation to the country's manufacturing base or MVA. But the subject can also be addressed from an international perspective and in the second half of Chapter 4 that approach is adopted. Once the discussion is placed in an international framework marked contrasts between different industries emerge, which make the search for similarities in structural patterns even more problematic. However, the advantages of this approach are several in view of the unmistakably international character of today's industries and the significance which public officials and governments attach to this dimension.

Interpretations and Evidence

An account of the several interpretations offered to explain structural patterns within the manufacturing sector can begin with a look at the actual composition of world MVA. Table 4.1 represents the industrial structure in terms of weighted averages for each of the three groups of countries: LDCs, socialist countries and Western countries. An examination of the figures provides a basis for several inferences. First, there is some evidence pointing to systematic differences in the industrial structure, depending on the level of development. In the LDCs, for instance, a comparatively large portion of MVA is accounted for by industries supplying consumer goods (for example, food, beverages or textiles) while, in developed countries, industries producing capital goods are most prominent. Second, in a majority of cases, the share of a specific industry followed a consistent trend – either upward or downward – during the period considered. Although the composition of MVA may be subject to cyclical factors, long-term changes would seem to depend on other, more fundamental, determinants as well. Third, the direction of change was usually (but not always) repeated in each of the country groupings. The evidence is not sufficient to support broad generalizations about structural patterns but it does suggest some similarities in the rise and fall of specific industries.

Based on such impressions, economists undertook more systematic investigations into the international composition of MVA. Early studies on industrial structure took their inspiration from the theoretical distinction between consumption and investment. The manufacturing sector was divided into two groups of industries: those producing consumption goods and those producing capital goods (Hoffman, 1958). This characterization highlighted broad differences in the factor requirements and demand patterns of the two industrial groups. Industries producing consumer goods were thought to be relatively labour-intensive, while those supplying capital goods were regarded as requiring correspondingly large investments in plant and equipment.

And because the share of investment in GDP generally rose as economic progress continued, domestic demand for capital goods was expected to grow more rapidly than demand for consumer goods. However, the growth of various industries was subsequently seen to be determined by other considerations as well – investments in R and D, the availability of skilled labour or considerations relating to marketing or organization. The theoretical distinction between consumption and investment goods was eventually dropped and the term 'light' and 'heavy' industry are now used in their place.

A second, closely related, interpretation of structural change provided for a more detailed breakdown. The classification, which was demand-inspired, arranged industries in three groups according to the nature of the final product: consumer goods, industrial supplies or intermediates and capital goods. Once the structure of the manufacturing sector was depicted in these terms the statistical analysis of trends in both Western countries and LDCs pointed to certain similarities in the changing composition of manufacturing output (Chenery, 1960; UNIDO, 1974, Chapter 1). Like the study of sectoral patterns, inferences were drawn from data spanning only a limited period of time but a large number of countries at different levels of income were included in the survey. Thus, in countries with a per capita income level of US$100, over two-thirds of MVA was typically devoted to the production of consumer goods, while only 12 per cent was accounted for by capital goods. At a per capita income of US$600, the respective shares were 43 per cent and 35 per cent. Intermediate industries were found to have a fairly constant (or only slightly increasing) share of MVA among countries at different levels of income (Chenery, 1960, pp. 630–39).

The suggestion that the composition of the manufacturing sector changed in a fairly uniform way in different countries was not made without qualifications. Economies of scale were known to be particularly important for some industries (paper, petroleum refining, steel or non-ferrous metals, for example). These industries could be expected to be of comparatively greater importance in countries with domestic

Table 4.1 Structure of MVA[a], by Country Grouping (percentage)

Branch	ISIC code	LDCs[b]			Socialist countries			Western countries		
		1963	1973	1982	1963	1973	1982	1963	1973	1982
Food products	311/2	19.0	14.5	14.6	15.2	11.8	9.2	10.4	8.4	9.5
Beverages	313	3.3	2.8	3.6	2.7	2.0	1.9	2.0	1.9	2.1
Tobacco	314	3.6	2.7	2.8	1.0	0.7	0.5	1.0	0.8	0.8
Textiles	321	14.0	10.6	8.5	8.7	6.9	5.5	5.4	4.5	3.7
Clothing	322	3.7	2.6	2.4	5.4	4.7	4.3	3.5	2.8	2.4
Leather and fur products	323	0.9	0.6	0.5	1.0	0.7	0.6	0.7	0.4	0.4
Footwear	324	1.5	1.0	0.9	2.1	1.5	1.3	1.0	0.6	0.6
Wood and cork products	331	2.6	2.1	2.1	2.7	1.9	1.4	2.4	2.1	1.7
Furniture and fixtures excluding metal	332	1.4	1.1	0.9	1.4	1.4	1.4	2.0	2.1	1.9
Paper	341	2.3	2.5	2.4	1.2	1.1	0.9	3.8	3.8	3.8
Printing and publishing	342	3.0	2.4	1.9	1.0	1.0	0.8	5.1	4.3	4.7
Industrial chemicals	351	2.4	3.7	4.1	3.8	5.4	5.8	3.8	5.3	5.2
Other chemicals	352	4.5	5.9	7.7	0.9	1.1	1.0	3.4	3.8	4.7
Petroleum refineries	353	6.8	9.1	9.5	0.9	1.4	1.2	1.5	1.7	1.5
Miscellaneous products of petroleum and coal	354	0.5	0.7	0.6	1.2	0.8	0.6	0.6	0.3	0.3

Industry	ISIC									
Rubber products	355	1.7	1.8	1.6	1.1	1.2	1.1	1.4	1.5	1.3
Plastic products	356	0.9	1.4	1.2	0.3	0.7	0.8	0.9	2.0	2.4
Pottery, china and earthenware	361	0.9	0.7	0.6	0.8	0.8	0.9	0.6	0.5	0.4
Glass	362	0.7	1.0	1.0	0.8	0.9	1.1	0.9	0.9	1.0
Other non-metallic mineral products	369	3.2	3.5	4.6	5.2	5.1	4.0	3.0	3.0	2.5
Iron and steel	371	4.2	4.7	5.0	7.5	5.8	4.3	6.7	6.6	4.7
Non-ferrous metals	372	1.8	1.9	1.7	2.6	2.8	2.5	1.7	1.8	1.5
Metal products, excluding machinery	381	4.0	4.6	4.3	...	...	...	7.2	7.3	6.7
Non-electrical machinery	382	2.7	5.1	4.2	...[c]	...[c]	...[c]	10.4	11.0	11.5
Electrical machinery	383	3.1	4.4	5.5	30.5	37.6	45.8	6.7	8.7	10.6
Transport equipment	384	5.2	7.0	6.1	...	...	...	10.3	10.3	10.0
Professional and scientific equipment, photographic and optical goods	385	0.4	0.4	0.4	...	...	...	1.7	1.9	2.3
Other manufactures	390	1.7	1.2	1.3	2.0	2.7	3.1	1.9	1.7	1.8
Total manufacturing	3	100.0	100.0	100.0	100.0	100.0	100.0	100.0	100.0	100.0

Sources: UNIDO, 1986a, Table 9.

[a] Excluding Albania, China, Iceland and Luxembourg.

[b] The date for 1963 cover seventy-three countries, which, in 1975, accounted for 97 per cent of the MVA of all LDCs; the data for 1973 and 1982 cover sixty-four countries, which, in 1975, accounted for 92 per cent of the MVA of all LDCs. Therefore, although the structures for all years are probably representative of LDCs as a whole, the variation in country composition should be noted. All estimates are based on data stated at constant prices.

[c] Percentages refer to all industries within the group ISIC 38.

markets which were of sufficient size to absorb high levels of output. The attention to other group factors was also retained. For instance, country differences in factor endowments, in the distribution of income and cultural or political factors were other elements which could result in departures from the typical pattern of structural change.

A more elaborate attempt to identify similarities in the changing composition of manufacturing output was subsequently offered by Chenery and Taylor (1968). They distinguished between industries in terms of the *relative* change in income elasticities as the level of income rose. This approach focused on the level of per capita income at which each industry makes its major contribution to growth of the manufacturing sector. At the same time, analysts attempted to take account of some of the more important differences between countries by arranging them into groups according to the size of the domestic market, the country's policy orientation and its level of resource endowment (Chenery and Taylor, 1968; UNIDO, 1979a, Chapter 2).

Three types of industries were identified on this basis. 'Early' industries were those which supplied necessities (for example, food, textiles, clothing or footwear) and were regarded as using fairly simple production technologies. Because demand for these products tended to rise more slowly than the growth of income their share in total MVA declined over time. 'Middle' industries were those whose share of MVA expanded rapidly at low-to-intermediate levels of per capita income. Rubber products, wood products and some chemicals were offered as examples of middle industries. As incomes rose, the growth of domestic demand for these goods would slacken and opportunities for supplanting imports would be exhausted. Eventually, domestic consumers and industries would demand a more sophisticated range of products and 'late' industries, such as printing, paper and metal products, would emerge as the most rapidly expanding parts of the manufacturing sector.

Table 4.2 gives a global picture of long-run changes in the composition of MVA according to each of these overlapping interpretations. Such figures are more useful for describing broad trends rather than serving as precise indicators of the composition of MVA at any point in time. When total MVA is considered in terms of light and heavy industry (according to two different sources of data), the direction of change is clear. Heavy industry predominates in both socialist and Western countries and its share has risen over time, albeit at a declining rate. In fact, studies of individual Western countries – Australia, Canada and the USA – are reported to have found a tendency for the share of heavy industry to stabilize at roughly 50 per cent of MVA (Batchelor, Major and Morgan, 1980, p. 131). While light industry accounts for a comparatively larger portion of total MVA in LDCs, a similar shift in favour of heavy industry is clearly evident.

The more detailed breakdowns of MVA according to end use and income elasticity give some additional insights. Among industrialized countries the impetus for the shift away from light industry was largely due to the expansion of industries producing capital goods and late industries. The contribution of industries providing intermediate products and/or those regarded as having moderate income elasticities were of less significance. Again, the figures for LDCs offer a slight contrast. Middle industries and those producing industrial intermediates have expanded comparatively rapidly in LDCs and now account for a sizeable proportion of total MVA.

Like the wider ranging study of sectoral patterns of structural change, the analysis of industry groups within the manufacturing sector extends our knowledge of general trends, but suffers from several obvious drawbacks. First, the framework of empirical studies relies on a 'broad brush' technique by classifying industries according to very general impressions about their input requirements and demand characteristics. The actual circumstances which a particular industry faces in different countries, however, can vary widely and may limit the general applicability of these impressions. Second, the significance of individual country characteristics is accentuated when the subject of analysis is shifted away from a sector-wide discussion to specific industries. The approach may therefore underestimate the importance of country differences in domestic demand,

Table 4.2 Estimates of the Changing Composition of MVA[a] (percentage)

Industrial subgroup[b]	Advanced socialist countries				Advanced market economies				LDCs			
	1963	1970	1978	1982	1963	1970	1978	1982	1963	1970	1978	1982
I Industrial sub-sector (as compiled from country data)												
light industry	44.6	39.8	33.5	31.8	37.7	34.1	33.0	33.2	56.7	48.6	42.2	42.3
heavy industry	55.4	60.2	66.5	68.2	62.3	65.9	67.0	66.8	43.3	51.4	57.8	57.7
II Industrial sub-sector[c] (as compiled from indices for sub-sector)												
light industry	36.0[d]	33.0	33.3	31.5	35.2[d]	33.0	32.8	32.9	56.8[d]	52.8	43.4	42.8
heavy industry	64.0[d]	67.0	66.7	68.5	64.8[d]	67.0	67.2	67.1	43.2[d]	47.2	56.6	57.2

III End use

consumer non-durables	48.1	43.8	38.7	37.7	37.1	33.0	31.5	31.8	54.5	45.9	39.5	39.8
industrial intermediates	16.2	18.0	18.2	17.4	19.9	21.8	23.3	23.2	24.6	28.2	31.5	33.3
capital goods (including consumer durables)	35.7	38.2	43.1	44.9	43.0	45.2	45.2	45.0	20.9	25.9	29.0	26.9

IV Income elasticity

early industries	29.7	25.2	20.0	18.4	19.8	17.1	16.1	16.6	40.7	34.7	29.7	30.4
middle industries	15.0	14.7	13.6	12.7	15.8	15.5	15.8	15.3	23.0	24.7	27.1	28.6
late industries	53.3	57.6	63.5	65.8	62.5	65.6	66.3	66.3	34.5	39.4	41.9	39.7

Sources: UNIDO (1985c) and (1986a).

[a] All calculations are based on data at constant prices.

[b] For definitions of these industry classifications see the statistical appendix.

[c] Percentages were originally derived from United Nations indices for the two sub-sectors and country coverage was more complete than data compiled from individual country information.

[d] 1965.

resource endowments or the impact of industrial policies. Third, the product range and the extent of product specialization in a given industry can also vary – even among countries at similar levels of development. In the steel industry, for instance, Swedish producers of special steels accounted for one-third of the country's output in the early 1980s, while the corresponding figure for the UK was 1 per cent (Ballance and Sinclair, 1983, p. 121). Demand patterns, production technologies and factor requirements for the two sets of firms differed accordingly. And the contrasts are likely to be even more marked if comparisons are made between a Western country and a LDC. Fourth, there is a network of other determinants which are not easily incorporated into such studies. Examples include the influence of the multinationals, the degree and form of state involvement, the nature of technological advancement and the extent of technology transfer. The influence of each of these determinants can differ between industries and among countries, making it difficult to generalize about their impact on industrial structure.

Industrial Structure in a Global Framework

Our understanding of structural change can be carried one step further by recasting the discussion in an international framework. Previous chapters have stressed the importance of internationalization for firms and policy-makers alike. Whatever their particular concern, industrial strategists cannot afford to adopt a parochial attitude in decisions involving the location of additional capacity, the development of new products, or other competitive moves. Likewise, in the current environment of interdependence and competitive coexistence, countries rather than industries or firms are typically regarded as the real competitors in world markets.

Although an international perspective adds to our understanding of structural patterns, the importance of this approach should not be overdrawn. Conventional economic factors will still influence the global distribution of output in a given industry. Some of the more obvious examples are the availability and cost of various inputs – for example, labour (unskilled, semi-skilled and skilled), domestic resources and production technologies and the nature of demand for the industry's products, in both the home market and abroad. For instance, the rising importance of textile production in LDCs can be partly attributed to the cost advantages which these firms enjoy as a result of the low wage rates which prevail in these countries. Similarly, steel producers in LDCs have benefited from the comparatively rapid growth in domestic demand for that industry's products, while global shifts in the petroleum refining industry reflect the distribution of natural resources and the efforts of major oil-producing countries to move downstream into the production of chemicals and other oil using industries. (Several of these determinants will be considered in more detail in subsequent chapters.) Nevertheless, to the extent that industries have gradually become more politicized and markets have been internationalized, the global configuration of major industries has come to reflect much more than Adam Smith's 'invisible hand'.

Table 4.3 gives an overview of recent shifts in the global pattern of production for several specific industries. When pictured in these terms, the LDCs are a relatively important force in only one industry: petroleum refining. They account for a moderate proportion of world MVA in several consumer goods' industries (food, beverages, tobacco, textiles) and in others which are resource-dependent (products of wood, rubber and non-metallic minerals). Producers in LDCs claim only a minor share of world MVA in various large industries, such as paper, industrial chemicals, electrical and non-electrical machinery and transport equipment, and their relative position in these industries has changed very little since 1970. In the industrialized world, socialist countries are moderately important producers of some consumer goods, resource-based products and certain capital goods (machinery and transport equipment). Curiously, they are of relatively minor significance in several intermediate industries such as paper, printing and other chemicals. Although there are few industries where Western countries have not lost ground relative to producers in other

Table 4.3 Global Distribution of Value Added in Selected Industries (percentage)

Branch	ISIC code	LDCs			Socialist countries			Western countries		
		1970	1975	1982	1970	1975	1982	1970	1975	1982
Food products	311/2	13.9	13.8	16.4	25.4	27.8	26.2	60.7	58.4	57.4
Beverages	313	12.8	14.6	19.1	21.7	23.6	24.2	65.5	61.8	56.7
Tobacco	314	28.1	29.0	33.6	14.7	16.3	16.6	57.2	54.7	49.8
Textiles	321	17.4	18.8	19.9	26.4	30.7	32.9	56.2	50.5	47.2
Footwear	324	10.0	11.3	12.0	36.5	41.4	46.3	53.5	47.3	41.7
Wood and cork products	331	9.8	11.1	13.8	20.0	23.3	24.6	70.2	65.6	61.6
Paper	341	6.7	7.7	9.0	7.2	9.6	9.1	86.1	82.7	81.9
Printing and publishing	342	6.4	6.9	6.4	5.7	7.3	7.3	87.9	85.8	86.3
Industrial chemicals	351	6.0	7.6	8.7	21.7	28.3	31.5	72.3	64.1	59.8
Other chemicals	352	13.4	17.4	21.4	6.5	8.0	7.3	80.1	74.6	71.3
Petroleum refineries	353	35.5	38.3	45.3	13.2	16.0	15.0	51.3	45.7	39.7
Rubber products	355	10.8	12.6	13.9	16.5	21.1	23.6	72.7	66.3	62.5
Pottery, china and earthenware	361	12.2	12.9	11.8	27.0	35.4	43.9	60.8	51.7	44.3
Glass	362	8.2	9.7	11.0	19.1	26.1	30.0	72.7	64.2	59.0
Other non-metallic mineral products	369	8.7	10.7	15.6	31.1	36.1	36.0	60.2	53.2	48.4
Iron and steel	371	6.2	8.1	11.4	19.5	23.9	26.6	74.3	68.0	62.0
Non-ferrous metals	372	8.6	9.2	10.1	29.7	36.6	38.9	61.7	54.2	51.0
Metal products, excluding machinery	381[a]	5.9	6.9	7.1	18.7	26.6	33.6	75.4	66.5	59.3
Non-electrical machinery	382[a]	3.0	4.9	4.3	17.6	23.8	29.6	79.4	71.3	66.1
Electrical machinery	383[a]	5.1	6.3	6.3	18.6	25.3	27.4	76.3	68.4	66.3
Transport equipment	384[c]	5.8	7.5	6.8	16.9	23.1	29.7	77.3	69.4	63.5

Source: UNIDO, 1986a, Table 6.
[a] Shares for branches within ISIC 38 may be somewhat distorted owing to variations in the national reporting practices of several important producers of fabricated metal products, machinery and transport equipment.

parts of the world, they nevertheless continue to be the predominant suppliers in almost every case.

Aside from providing a rough picture of the changing world map, the data yield several useful inferences. First, in contrast to sectoral patterns of structural change, global shifts in industrial activity occur with surprising rapidity. Second, the figures reflect fairly well-defined trends and are not random fluctuations. The nature of these shifts, however, differ among the industries shown. Contractive pressures are unequally dispersed among industries and countries. Some industries are required to undertake considerable adjustment, while others carry on business as usual. The intensity of interest group pressures and the resultant policies vary accordingly. Third, the redistribution of manufacturing activities has generally occurred at the expense of Western industries but the source of external pressure can vary. The impetus may originate in the LDCs, in socialist countries, or result from new capacity being established in both groups of countries. Alternatively, the source of adjustment pressure can be found in Western countries themselves. This last possibility is obvious for industries which are largely confined to the West – for example, paper, printing and publishing and non-industrial chemicals. Such an occurrence, however, is an equally important source of adjustment problems in other cases (notably steel, transport and several industries not shown in the table owing to lack of data for LDCs) and can overshadow the impact of new competitors in LDCs or socialist countries.

In order to be clear about the source and nature of adjustment pressures, a more detailed investigation of each industry would be required. However, the sheer volume of the data and the heterogeneity of each industry would make this exercise a formidable task. A compromise is to limit the discussion to a few, narrowly defined, product groups (or industries), subjectively chosen for illustrative purposes. Table 4.4 provides the basis for such an approach, giving a partial picture of the changing pattern of global production for six product groups. Because data for a single year may be sensitive to random events (for instance, a fall in demand, supply bottlenecks or an abrupt policy change), three-year averages were calculated for each manufacture and for two periods of time. However, before examining the results, two qualifications should be noted. First, the list of manufactures shown in each product category is not necessarily a representative one, as it was selected purely on the basis of available data for a large number of countries. Second, the products considered are all fairly simple manufactures produced with standardized technologies. For this reason, the importance of suppliers in LDCs will tend to be exaggerated relative to their contribution to total MVA. Despite these qualifications, the results suggest the extent to which various factors – public policy, the role of the multinational or the prevalence of state ownership – may influence the international distribution of production in various industries.

A first impression of global shifts in production can be obtained through a comparison of the unweighted averages for each product category. In every case averages for the USA and the EC fell between 1972 and 1981. More remarkable is the fact that, with the exception of the transport industry, the corresponding figures for Japan also declined during this period. Averages for LDCs and a residual group of 'other industrialized countries' (socialist countries and members of OECD not shown elsewhere) all rose during this period. Figures for specific items reveal several instances where drastic shifts in production patterns have occurred. A notable example is the precipitous decline in the US share of world production of automobiles. The fall is partly attributable to the rapid emergence of Japan as an international competitor. In 1960, that country accounted for less than 1 per cent of world production (Ballance and Sinclair, 1983, p. 74), but by the beginning of the 1980s Japanese firms were producing more than one-quarter of the world's automobiles – most of them for export. The repercussions of the decline were significant. US automakers occupy a prominent position within the country's manufacturing sector. They have extensive links with suppliers of steel, machine tools, and other industries, as well as a comprehensive network of satellite firms performing sub-

Table 4.4 Global Distribution of Production of Selected Manufactured Commodities (percentage)

Commodity	1972–74					1979–81				
	USA	Japan	EC	LDCs	Other	USA	Japan	EC	LDCs	Other
Processed foods										
Tinned meat	40.8	0.9	20.4	5.5	32.5	44.6	0.9	17.3	5.5	31.7
Condensed milk and cream	17.4	1.1	24.1	39.0	18.4	12.2	1.3	24.9	38.5	23.0
Dried milk and cream	14.9	4.0	44.5	6.9	29.7	10.8	3.9	47.9	8.7	28.6
Tinned or bottled fruits	31.7	6.5	11.2	22.4	28.2	32.4	6.7	12.8	12.4	35.7
Tinned or bottled vegetables	39.5	1.4	21.5	3.2	34.3	37.6	1.5	19.8	3.8	37.2
Tinned fish	15.0	13.7	9.3	22.6	39.5	13.6	12.4	7.8	22.7	43.4
Margarine, imitation lard, etc.	33.8	4.3	22.5	12.4	27.1	31.5	4.9	19.6	14.5	29.5
Crude oil, soya bean	52.8	6.9	18.7	15.1	6.5	46.7	5.5	17.7	23.1	7.0
Crude oil, cotton-seed	30.3	1.4	1.7	37.5	29.1	26.9	0.6	1.1	37.0	34.4
Crude oil, groundnut	4.4	0.0	5.2	87.6	2.7	3.4	0.0	2.1	92.2	2.3
Other crude oils, vegetable origin	5.7	7.0	16.9	56.1	14.3	1.1	6.4	13.8	63.2	15.4
Wheat flour	9.0	2.9	15.2	21.4	51.5	9.7	3.1	16.0	25.7	45.4
Refined sugar	18.8	5.2	12.2	28.4	35.5	15.2	4.2	14.6	32.7	33.3
Cocoa powder	44.0	0.9	35.0	9.3	10.9	41.5	1.0	33.7	14.1	9.7
Prepared animal feeds	19.2	12.0	34.8	10.0	24.0	18.0	11.2	32.2	12.5	26.1
Average (unweighted)	25.2	4.5	19.5	25.2	25.6	23.0	4.2	18.8	27.1	26.9
Textiles, clothing										
Wool yarn	4.4	8.8	33.7	8.8	44.3	3.0	5.7	32.8	10.2	48.3
Cotton yarn	16.2	6.3	11.4	32.2	34.0	11.3	5.2	8.8	43.5	31.2
Cotton woven fabrics	12.5	5.2	10.5	42.8	29.0	8.6	5.1	10.2	44.4	31.7
Woollen woven fabrics	4.2	13.2	27.5	4.7	50.3	4.8	9.1	24.8	8.4	52.9

continued

Table 4.4 (continued)

Commodity	1972–74					1979–81				
	USA	Japan	EC	LDCs	Other	USA	Japan	EC	LDCs	Other
Textiles, clothing (continued)										
Woven fabrics of cellular fibres	18.8	15.1	19.4	25.5	21.3	9.6	10.9	14.5	42.4	22.5
Men's and boys' suits	20.4	15.6	31.4	13.6	19.0	20.8	13.9	24.1	18.3	22.9
Women's and girls' dresses	48.4	3.1	27.1	7.2	14.2	42.9	3.6	25.8	12.0	15.8
Men's and boys' shirts	32.3	10.5	20.1	18.8	18.4	31.5	1.1	17.7	25.4	24.3
Average (unweighted)	19.7	9.7	22.6	19.2	28.3	16.6	6.8	19.8	25.6	31.2
Industrial chemicals										
Chlorine	48.6	2.5	31.3	2.9	14.8	45.8	3.3	29.2	5.6	16.1
Sulphuric acid	29.1	7.0	21.3	7.9	34.7	31.1	5.3	16.6	10.5	36.3
Ammonia	35.6	1.8	26.8	5.3	30.5	33.4	0.3	19.6	14.7	32.1
Caustic soda	38.0	11.8	22.2	5.1	22.9	35.0	9.7	21.1	7.1	27.0
Synthetic dyestuffs	19.3	9.1	37.9	5.9	27.8	18.0	8.4	36.8	9.6	27.2
Nitrogenous fertilizers	25.3	6.2	16.0	11.5	40.9	22.0	3.2	16.0	17.3	41.4
Superphosphates	15.7	1.2	10.0	11.8	61.3	10.8	0.8	9.9	15.2	63.3
Non-cellulosic staple and tow	34.8	18.3	26.7	6.2	14.1	33.7	13.6	20.4	13.9	18.3
Cellulosic staple and tow	14.3	17.2	21.7	6.1	40.6	10.9	15.5	16.8	9.2	47.7
Polyvinylchloride	27.6	17.2	38.9	5.7	10.6	28.0	14.8	32.6	8.1	16.5
Non-cellulosic fibres	38.8	14.5	24.3	8.5	14.0	33.8	13.6	17.8	16.5	18.2
Cellulosic filaments	21.3	9.3	23.1	12.3	34.0	14.8	11.1	19.3	13.0	41.9
Average (unweighted)	29.0	9.7	25.0	7.4	28.9	26.5	8.3	21.3	11.7	32.2

Iron and steel

Pig iron (for casting)	12.2	7.8	19.6	12.0	48.4	9.3	4.9	15.0	15.2	55.6
Pig iron (for making crude steel)	19.1	19.0	22.9	5.0	33.9	14.5	17.8	19.0	9.1	39.5
Ingots of crude steel	20.3	17.1	22.9	4.6	35.1	17.0	16.3	19.7	7.0	40.0
Wire rods	11.7	16.2	30.5	5.6	35.9	10.2	14.7	27.4	9.5	38.2
Angles, shapes and sections	15.8	19.4	23.8	1.8	39.3	12.9	21.1	18.7	2.8	44.5
Plates (heavy), over 4.75 mm	12.7	24.7	20.4	6.4	35.9	10.7	18.2	18.5	10.3	42.3
Average (unweighted)	15.3	17.4	23.3	5.9	38.1	12.4	15.5	19.7	9.0	43.4

Household appliances

Stoves, ranges, cookers	14.1	41.5	15.7	9.9	18.9	10.4	41.7	15.0	14.7	18.3
Sewing machines	1.0	39.7	15.4	17.7	26.2	1.0	31.2	13.5	27.2	27.1
Household refrigerators	18.0	11.0	28.8	9.6	32.6	13.8	11.2	24.2	18.1	32.7
Washing machines (household use)	19.8	16.1	33.4	4.1	26.6	16.3	16.2	30.0	7.4	30.1
Television receivers	19.8	24.0	22.6	9.3	24.4	15.0	21.6	17.1	24.3	22.0
Radio receivers	11.5	18.3	11.4	44.8	14.0	6.8	11.2	7.7	61.6	12.8
Average (unweighted)	14.0	25.1	21.2	15.9	23.8	10.6	22.2	17.9	25.5	23.9

Transport

Passenger cars	31.4	14.8	35.6	3.5	14.7	24.0	23.0	32.6	3.9	16.4
Buses and motor coaches	13.5	14.9	21.2	10.3	40.0	9.1	24.8	14.0	9.1	43.0
Motor-cycles, scooters, etc.	1.9	40.3	26.7	8.4	22.7	1.6	48.0	17.7	14.7	18.0
Bicycles	22.8	19.1	22.3	11.5	24.3	16.7	14.6	26.0	16.9	25.7
Average (unweighted)	17.4	22.3	26.5	8.4	25.4	12.9	27.6	22.6	11.1	25.8

Source: United Nations, *Yearbook of Industrial Statistics*, Vol. 2 (various issues).

contracting work, supplying components and sub-assemblies. As a result the government was quick to impose policies to stem the flow of automobile imports. American automakers also began a search for ways to cut costs and were eventually forced to rethink some of their long-term strategies.

Figures on the world production of industrial chemicals suggest that the source of adjustment pressure can be attributed to the creation of new capacity, both in the LDCs and industrialized countries. With very few exceptions, the shares of world production claimed by European, Japanese and American chemical firms declined after 1972. Several governments have attempted to assist their producers of industrial chemicals through various means, such as re-straining the prices of natural gas feedstock in the USA or subsidizing capital investment in some European countries. At the same time, however, other considerations worked against Western producers. New environmental regulations, for example, have limited the industry's growth of production in Western countries. Firms operating plants designed in the early 1970s have also suffered because of their high energy costs. For these and other reasons the share of the LDCs has risen, sometimes substantially, in all the chemicals included in Table 4.4. However, chemical producers in other countries (in this case mainly socialist countries) are now the predominant suppliers of many chemicals.

The achievements recorded by producers in the LDCs represent a fragmented pattern, cutting across several industries. Prominent examples include cotton yarn, woven fabrics, synthetic fibres for use in textiles (for example, non-cellulosic staple and continuous fibres) and various household appliances. In most of these products the extent of the global redistribution was of no significance for the over-whelming majority of LDCs. The changes were the result of investments and policy decisions in a very few of these countries. The production of synthetic fibres is a typical example. Between 1972 and 1981 only four LDCs – India, Indonesia, South Korea and Thailand – accounted for 14 per cent of the increase in world production of non-cellulosic staple and tow, while the corresponding figure for non-cellulosic (continuous) fibres was even higher (35 per cent). Stated another way, between 1979–1981 these four countries claimed two-thirds of all production of LDCs in the first item and 51 per cent in the second. A general feature of the underlying data is that the gains recorded by LDCs often tend to be confined to specific manufactures and are concentrated in a few countries.

Further evidence regarding the impact of government policies on the international composition of industrial production can be found in the data for production of processed foods, where the predominance of the USA and EC combined cannot be overlooked. The combined share of these two producers amounts to more than one-half of the world total for a number of items. A highly efficient agricultural sector, coupled with the necessary processing facilities, would partly explain this prominence – particularly for the USA. But world leadership is also due to the generous subsidies provided to agriculture and to various agro-industries in the two markets. In the EC, export subsidies alone were valued at $5.8 billion in 1981. A further $12.8 billion was spent to bolster European farm incomes, while $15.4 billion was used for this purpose in the USA during 1981/82 (*The Economist*, 8 January 1983). Such largesse, supplemented by an array of policies to restrain imports, would ensure that the two sets of producers continue to dominate the world food industry production and mean that the likelihood of a contraction in domestic importance is remote.

Figures on the production of household appliances serve to illustrate the important role sometimes played by the multinational in determining changes in the global pattern. As in other industries, American, Japanese and European producers have all experienced a long-term decline, while manufacturers in LDCs have emerged as the world's major suppliers of many household appliances. But the relationship between these firms and their counterparts in Western countries differs markedly from that found in industries such as industrial chemicals or food processing. Many of the firms based in LDCs are subsidiaries or affiliates of multinationals located in Europe, Japan or the USA. Their operations are often regarded as no more than appendages to the multinationals. For instance, in the production of colour television sets, Singapore has been described as a 'front' for Japanese firms, while Taiwan depends heavily on Philips and RCA (Turner and McMullen, 1982, p. 55). One result of this arrangement is the high priority given to exports. Foreign markets absorb more than 90 per cent of all production in Hong Kong, Singapore and Taiwan and over 70 per cent in South Korea (IDE, 1980, p. 56). Malaysia, too, may soon join this group, as producers elsewhere are shifting the labour-intensive portion of their operations to that country to take advantage of its relatively low wage rates.

Finally, global trends in the steel industry are similar to those sketched above. Nevertheless, the circumstances leading to a relative decline among major producers are again distinct from those noted in other industries. First, the predominance of the steel industry in most Western countries was the result of a full century of growth and expansion, spurred by the construction of vast shipping fleets, railway systems and huge machines. By the 1970s, however, the impetus for growth had shifted to other industries such as telecommunications, energy, aerospace and computers. Unlike their predecessors, these new growth industries are not intensive users of steel. Steel-makers in Western countries are dependent on user industries, which themselves are losing ground relative to overall economic activity. The world decline in demand for steel products was aggravated by other factors. For example, the introduction of new production techniques has hastened the substitution of aluminium, plastics and highly resistant glass for steel, while technical advances have reduced the steel requirements of some users. Second, in comparison with other industries, steel producers have maintained an insular or inward-looking orientation (Ballance, 1985, p. 15) which has restricted their alternatives when faced with a shrinking domestic market. The sparsity of international contacts is partly explained by the fact that the industry's development was everywhere geared to meet domestic needs. Widespread state ownership or control, particularly in Western Europe and in LDCs, has further limited the extent of internationalization (Ballance and Sinclair, 1983, p. 116–8). All these factors have made the steel industry's adjustment to its new circumstances a painful one.

This excursion into some of the international aspects of structural change reinforces opinions expressed in the preceding section of this chapter. There it was argued that attempts to generalize about structural patterns, associated public policies and corporate strategies are greatly compli-cated by the heterogeneity of industries concerned. The foregoing descriptions provide only the barest outline of the considerations and forces which lie behind the changing patterns of world production. Nevertheless they are suf-ficient to demonstrate the need to take account of the interaction between a complex and varied set of international and national factors in each industry. When set in this framework, the heterogeneous nature of manufacturing activities would seem to demand a fairly detailed or industry-specific focus. A description of industrial structure that is essentially 'domestic' in scope serves only as a starting point and cannot do justice to the international dimensions of structure and policy which now dominate world industry. Once the investigation of the industrial structure is extended into the international sphere an improved understanding of policy motives and industry strategies can be expected to outweigh any loss in ability to generalize about structural similarities which apply to groups of industries. The basis for this approach is carried one step further in the following chapter which looks at the determinants of international competitive abilities in terms of the economic concept of comparative advantage.

Supplementary Reading

The work of Chenery and Taylor (1968) continues to be one of the most widely cited studies of structural change within the manufacturing sector. Guisinger (1977) and Fattah (1979) provide examples of country studies which apply Chenery's approach in this context. For an application of the approach to Association of South East Asian Nations (ASEAN) countries see Ariff and Hill (1985, Chapter 5). Gupta (1971) adopts these methods in his study of structural change in different states of India. A similar study using Brazilian states as the unit of observation illustrates some of the weaknesses of the structural approach (Jameson, 1975). Kirkpatrick, Lee and Nixson (1984, pp. 12–45) provide a good summary of both the defence and criticism of the model for analysis of structural change within the manufacturing sector.

CHAPTER FIVE

International Differences in Competitive Ability

The growing involvement of the state in manufacturing has been a recurrent theme of previous chapters. One consequence of state involvement has been the tendency for government intervention to assume a narrow focus, the intervention being tailor-made to suit the needs of individual industries or even firms. The new concern with industry-specific conditions is explained by several factors. They include: fears of de-industrialization and the hope that such trends can be reversed through efforts to re-industrialize; a growing acceptance of government responsibility to 'pick winners' or 'national champions' among industries, firms or even products; and a widening range of other policy initiatives, implemented against a background of industry-level disputes in steel, petrochemicals, textiles, clothing, automobiles, and so forth.

A feature shared by all the associated policies is that their efficacy is partly judged in terms of the impact on the international competitive position of the 'target' industries. Policy-makers in Western countries and LDCs alike are increasingly called upon to pinpoint new industries with a competitive potential, or to identify the necessary steps needed to revitalize competitive abilities in others. Such exercises demand a fairly high degree of analytical precision. Success would require the policy-makers to carry out an accurate assessment of competitive ability in various industries, to anticipate international changes in these conditions over time and to make use of all these facts in formulating their recommendations. The available resources, however, will always be limited and can be redirected to favoured industries only by discriminating against other, less favoured industries.

One purpose of this chapter is to illustrate the comparative nature of economies. The appropriate framework for such a discussion is offered by the law of comparative advantage. This law maintains that trade simultaneously benefits all participants. A country gains by specializing in industries where it has a comparative advantage and exchanging (exporting) these products for others where it lacks such an advantage. The principle of comparative advantage is widely accepted, but the implications for a country's pattern of specialization and trade receive less attention. For instance, a country's international standing in a particular industry will be determined by that industry's efficiency relative to the same measure in other countries which are its trading partners. Each industry's ability to compete in international markets depends not on its absolute cost advantage but on its relative advantage. And in a world economy, where countries trade extensively, no single country can be expected to be internationally competitive in every product and industry. Although a country might be more efficient than its trading partners in all fields of manufacturing, it would still export only those products in which its relative efficiency is greatest, that is, the products in which the country has a comparative advantage. Simultaneously, the country would import products in which it is (relatively) less efficient and the domestic market share of the latter industries will be small.

By definition, a country's declining industries will not be efficient relative to other industries. Even if, by some extraordinary effort, the competitive status of an ailing industry could be reversed through modernization, ration-alization of excess capacity, upgrading labour skills, or by other means, the results are unlikely to restore the industry to a position of relative efficiency. For similar reasons, the task of developing new and promising areas for industrial expansion may be all too casually underestimated.

110

If a full appreciation of comparative dicta were sufficient for policy and planning purposes, the responsibilities which governments have assumed would be arduous but relatively straightforward. Further ambiguities arise because the law itself says nothing about the determinants of comparative advantage. However, a number of theories have been advanced to identify these determinants. A full exposition of trade theory is outside the scope of this book but the intuitive content of several theories is fairly simple and a few are briefly described in the following section. With this background, the discussion turns to some of the empirical issues which arise when attempting to estimate comparative advantage. The chapter concludes with a review of recent evidence.

A Descriptive Look at Trade Theories

Classical Ricardian theory pictured trade as a consequence of different sets of production costs that were incurred by producing in alternative locations. Persistent differences in production costs were attributed to the fact that certain inputs were not internationally transferable. Labour was regarded as the crucial input while other factors, such as technology, capital or domestic consumption patterns, received little attention. International variations in levels of labour productivity were thought to depend on the country of production and the quality and availability of associated inputs. Thus, the basis for trade was originally stated in terms of its proximate cause – the comparative costs of production – which, in turn, were explained by international differences in a single scarce factor of production, that is, labour.

Despite the fact that the Ricardian explanation clearly ignores many potentially important determinants of comparative advantage, it continues to serve as a basis for analyzing patterns of trade and production. The popularity of the approach derives not from an acceptance of a labour theory of value but from other lines of reasoning. One justification is the empirical fact that in Western countries labour usually accounts for a large proportion of a manufacturer's total costs. Small deviations in this cost component may alter the international pattern of comparative advantage. Another justification is the expectation that the relative usage of various factors of production would have to differ widely among industries if the prominent role attributed to labour were to be undermined (Johnson, 1966). In the opinion of some researchers, the relative usage of different factors of production within the manufacturing sector is not so great as to obviate the use of a 'pure labour cost' approach.

Subsequent theoretical work has, nevertheless, elaborated on the determinants of comparative advantage. The importance of factors of production other than labour were recognized. The relative availability of these factors (including skills and capital equipment) was seen to be the ultimate cause of international trade. This theory, attributed to E. Heckscher and G. Ohlin, has received the most attention in the literature on the subject and is actually available in two versions. One, known as the 'commodity' version, suggests that a country will tend to export goods which require comparatively large amounts of those factors of production which are relatively abundant in the country. Thus, a country which is rich in capital would be expected to produce and export goods which require relatively large amounts of capital. However, a practical application of the proposition is not simple. It requires detailed knowledge of factor endowments and the intensity of factor usage in various industries, as well as the trade patterns of the country concerned. In other words, a three-way relationship between factor abundance, factor intensity and trade is stipulated for each country and its trading partners. As a result of these complexities, attention has focused on an alternative assessment of the theorem – the 'factor content' version. This assessment depicts trade as an implicit exchange of the factors of production embodied in traded goods. A country will tend to 'export' its relatively abundant factors in the sense that the amounts of these factors embodied in its exports will exceed the corresponding amounts used in alternative bundles of goods produced for home consumption and in competition with foreign suppliers.

More recently, recognition of significant technological differences between countries has given rise to other trade theories which focus on this attribute. One version, suggested by Posner (1961), emphasizes the role of technical progress as a determinant of trade. New products and production processes are constantly being developed and the innovating country will, for a time, enjoy a technological superiority over its trading partners. New technologies will eventually be replicated elsewhere but the process of technological advancement is continuously renewed as innovations occur and existing technologies are transferred elsewhere. However, the explanation leaves open the question of why new technologies are not transferred to the least cost location very quickly. That consideration may be particularly relevant for industries dominated by multinationals with far-flung networks of subsidiaries. Hirsch (1967) suggested that products pass through a cycle of systematic change. The production of new items initially requires large amounts of skilled labour. As demand increases, however, the opportunity to realize greater economies of scale will emerge and production becomes more capital-intensive. Eventually, production processes will be standardized and will then require a proportionately large labour force – much of it unskilled. Another variation on this approach (Vernon, 1979) proposes that the development of new products is contingent on the nature of demand in the richer countries. Production – and exports – will first occur in these countries and will only later be transferred to lower cost locations.

If the scope of analysis is confined to an individual product rather than a category of products, major innovations are seen to occur at infrequent points in time and represent 'discontinuations' in the history of each product. Majumdar (1979), for example, documents the way comparative advantage in electronic calculators switched back and forth between the USA and Japan in the 1960s and 1970s. Each shift was the result of a major innovation. The development of the transistorized calculators by American firms in 1962 was followed by the introduction of integrated circuits and semiconductor technology by Japanese competitors in 1967. US firms began to supply the single chip calculator in 1971 while the calculator-on-a-substrate was introduced by Japanese producers in 1973. Clearly, though, a considerable period of time may elapse before technologies mature and the ability to generalize about such erratic shifts in techological leadership is limited.

Several other general trade theories could be mentioned, as well as more specific statements given to explain observed paradoxes or to highlight additional determinants. The diligence of trade specialists can be partly attributed to the fact that the major theories provide a less than complete explanation of world trade and, thus, comparative advantage. One impression which does emerge, even from a cursory review, is that efforts to develop a theory which convincingly explains the determinants of comparative advantage have, so far, yielded only mixed results. In some instances trade patterns can be explained by more than one version of a theory and the precise nature of the underlying determinants of comparative advantage can be only vaguely identified. In others, theories have proven to be so complex – often involving a multiple or compound hypothesis – that they defy adaptation to the real world. Other problems include: the application of any theory to a trading world populated by many countries, many commodities and many factors; the specification of what actually constitutes a factor of production; and the appropriate treatment of trade in intermediate products. The inability to provide an unambiguous specification of the determinants of comparative advantage has meant that public authorities also lack the precise economic information needed to fashion a set of policies which would force firms to behave in conformity with the wishes of the governments concerned. Despite these difficulties, attempts to measure comparative advantage have proceeded along fairly pragmatic lines. The following section looks at some of these approaches and underlines some of the practical difficulties.

Measuring International Differences in Comparative Advantage

Attempts to quantify international differences in comparative advantage were first prompted by the desire to assess the long-term effects on trade liberalization resulting from tariff reductions in the Dillon and Kennedy Rounds (Balassa, 1965). As the focus of industrial policy has become more industry-specific, economists have redoubled their efforts to measure comparative advantage.

Despite extensive analysis, the quantification of comparative advantage has proved to be elusive. The inability to develop a generally accepted methodology is partly explained by the fact that comparative advantage is based on price relationships that would prevail in the absence of trade. Because trade itself influences prices, pre-trade prices (also called autarky prices) cannot be observed and comparative advantage cannot be measured directly. An alternative technique is required that indirectly draws implications about comparative advantage using post-trade observations.

The primary problem in measuring comparative advantage relates to the availability of the required data as well as conceptual difficulties. For instance, countries are of widely differing sizes. A large country with a relatively minor cost advantage, that is, a small degree of comparative advantage could be an important exporter relative to a smaller country that enjoys a larger cost advantage. Thus, measures of comparative advantage must be adjusted to account for differences in country size. At least two alternatives are available: to relate exports to domestic production or to relate imports to domestic consumption. The first of these measures would provide a crude representation of comparative advantage and the second comparative disadvantage.

While such an approach might account for different country sizes, it does not address other problems of measurement. Paramount among these is the fact that information is not available for each and every traded product. Trade statistics, for instance, refer to categories of products, a practice which means that most countries are shown simultaneously as importers and exporters of the same product category. In such cases crude measures of trade performance might very well show a country to have a comparative advantage and a comparative disadvantage in the same product category or industry. Thus, in addition to standardizing for country size, account must be taken of two-way or 'intra-industry' trade. The most common method of adjustment is to express a country's trade in net terms (that is, exports minus imports). If a country's comparative advantage in certain items included in an industry's product range outweighs its comparative disadvantage in the remaining items, net exports would be positive.

The following example illustrates some of the problems encountered in the measurement of comparative advantage. Table 5.1 shows production, exports and imports of iron and steel for Japan and Sweden in 1980. In Japan exports exceed imports and the country produces more steel than it consumes. Thus the country could be expected to have a net comparative advantage in the industry as the comparative advantage it enjoys in exported articles outweighs the comparative disadvantage associated with imported steel items. Data for Sweden reveal a similar outcome. But which country enjoys the greater degree of comparative advantage? To answer this question the data must be made comparable or standardized. A number of different measures are available for this purpose, four of which are shown in Table 5.1. The first measure, exports as a share of production, indicates that Sweden has a greater comparative advantage in iron and steel than Japan. However, the other formulations listed indicate the reverse. These results are indicative of the problems encountered in assessing the degree of comparative advantage. All four measures are derived from the most basic interpretation of the concept. Yet when they are applied to actual data on trade, production and consumption, inconsistencies arise.

There are at least two reasons for these inconsistencies. First, the level of data aggregation may be so great that the true pattern of comparative advantage is obscured. Japan has a comparative advantage across the industry's entire product spectrum but Sweden has specialized in the

Table 5.1 Competitive Performance and 'Measures' of Comparative Advantage: Illustrative Data on Production and Trade in Steel by Japan and Sweden, 1980

| | Production and trade performance (US$ millions) | | Alternative 'measure' of comparative advantage (in percentage) | | |
	Japan	Sweden	Ratio	Japan	Sweden
Production	107,535	4,283	Exports as a share of production	28	50
+ Imports	1,165	1,981	Imports as a share of consumption	1	48
= New supply	108,700	6,264	Net exports as a share of production	27	3
− Exports	29,693	2,125	Production as a share of consumption	136	103
= Consumption	79,007	4,139			

Source: UNIDO, 1985b, p. 78.

production of relatively sophisticated steel products. Unlike Japan, which imports iron ore and coal, Sweden satisfies its raw material needs by importing crude iron and steel. Thus, the statistics mask the fact that Sweden attains a comparative advantage at the higher stages of processing steel only. Second, due to government policies in support of an industry (such as subsidies to stimulate production or measures to limit imports) trade performance may not reflect the 'true' pattern of comparative advantage which would prevail in a world of completely free trade. It may be that the government of Japan has introduced policies which restrict imports to a very low share in consumption.

Researchers have attempted to minimize the first problem by using data for more narrowly defined product categories. A major difficulty with this solution is that most countries employ a classificatory system for compiling production statistics that is different from that used for trade statistics. Often, it is possible to obtain comparable data for production, imports and exports only by combining products into highly aggregated categories. In order to study comparative advantages for narrowly defined product ranges, it is necessary to construct measures which utilize only one set of data (usually trade statistics since these are collected at a more detailed level).

Ambiguities attributable to government policies have been dealt with in two ways. Some analysts have chosen to exclude imports from the measurement of comparative advantage. Because imports are subject to so many types of trade restrictions, they fear that using these data may lead to a biased estimate (Balassa 1977 and 1979a). Other observers contend that governments which protect a particular industry through import limitations are also prone to provide additional forms of support by subsidizing R and D and plant construction and by offering preferred credit terms, tax incentives and similar measures. These investigators favour indices based on net trade flows (Donges and Riedel, 1977).

A final point which should be mentioned concerns the appropriate interpretation of any measure. The theory implies that any set of estimates for a particular product or industry should yield precise indications of the absolute differences in the comparative advantage between each country. Such indicators would be described as 'cardinal' measures of comparative advantage. Less stringent interpretations of the results are sometimes necessary however. One alternative is to treat the measures as indicators of the degree of comparative advantage enjoyed by one country relative to another, without drawing inferences about absolute differences in the magnitudes of the two measures (e.g. Balassa, 1979a; UNCTAD, 1983). This interpretation would result in a ranking of industries according to their degree of comparative advantage and is referred to as an 'ordinal' measure. Still another possibility, suggested by Yeats (1985), is to regard each estimate as a dichotomous indicator that merely distinguishes between those countries which have a comparative advantage in a particular commodity or industry and those which do not.

International Patterns of Comparative Advantage

The difficulties encountered in applying the concept of comparative advantage are many. The precise determinants can be only vaguely described and the available measurement techniques can yield no more than notional results. Despite these drawbacks, pragmatic studies of comparative advantage can still provide general impressions of trends in broad product aggregates. Owing to the theoretical and statistical difficulties involved, most of the empirical work has been confined to tests of various theories, or parts of theories or hypotheses, and has been ably summarized elsewhere (Deardorff, 1984). The following discussion leaves these theoretical issues aside in order to gain some impressions (however tentative) of actual patterns of comparative advantage.

One of the widest-ranging investigations utilized three alternative indicators of comparative advantage and dealt with 129 industries and 47 countries (UNIDO, 1982). The results showed that in the majority of the LDCs comparative advantage was limited to the production of simply processed manufactures, most of which were closely linked to agriculture or were otherwise resource-based. LDCs at comparatively high levels of development were found to be less dependent on the availability of natural resources; some of the industries in which they excelled were clearly labour-intensive (for example, articles of clothing, textiles, footwear) while others, such as electrical machinery, equipment and supplies, were labour-intensive and/or used fairly standard, mature technologies.

These findings, of course, are not surprising in view of the large amounts of unskilled labour and limited techno-logical expertise available in LDCs relative to Western countries. Other, more narrowly focused, studies have provided additional contrasts. Several have considered specific industries such as steel, wood products and petroleum refining (UNIDO, 1983, Chapter 12) or textiles and clothing, steel products and electronic components (UNIDO, 1985b, Chapter 5). Once countries are divided into those having a comparative advantage and those which do not, two distinct patterns emerge depending on the industries involved. First, in the case of textiles, clothing and wood and wood products, the countries which appear to have a comparative advantage have developed their industries primarily by supplying foreign markets; domestic consumption is not of paramount importance. Countries lacking a comparative advantage have nevertheless met the bulk of their needs through domestic production, while satisfying the remainder through imports. Second, in other industries, such as steel and electronics, the tendency has been to exploit a comparative advantage only as an extension of the domestic market. For instance, although Japan is regarded as having a comparative advantage in a wide range of steel products, the country still consumes more than 80 per cent of its own production of steel (UNIDO, 1985b, p. 87). Again, countries with a comparative disadvantage have satisfied most of their needs through domestic industries.

International trade, however, can be pictured as more than the result of a simple pattern of comparative advantage by which countries export products produced by one or more industries and other countries export products of other industries. It is a highly interdependent process, whereby some countries produce and export raw materials to others which process the materials into intermediate products for export to third countries for yet further processing. The degree of interdependence, the number of processing stages and the international location of these stages will vary among industries. And in some cases more than one stage of processing will occur in the same country; production efficiencies may dictate that subsequent processing occurs in the same plant.

When patterns of trade and comparative advantage are analyzed in this fashion, a more elaborate picture emerges. Instead of using indigenous raw materials to make final goods, countries endowed with raw materials excel in the extraction and simple processing of these materials into intermediate products which are then exported (UNIDO, 1985b, pp. 93–103). Other countries import the intermediate products for processing into higher-staged intermediate products which in turn are exported. Eventually, a final good emerges from this chain of processing. An extreme example is the case of Hong Kong which, in 1980, accounted for 17 per cent of all exports of clothing by Western countries and LDCs combined but which at the same time was a large importer of textiles (UNIDO, 1985b, p. 92). One implication is that for countries which have chosen to enter an industry at an intermediate stage, success requires a close integration of their processing operations with both foreign suppliers and export markets. Such countries will definitely not be simply importers of raw materials and exporters of final goods but will have established themselves as processors of imported materials into higher staged goods. They will have rationalized their industrial structures to suit industrial interdependence.

Because all these impressions are based on industry-wide statistics, they conceal many variations among different product groups. Even countries that appear to enjoy an overall comparative advantage in an industry tend to specialize, to some degree, in sub-sectors of that industry. Specialization is particularly obvious in the steel industry. Although Japan has a comparative advantage in many items, its ability to compete in the production of ferro-alloys and similar products is limited. In addition to substantial intra-industry trade, the EC is an important exporter of pipes, fittings and a variety of steel plates and sheets. Other Western countries are specialized in the export of alloy and high-carbon steels. India, one of the few LDCs with an overall comparative advantage in steel, exports pig iron, roughly forged slabs, rails and welded pipes.

Extensive specialization can be found in almost any industry. Another example is the wood products, an industry defined to include the manufacture of shaped and simply-worked wood items, plywoods, veneers and products made chiefly from wood. Here, most LDCs tend to specialize in a rather narrow range of products. The exports of South Korea, for instance, consist mainly of plywood and veneer panelling, while other LDCs supply lumber (either coniferous or non-coniferous), builders' products, moldings, and so on. Although usually embracing a wider product range, evidence of specialization is equally apparent in Western countries. Australia is a competitive supplier of chipwood, hoopwood, poles and pilings; Japan exports various types of plywood and veneer panelling; Spain and Italy excel in a wide range of decorative items; and the USA supplies coniferous lumber, hoopwood and builders' products.

Such studies demonstrate that the concept of comparative advantage can be of use for empirical analysis. The results, however, offer little assistance to policy-makers who might wish to base their recommendations on some notion of comparative advantage. First, owing to the fact that an ordinal or dichotomous interpretation must be employed, the evidence is necessarily stated in very tentative terms. The available methods provide little basis to specify absolute differences in comparative advantage (that is, a cardinal evaluation) – yet such information would be of most use to the policy-maker. Second, impressions gained are necessarily pragmatic and are limited in their application. The studies draw upon comparisons across fairly broad product aggregates and refer only to limited time periods, but comparative advantage is very specific in scope and is likely to change over time. Finally, the limited evidence which has been compiled clearly points to an underlying pattern of comparative advantage which is highly intricate. Thus, the search for comparative advantage could not merely be conducted in terms of one particular group of industries to the exclusion of others; the extent of specialization may be so great that an assessment might have to be carried out in terms of individual products and even different stages in the production of a given product.

In conclusion, comparative advantage is an extremely complex subject and this discussion has touched only selected issues. Problems of both a theoretical and statistical nature seriously limit its usefulness as a policy guide. These drawbacks, however, do not extend to the validity of the concept itself. International competitiveness continues to be governed by a criterion of relative rather than absolute advantage. A preoccupation with the prospects of individual industries, however, can lead to policies and recommendations which are so narrowly formulated that they are unlikely to meet their intended aim.

The following chapter looks at some of the potential determinants of comparative advantage in greater detail.

Supplementary Reading

Deardorff (1984) offers an excellent review of the relationships between trade theories and empirical analysis, which can be read with benefit by students at all levels. Bowden (1983) examines the difficulties encountered by the empiricist in testing many of these theories. Many of the empirical and policy-related aspects of trade theory are clearly discussed in Greenaway (1985). For a simple application of the law of comparative advantage using trade statistics, see UNIDO (1982) and the sources cited there. Both production and trade data are utilized in later studies (UNIDO, 1985b, pp. 77–104 and UNIDO, 1986c). The possible relationships between comparative advantage and patterns of structural change have been studied by UNIDO (1986b).

Literature on the product cycle is particularly relevant to the issue of structural change and the maturity of industries.

Kindleberger (1978) uses the concept to explain economy-wide trends in the USA. At the other extreme is Magee (1980) who has applied the product cycle theory to products and has incorporated the influence of raw materials. Finger (1975) has suggested another interpretation which has been tested by UNIDO (1981a, pp. 75–82).

With regard to the policy implications, Lindbeck (1981) provides an introduction to the limitations of comparative advantage as a guide to policy-makers. A related – and rapidly growing – body of literature concerns the feasibility and criteria for singling out certain industries for government support. Arguing in the context of the American economy, Magaziner and Reich (1982), Hadley (1983) and Adams (1983) endorse this approach and suggest various criteria for implementation – among them, competitiveness. Krugman (1983, 1984) is one of the most influential critics of the tactic.

CHAPTER SIX

Factor Intensities and Technological Change

Comparative advantage can be pictured as the outcome of two distinct sets of determinants. One set is composed of factor endowments which will differ between countries but at least in the short run will remain unchanged. The second set, factor intensities, represent technological parameters which vary from one industry to another and change over time as a result of technological improvements in production processes. This chapter leaves aside the role of factor endowments to focus on the concept of factor intensities.

The extent to which technological advancement may alter international patterns of factor usage (and, therefore, comparative advantage) has been the subject of much study. Most innovations originate in Western countries where labour costs are comparatively high and where other factors of production (for example, capital) are relatively abundant. For this reason, they are often thought to have a labour-saving bias which will reduce the amount of labour input required to manufacture various products. Some analysts have suggested that the scope for replacement of labour could be so great as to cause 'factor intensity reversals', meaning that production processes which relied heavily on unskilled labour could be transformed into operations which were relatively capital-intensive.

The search for labour-saving innovations received added impetus as the result of various trends during the 1970s. First, with the emergence of certain LDCs as major exporters of a variety of manufactures, world markets became subject to additional competitive pressures. Because of their abundant supplies of cheap labour many observers expect LDCs to excel in production processes that are relatively labour-intensive (Lary, 1968; Tuong and Yeats, 1980). Western firms might respond by modernizing their operations in an effort to reduce any cost disadvantage due to their higher pay scales. An emphasis on labour-saving innovations would be re-enforced by the fact that the wages paid to unskilled labour have risen in most Western countries as a result of egalitarian wage policies. Second, the capabilities of automated machine tools, microcomputers, industrial robots and similar types of capital goods were greatly improved in the 1970s. Some Western governments actively encourage the use of these products in the hopes of bringing about a realignment of factor intensities in certain industries. Finally, established patterns of factor usage were altered as a result of unrelated events, such as the rise in energy prices and increased specialization as major firms narrowed their product lines in order to compete in international markets. The turbulence and disruption experienced during this period made the application of numerous technological advances economically feasible and may have led to all sorts of changes in production processes including labour-saving innovations.

Even if technological innovations have led to significant shifts in factor intensities, the use of the 'old technologies' which employ more labour could still be feasible – particularly in populous LDCs with comparatively low wage rates. Manufacturers which continue to use these technologies may retain a comparative advantage, albeit a reduced one. However, the productivity differential resulting from a technological innovation could be of such a magnitude that despite substantially lower wages, firms depending on 'old technologies' might find it difficult to compete with manufacturers in higher-wage countries relying on the new technology. Clear evidence to support or reject sweeping generalizations such as these, however, cannot be assembled. Like other theoretical tools, the concept of factor intensities is subject to certain ambiguities and shortcomings. Following a brief survey of these issues, evidence for selected industries is examined.

The Measurement of Factor Intensity

Interest in the subject of factor intensities has received its primary impetus from the work of trade theorists. Economists wishing to test a particular theory, or to explain variations in some measure of the trade performance, will often make use of the concept. Although factor intensities are a recognized determinant of comparative advantage, general trade theories have treated the subject in a highly simplified fashion. Trade models have typically assumed the existence of only two factors of production and much of the associated empirical research has been conducted within this framework. Various theories of international trade can be extended to a multi-factor world but considerable problems are encountered by empiricists who wish to study factor intensities in this context. Additional clarification may be sought from other realms of economic theory (for instance, the theory of production), although much of the rationale for development of an analytical framework will ultimately depend on the analyst's intuition and supposition (e.g. Bowden, 1983). In addition to the theoretical complexities involved, obvious practical problems will emerge when several factors of production are simultaneously incorporated in any study.

For all these reasons empiricists have been forced to search for ways to simplify their task. Justification for the study of only a limited number of factors is largely based on pragmatic reasoning. First, it may be argued that the inclusion of several factors will not necessarily lead to a better understanding of international differences in competitive ability or operating conditions. Second, the list of factors which are of paramount importance will presumably vary, depending on the industry studied. The omission of some factors can be justified on the grounds that they are of limited significance. Finally, the scope of study can be reduced by first identifying sets of goods or industries which share certain input requirements.

127

An obvious means of simplification is to exclude from study those industries whose inputs have a particularly high resource content. For instance, the location and competitive ability of industries which are specialized in the transformation or processing of raw materials are more likely to be determined by the quality and local availability of material inputs than by the relative requirements of capital and labour used to process these materials. For other industries, which are not so resource-dependent, the necessary inputs are readily transported and are widely available in international markets; manufacturers operating in countries which do not have local sources of supply can easily import them (Lary, 1968, p. 48).

The selection of factors to be studied is open to the researcher, but the most common practice is to focus on labour and capital. Even in this restricted framework, however, the issue of the appropriate specification of factors has re-emerged in another form. Several analysts, notably Kravis (1956) and Keesing (1966), observed that wage rates in export-oriented industries significantly exceeded those in import-competing industries. The existence of persistent wage differentials was attributed to the fact that some industries required workers with greater skills, education and training than others (Waehrer, 1968). All these requirements were lumped together under the heading of 'human capital' and were used to explain wage differentials between industries.

This interpretation cast doubt on the practice of treating labour as a single 'homogeneous' input. Further reasons for doubt came from studies showing that accumulations of physical capital and expansion of the labour force could explain only a part of total economic growth. A substantial residual was left to be attributed to other sources, such as technological advancement and human capital formation (Solow, 1957; Denison, 1963). Subsequent research (Branson and Junz, 1971; Keesing, 1971; and Baldwin, 1971) confirmed that human capital, that is, accumulated skills, exerted an important influence on trade patterns and should be analyzed in a more explicit fashion. A general impression emerging from all this work was that the availability and/or usage of human capital (accumulated skills) may be a more important determinant of international differences in competitive abilities than physical capital. This was thought to be particularly true for manufactures and implied that human capital is a relatively scarce and immobile factor of production.

Recognition of the need to distinguish between different types of labour complicated the work of empiricists. If the possibility of factor reversals is excluded, industries can be meaningfully ranked according to their relative use of the two inputs, that is, labour and capital and the results compared across countries. But once the existence of three or more factors is acknowledged, the practice loses some of its rigor. When physical capital, human capital and unskilled labour are all considered simultaneously, industries may be ranked according to either one of two sets of relationships: physical capital per unit of labour or human capital per unit of labour.

Under certain conditions, however, retention of the simple, two-factor framework may still be possible. For example, if two inputs can be used interchangeably, that is, the inputs are perfect substitutes, they may be regarded as a single factor of production. Likewise, if two inputs are used in a fixed and unchanging proportion (meaning that there is no substitution), only one need be considered. Thus the criterion for compressing three inputs into a two-factor world depends on the degree of substitution. However, the large number of empirical studies which have addressed this subject have led to no general conclusion regarding substitutability between the three factors. There is limited evidence to support a practice of combining human and physical capital (Berndt and Christensen, 1973) although other studies have implied that for most industries it makes little difference how the three factors are combined (Corbo and Meller, 1982). A variety of reasons may be offered to explain the lack of agreement on this point. It is possible that elasticities are so unstable – varying widely between countries and fluctuating greatly over time – as to make the estimates meaningless. Alternatively, the combined effect of theoretical, econometric and statistical problems may be so severe as to make the estimates unreliable. In practice, analysts have either made a subjective decision to combine two of the three factors or have ranked industries by each possible combination between pairs of factors (Erzan, 1983).

To incorporate the influence of additional factors of production without further complicating the underlying issues of theory and measurement, recent studies (Krause, 1982; Tyers and Phillips, 1984) have adopted a slightly different tactic. They classify industries according to the 'dominant' input, which is defined to be either the factor used most intensively or the factor which is the major determinant for the location of production. Using this line of reasoning the list of factors to be considered in the classification exercise can be extended to include agricultural resources, mineral resources, unskilled labour, technology, physical capital, human capital, or other inputs. Simplification of the list of factors to be considered is still possible. For example, following Lary (1968), analysts may choose to exclude one or more factors from their classification scheme. Depending on the countries and industries which are the subject of study, the investigator may argue that a particular factor (for example, physical capital) is internationally mobile. When this argument applies, the input can be expected to be available at similar prices in different countries and would not be likely to determine the choice of a production site. Whatever the eventual choice of factors, most studies relate their classification results to some measures of factor endowments to arrive at some assessment of comparative advantage.

Aside from the choice of factors to be included in any study, two other issues are relevant and can be briefly mentioned. One concerns the definition of factor intensity. The concept may be defined to include only inputs directly entering into the production process. For example, the measurement of direct factor intensities might take account of the amounts of labour and capital actually employed in the industry, but the labour and capital embodied in the intermediate inputs used by the industry would be ignored. An alternative approach is to construct a measure of 'total' factor intensity which would incorporate not only direct factor usage but also the labour and capital that enter with the production process indirectly via intermediate inputs. With certain qualifications, there is general agreement that total factor intensities are the appropriate choice for studies intended to explain patterns of trade, while direct factor intensities are more relevant for an analysis of the international pattern of production (Hamilton and Svensson, 1983, p. 453). This recommendation depends mainly on the extent to which intermediate inputs are traded. If they are widely available, the relevant factor requirements are only those which apply to each particular stage of production.

Finally, there are differences of opinion regarding the method of measurement. One possibility is to express the measure in terms of a 'stock' – for instance, the total amount of capital or labour available in the industry. Examples of stock measures would be the accumulated physical capital per employee or an aggregation of man-years used in the industry. Alternatively, factor intensities can be pictured as a 'flow' expressed in terms of the payments to labour and capital for services rendered during the accounting period. Both measures are proxies involving certain drawbacks and have been debated extensively in the relevant literature (Lary, 1968; Balassa, 1979b). For instance, estimates of capital stock are derived from data on capital assets (buildings, machinery and equipment) and are expressed at different price levels depending on their date of acquisition. Differences in rates of depreciation and obsolescence, as well as the use of historical rather than replacement values for physical capital, represent disadvantages of the stock measure.

Because the estimates considered later in this chapter are flow measures, their construction can be described in more detail. With regard to the actual measurement of factor intensity, the income or value added generated in any productive activity is attributed to the use of physical capital (for example, machines and equipment) and to labour. Human participation in the production process represents the contribution of rudimentary labour and application of special skills. Accordingly, the share of wages and salaries in value added can be pictured as consisting of two components, that is, the compensation for unskilled labour and the returns to skills. Furthermore, the difference in pay of an unskilled labourer (one with only minimal education and training) and that of a skilled labourer represents the returns paid for the skills acquired through education and training. To the extent that differences in wages and salaries reflect differences in productive skills, an industry offering relatively high average wages and salaries per employee may be regarded as one which is intensive in its human capital requirements. Similarly, in the absence of excessive profits the relative level of the non-wage and salary component of value added per employee in an industry reflects the intensity of the use of physical capital.

Like the use of stock measures, estimates of factor intensities that are based on the contribution of each input to total value added have several shortcomings. The degree of hardship associated with different occupations will affect the level of wages and salaries. Variations due to this characteristic cannot be distinguished from variations arising from differences in skill requirements. The most prominent distortions, however, stem from non-competitive character-istics that may prevail in various markets. In some industries excessive profits can persist for extended periods and lead to an over-estimation of the contribution of physical capital. Similarly, employees in certain industries may have a greater bargaining power than those in other industries, resulting in relative levels of wages and salaries which do not reflect differences in skill requirements. Finally, inter-national comparisons of relative factor intensities in different industries may suffer from problems that are mainly statistical in nature. The product mix of an industry will differ among countries and the effects can be pronounced when industry estimates are carried out in a highly aggregated form. The discussion clearly implies that the empiricist's tools for determining factor intensities are limited. At best only approximations can be expected. Despite the drawbacks, however, many studies have con-cluded that such measures provide a useful basis for examining international trends in the use of labour and capital.

Estimates of Factor Intensity

In line with the foregoing description, measures of relative factor intensity for both human and physical capital for a selected group of industries and countries are examined in this section.

The estimates are based on a concept of direct factor usage and are expressed as a flow rather than a stock. Two variables are used in the analysis: wages and salaries per employee are regarded as a measure of skill intensity, while non-wage value added per employee is treated as a measure of capital intensity. A measure of relative factor intensity was obtained by expressing the figures as a percentage of the corresponding total for the country's manufacturing sector. Two-year averages were calculated as a means of reducing the impact of cyclical factors. Finally, in order to minimize distortions due to variations in product mix, industries were defined at the most detailed level possible using international data sources. This step limits the number of industries for which data are readily available, but would seem to be essential if comparable figures are to be assembled for several countries.

Textiles

Table 6.1 summarizes the results of this exercise for the textile fabrics industry, which comprises a range of activities which includes the spinning, weaving and finishing of fabrics. Before examining the results several general characteristics can be noted. First, with very few exceptions, the share of employment in each country exceeded the contribution to MVA. This relationship suggests that productivity tends to be somewhat lower than the average for the manufacturing sector. Second, patterns of structural change are remarkably similar among the countries in each respective group. The production of textile fabrics experienced a relative decline in all Western countries. Although the industry is of considerable importance for LDCs, a contraction occurred in many of these countries as well. Finally, despite the use of a fairly

Table 6.1 Industrial Structure and Relative Factor Intensities of the Textile Fabrics[a] Industry, 1970–1971 and 1979–1980 (percentage)

| | Share in total manufacturing | | | | Relative skill intensity[b] | | Relative physical capital intensity[c] | |
| | Employment | | Value added | | | | | |
	1970–1971	1979–1980	1970–1971	1979–1980	1970–1971	1979–1980	1970–1971	1979–1980
Western countries								
Australia	3.5	2.1	2.7	1.8	85	95	70	74
Austria	5.1	4.7	3.8	2.8	83	83	69	72
Canada	2.8	2.0	2.1	1.5	81	82	63	70
Denmark	1.8	1.2	1.6	1.0	92	90	82	72
Finland	3.1	1.9	2.4	1.3	80	83	76	59
Japan	7.3	4.6	5.0	3.1	78	79	56	59
Sweden	1.7	1.1	1.3	0.8	88	89	64	66
UK	4.3	2.9	2.9	1.8	77	77	56	50
USA	3.1	2.6	1.8	1.5	71	71	47	49
Average (unweighted)	3.6	2.6	2.6	1.7	82	83	65	63

LDCs								
Chile	10.9	9.9	6.0	4.1	85	68	47	33
Colombia	3.1	4.7	3.6	4.0	101	107	105	78
Turkey	19.7	13.5	11.1	12.2	90	103	46	90
Ethiopia	34.4	31.5	25.1	19.9	84	90	69	57
Ghana	16.0	17.6	10.1	7.7	100	90	54	34
Hong Kong	11.3	7.8	18.6	9.2	118	115	212	121
Singapore	2.7	2.0	1.5	1.3	71	86	44	53
South Korea	16.2	15.6	9.8	10.9	83	82	53	63
Tunisia	11.3	8.4	8.6	5.5	85	98	70	42
Average (unweighted)	14.0	12.3	10.5	8.3	91	93	78	63

Sources: United Nations, *Yearbook of Industrial Statistics*, Vol. 1 (various issues).

[a] Involves the spinning, weaving and finishing of textiles. The industry consists of ISIC 3211.

[b] Relative skill intensity is represented by wages and salaries per employee in the industry divided by the corresponding ratio for the manufacturing sector.

[c] Relative capital intensity is defined as non-wage value added per employee divided by the corresponding expression for the manufacturing sector.

narrow statistical definition, the 'industry' includes various products that are not closely comparable in terms of their respective factor requirements. The production of textiles includes not only the formation but also the finishing (other than knitting) of fabric from both man-made and natural fibres. Spinning and weaving are generally regarded as labour-intensive operations, but parts of the finishing process – for example, permanent press treatment for shirts or slacks – can be both skill and capital-intensive (Toyne, et al., 1984, p. 13). Thus the estimates provide only a composite picture for a set of activities which are, at best, loosely related.

Table 6.1 shows that relative factor intensities in Western countries were similar and changed very little between 1970 and 1980. A much wider variation can be seen in the estimates for LDCs, a fact which suggests corresponding differences in production technologies and product mix. Physical capital is used relatively sparingly and skill requirements are only moderate. Moreover, the estimates provide little indication of an upgrading in the relative requirements for labour skills or physical capital during the decade – neither in Western countries nor in LDCs.

The results agree with the casual impressions of the industry formed by most analysts, but they are contrary to the claims of some industry spokesmen and much of the anecdotal evidence found in the literature. The latter sources point to the availability of various innovations, most of which entail greater applications of physical capital. The use of automatic looms and robots in the spinning and weaving of yarn and cloth, for example, can have a dramatic impact on labour productivity, on the size of the firm's work force and on its wage bill. In a fully robotized plant producing yarn for shirts, labour may account for no more than 10 per cent of manufacturing costs (down from 50 per cent in 1975) and even in the production of a traditionally labour-intensive product like denim, labour costs could be reduced to as little as 15 per cent of manufacturing costs (*The Economist*, 27 July 1985). Such opportunities are certainly available to textile producers and, if they were widely adopted, should result in an industry which made greater use of physical capital (and perhaps skilled labour) than can be inferred from the estimates in Table 6.1. A closer look at trends in technological innovation, however, reveals a pattern of innovation which is fragmented, diverse and does not reflect a single-minded concern with labour-saving innovations.

Beginning in the mid–1930s, the development of new technologies was concerned with the manufacture of synthetic and blended-fibres. In comparison with technologies used in other industries, these were predominantly labour-intensive (Toyne, et al., 1984, p. 43). A reorientation of the industry's priorities had taken place by the mid–1960s as a result of growing competition. However, the objectives were varied. New advances emphasized product development (for example, specialized fabrics) and improvements in product quality as well as technical innovations which improved production versatility and/or reduced the labour force.

One reason for this diversity of objectives is that the industry's research programmes are mainly concerned with very specific applications or problems. Because textile producers depend on their suppliers of fibres and the manufacturers of textile equipment for major technological developments (Toyne, et al., 1984, p. 35), innovations intended to reduce the labour costs of the textile industry do not receive a high priority. An even more important explanation is that many Western producers have sought to avoid direct competition with low-wage producers in LDCs. Some have moved up market into production of high-quality and high-fashion clothing where their proximity to the final consumer is an advantage. In doing this they may rely on modern computer networks to gather information on fashion changes, to produce only 'to order' (thus reducing the inventories and stocks to be carried), or to adjust production runs quickly in response to capricious shifts in demand. Other producers have chosen to specialize in items such as carpets or furniture coverings where competition from LDCs is less intense. Any of these moves may result in some upgrading of technologies. But they are not primarily intended to redress cost disadvantages arising from international differences in pay scales or to reduce the amount of unskilled labour required by the firm. Instead, the moves emphasize the need to respond quickly to the vagaries of the market, to improve the firm's materials-handling capabilities, or to enable it to find a 'safe' market niche.

Textile producers have also found that the introduction of new technologies has reduced their flexibility. Some of the largest firms (mainly American ones) have embarked on investment programmes with the simple objective of producing more material. Such investments have also made their operations more capital intensive, with the result that the firms can no longer react quickly to changes in demand. For example, to make their investments pay, manufacturers have had to convince buyers to take fabric rolls exceeding 3,500 yards (3,200 m). In the past a typical roll would have been 100 yards (91.5 m). These types of changes impinge on the firm's ability to stay abreast of the fast-changing fashion market.

Another reason for the slow pace of modernization is that a majority of firms in both Western countries and LDCs are small and lack the finances to modernize. And as the rate of technological innovation has accelerated, the cost of textile machinery has risen. Only the largest and financially strongest firms have managed to stay abreast of these trends. The inability to modernize is a problem even in countries which are thought to be among the most efficient textile producers. For instance, in 1981 up to 60 per cent of Hong Kong's dyeing and finishing capacity was out of date, while 30 per cent of South Korea's textile machinery was regarded as obsolete (*The Economist*, 12 December 1981). Similar conditions prevail in the USA, where the rate of modernization (defined as the ratio of machines supplied to the number already installed) in spinning and weaving was less than one-half the EC average throughout most of the 1970s (*Far Eastern Economic Review*, 30 April 1982, p. 45). When all Western countries are considered as a group, investment by the textile industry has been found to have declined, both relatively and absolutely, after 1974 (GATT, 1984, p. 56).

Finally, the role of public policy is relevant. Textiles (along with clothing) have long been subject to a variety of trade restraints. The first 'voluntary' agreement to limit exports was signed by Japanese textile producers with the USA In 1936. After the Second World War the Asian textile industry rebuilt and resumed its exports to Western countries. And in 1962 a Long Term Arrangement for International Trade in Cotton Textiles (LTA) was concluded which restricted exports to most Western countries. The stated purpose of the LTA was to allow Western producers a temporary breathing space to adjust to increased imports from low-wage countries. But the breathing space proved to be too short and the LTA was periodically renewed before it was replaced in 1973 by an international agreement that covered not only cotton but all major textile fibres. Known as the Multifibre Arrangement (MFA), the present system is composed of an elaborate network of tariffs and quotas which has been periodically renewed by the signatories. Each version has been more restrictive than its predecessor (Shepherd, 1981, p. 2).

Justification for the MFA rests largely on the argument that the industry's dependence on unskilled labour gives producers in low-wage countries a decisive advantage over their competitors in high-wage countries. In principle, the MFA is still regarded as a 'temporary' measure intended to allow Western firms the time they need to modernize and regroup. It is a powerful instrument for restraint, however, applying as it does to 80 per cent of world trade in fibres, fabrics and clothes. It encompasses not only all the major textile products but also applies to every major consuming market. Consumer organizations have suggested that in Western Europe the restrictions have boosted the prices of textiles and garments by 10–15 per cent (*Far Eastern Economic Review*, 2 May 1985, p. 62). Patterns of trade, investment criteria, decisions regarding the products to be produced and many other aspects of the industry are influenced by the Arrangement. Because of the MFA, Western producers are under less pressure to innovate and modernize than would be the case if competition were less restrained.

Automobiles

Table 6.2 provides data on the production of motor vehicles, an industry with factor requirements which are quite different from textiles. A comparison of country data on employment and MVA shows that in most Western countries productivity exceeds the average for the manufacturing sector although this is not true for some of the LDCs listed. The automobile industry is an important one in all countries but, with few exceptions, its contribution to employment and MVA did not increase during the 1970s.

Production of passenger automobiles is clearly the dominant activity throughout the industry. However, international comparisons are complicated by wide variations in product specialization. Product lines range from small subcompacts to luxury cars. While major firms may choose to compete across the entire range, others specialize in the production of certain types of automobiles and factor intensities will vary as a result. Comparisons between Western countries and LDCs are particularly difficult. Automobile firms in only four of the latter countries – Argentina, Brazil, India and South Korea – are sufficiently developed so as to account for more than 90 per cent of the final product. In other LDCs the industry is limited to the assembly of complete kits (CKD) or local production of some parts and components along with the assembly of knocked-down kits (KD sets). One result is that the contribution of domestic firms, that is, the local content, in countries such as Chile and Colombia accounts for no more than 20–40 per cent of the final product (Jones and Womack, 1985, pp. 395–97). Furthermore, these operations are likely to require a different mix of factors (in particular, greater amounts of unskilled labour) than is the case for Western firms.

The estimates in Table 6.2 depict an industry which everywhere relies on a relatively skilled labour force. To some extent the results probably over-estimate the importance of skilled labour. High wages may also reflect the fact that auto-workers are widely unionized and have negotiated pay scales which are more generous than in other industries. This possibility would partly explain the significant rise in relative skill intensities in the USA during the 1970s. The relâtive use of physical capital varies more widely among Western countries but tended to decline during the 1970s. In the LDCs the evidence suggests a different pattern of factor usage. Skill intensities were high and remained fairly stable during the previous decade, while the use of physical capital often fell relative to the average for manufacturing. The latter trend may be due to the international pattern of specialization – expansion of assembly operations and the production of automobile parts and accessories – requiring less physical capital than would be the case for expanding industries in the LDCs.

The industry's history of technological advancement dates back to 1910 and has been pictured as consisting of at least three phases (Altshuler, *et al.*, 1984). The first phase began with the mass production of automobiles in the USA. American producers undercut European firms, which were geared to supply custom-built models. The European response was to impose heavy tariffs on both imported cars and components, a tactic which led the Americans to establish their own European facilities. A second phase began with the formation of the EC and the general decline in the Community's tariff barriers. Access to larger markets gave European producers the opportunity to realize greater economies of scale and led to more improvements in production techniques which further lowered the costs to firms using mass-production methods. A third phase occurred in the late 1960s when Japanese car makers emerged as major exporters. The Japanese success was founded on their ability to cut labour costs and simultaneously improve quality. Since the mid–1970s, Western governments have reacted by imposing variety of trade barriers, including tariffs, quotas, 'voluntary' export restraints and local content laws. The Japanese motor vehicle industry has nevertheless continued to modernize and for 1979–80 reported the highest relative usage of physical capital of any country as shown in Table 6.2. By 1985, Japanese producers were believed to have a cost advantage over American producers of at least $2,000 per car and a smaller, but distinct, advantage over European competitors.

Table 6.2 Industrial Structure and Relative Factor Intensities in the Motor Vehicle Industry,[a] 1970–1971 and 1797–1980 (percentage)

	Share in manufacturing employment		Share in MVA		Relative skill intensity[b]		Relative physical capital intensity[c]	
	1970–1971	1979–1980	1970–1971	1979–1980	1970–1971	1979–1980	1970–1971	1979–1980
Western countries								
Australia	6.2	7.1	7.2	6.3	108	101	124	76
Austria	1.8	1.9	1.9	2.1	115	115	90	101
Canada	5.7	6.2	8.1	7.1	124	115	161	115
Finland	1.5	1.7	1.2	1.5	105	103	56	75
Japan	5.2	6.4	6.6	7.7	112	122	134	118
Sweden	5.2	7.9	5.0	7.9	103	101	91	101
UK	6.2	5.9	5.5	5.2	119	113	56	67
USA	4.7	4.7	6.1	5.3	121	135	138	97
West Germany	...	9.2	...	9.5	...	116[d]	...	92[d]
Average (unweighted)	4.6	5.7	5.2	5.8	112	113	106	85

LDCs								
Chile	2.4	1.8	3.0	1.7	138	114	121	88
Colombia	1.9	3.1	2.2	2.1	102	121	107	86
Turkey	1.4	3.2	0.8	3.8	137	126	38	120
Ghana	2.1	2.3	2.7	1.5	94	93	139	60
Hong Kong	0.0	0.1	0.0	0.1	114	107	117	123
Singapore	1.5	0.6	1.6	0.5	111	119	105	59
South Korea	2.1	3.0	3.2	3.1	149	132	152	88
Tunisia	0.9	2.0	1.3	2.3	88	107	190	126
Average (unweighted)	1.5	2.0	1.9	1.9	117	115	121	94

Sources: For West Germany, OECD, 1984. For all other data, United Nations, *Yearbook of Industrial Statistics*, Vol. 1 (various issues).

[a] The industry refers to ISIC 3843. It includes passenger automobiles, commercial cars and buses and the specialized manufacture of motor vehicle parts such as engines, brakes, clutches, transmissions, wheels or frames.

[b] Relative skill intensity is represented by wages and salaries per employee in the industry divided by the corresponding ratio for the manufacturing sector.

[c] Relative capital intensity is defined as non-wage value added per employee divided by the corresponding expression for the manufacturing sector.

[d] Data refer only to 1980.

Unlike textiles and other labour-intensive industries, international competition in the motor vehicle industry is still confined to Japanese, European and American firms. The issue of factor intensity arises in this context, but more attention is focused on related aspects such as international differences in labour productivity and labour costs. Wage differentials are regarded as a major reason for variations in the competitive abilities of Western countries. The American auto industry entered the 1980s in a particularly difficult position. In 1970, average hourly earnings in the industry were the third highest in all of US manufacturing and during the next decade the increase in earnings was among the most rapid of any American industry.

Such a trend is perplexing, since that period was a particularly difficult one for American automobile producers. Lawrence and Lawrence (1985) offer one explanation. They suggest that the ability of trade unions to extract concessions depends partly on the industry's opportunities to substitute capital for labour. When output is rising this is not so difficult, as the industry's capacity must also be increased. But in a market which is stagnating or is subject to import penetration, such a tactic may not be feasible. The fact that the US automobile industry was already capital-intensive would mean that the possibilities for labour-saving adaptations were less numerous. But microeconomic theory also shows that, so long as the firms can cover some portion of their fixed costs, it would be logical to continue operations. The threat of closure would eventually undermine the position of the trade union. In the meantime, however, large wage increases could be expected. Such an end-game tactic may be applied repeatedly as the competitive edge between American, European and Japanese firms change.

Throughout most of the 1970s and early 1980s, conventional expectations for the industry highlighted the importance of international differences in labour costs. Small cars were picked to dominate world markets, as the pressures for energy conservation and environmental protection mounted. The number of models produced by major firms was expected to fall and the demand patterns in different national markets was expected to converge. Based on this line of reasoning, international differences in labour costs per unit of output would become the crucial determinant of competitive ability. Only firms with very high volumes and low production costs could hope to survive and they would have to relocate more and more of their operations to low-wage countries.

There are now several reasons why this scenario may not be realized. First, the conventional view was based on the assumption that a minimum scale of efficient production was approximately 500,000 vehicles per annum, but much smaller runs are now feasible with new, computer-controlled methods of production. These innovations should also permit specialized car makers to continue operation, although they may have to collaborate on certain items (for example, engines) where volume would still be crucial. Second, new technologies for the production of components are making it possible to produce a wider range of fuel-efficient models. Third, demand patterns in major markets have not converged as expected; consumers continue to want different cars. Fourth, with the eventual development of flexible manufac-turing systems – production systems relying on a computer-controlled network of automated machine tools and other computer aids – international differences in unit labour costs will become less important. The underlying change in cost components should permit the final assembly of automobiles to be located in the major consuming markets.

In conclusion, the industry's technological development is resulting in highly automated processes that require small amounts of direct labour. This is especially true for the production of engines or transmissions which are also very capital intensive. Only the production of minor mechanical components (such as starter-motors and alternators) con-tinues to be relatively labour intensive. On a cost basis the LDCs may still be competitive. As recently as 1984 the average wage of an assembly worker in South Korea was only one-tenth that earned by a member of the American automobile union. But the production of motor vehicles is not like textiles – wage costs are only one element and not an important one. Thus, even LDCs with aspirations for motor vehicle production are concerned with a wide range

145

of issues (a number of which are discussed in later chapters) that go far beyond the subjects addressed here.

Chemical industries

The last two industries to be considered in this chapter are basic industrial chemicals and polymers (synthetic resins, plastics and man-made fibres). The field of chemicals occupies a sprawling, but ill-defined, terrain at the heart of any large manufacturing sector and the two industries examined here are only a part of that complex.

Chemicals can be divided into two broad groups of products. One includes a diverse set of end-products consumed by households: paints, varnishes, drugs, soaps, cleaning preparations, perfumes, cosmetics and miscellaneous items ranging from polishes and glues to film and explosives. The second group consists of the two industries considered here, along with fertilizers and pesticides and industrial intermediates (for example, acids and solvents). Most firms are extremely large and supply a variety of products which include not only basic chemicals but also intermediate and end-products. At the same time, chemical firms have moved downstream to produce a score of products deep in the heart of other industries. The industry also has many immigrants. Heavy users, in industries such as textiles, steel, food and oil, now produce their own chemicals. Also, the production technologies in use offer a bewildering map of different routes from raw materials to end-products. For all these reasons the boundaries of each industry are extremely blurred and make any quantitative assessment a tentative one.

Table 6.3 provides data for basic industrial chemicals and polymers. Because the contribution of each industry to MVA usually exceeds the corresponding shares in employment, levels of productivity can be assumed to be relatively high. The work forces in the two industries are also highly skilled, reflected by the fact that wages and salaries per employee are 20–30 per cent above the average for manufacturing. The outstanding feature, however, is the heavy reliance on physical capital, which is often three to four times the level recorded for the manufacturing sector as a whole. Despite relatively high levels of productivity and capital intensity, neither industry has expanded significantly since the early 1970s. Production and employment have grown at rates equal to (or even less than) the rest of manufacturing.

The basis for the modern chemical industries was lain in the early part of this century. The raw materials originally used by chemical producers were animal fats, salt, limestone, pyrites and some coal and tar. Following the advent of petrochemicals (around 1920 in the USA), however, firms turned to oil and gas as the basic material inputs as they were easier to work with. The use of petrochemicals eventually led to a whole new range of production processes and products. During the 1950s and 1960s basic chemicals and polymers were consistently among the fastest growing industries in manufacturing. Annual rates of expansion were 8–10 per cent in Western countries, but were twice that level for certain plastics and fibres. Under these circumstances it is not surprising that programmes for R and D were predominantly concerned with the development of new products. Technological advances came rapidly as new molecular combinations were developed to make more kinds of chemicals and polymers. The emphasis was on bringing new goods to the market and the results were recognizable in fields as disparate as tyres and textiles or paint and plastic raincoats. With accelerating growth and rapid development of new markets there was little reason to be concerned with factor-saving innovations of any form.

By the beginning of the 1970s, the pace of technological development had begun to slacken. Increased competition for available funds, especially government support and industrial aids, was one explanation. Electronics and aerospace replaced chemicals as major recipients of government funds. Growing concern with environmental and toxicological problems also forced major firms to divert a significant portion of their funds for both R and D and capital spending to these purposes, with the result that the introduction of new products and processes has slowed. Also, advances in pure research began to slow down. Development of new molecular combinations for plastics and fibres became more

Table 6.3 Industrial Structure and Relative Factor Intensities in Chemical Industries, 1970–1971 and 1979–1980 (percentage)

	Share in total manufacturing				Relative skill intensity[a]		Relative physical capital intensity[b]	
	Employment		Value added					
	1970–1971	1979–1980	1970–1971	1979–1980	1970–1971	1979–1980	1970–1971	1979–1980
Manufacture of basic industrial chemicals except fertilizers (ISIC 3511)[c]								
Western countries								
Australia	0.9	0.9	1.5	1.5	111	134	217	210
Canada	1.4	1.4	2.2	2.9	134	138	175	266
Finland	1.2	0.9	2.2	1.4	127	115	241	180
Japan	1.2	1.1	2.5	2.4	145	150	253	259
Sweden	0.7	1.3	1.1	1.7	111	110	214	157
UK	1.7	2.0	3.2	3.5	131	137	254	216
USA	1.4	1.4	3.0	3.2	120	139	281	298
West Germany[d]	...	3.8	...	6.2	...	130	...	189
Average (unweighted)	1.2	1.4	2.2	2.9	126	132	234	222
LDCs								
Chile	0.5	0.3	0.3	0.3	150	72	47	102
Colombia	1.3	1.0	1.7	1.5	137	130	114	151
Ghana	0.2	0.3	0.2	0.3	79	228	108	67
Hong Kong	0.1	0.1	0.3	0.2	152	117	525	266
Indonesia	0.3	0.5	0.3	0.7	93	151	98	130
South Korea	0.4	0.7	0.6	1.6	198	165	179	249
Average (unweighted)	0.5	0.5	0.6	0.8	135	144	179	161

Manufacture of chemical polymers (ISIC 3513)[e]

Western countries								
Australia	0.3	0.4	0.6	0.8	132	192	220	260
Austria	1.2	1.1	1.5	1.5	121	119	123	148
Canada	0.2	0.3	0.4	0.6	129	141	211	259
Denmark	0.8	1.2	0.9	1.5	104	105	125	160
Finland	0.7	1.3	0.8	1.6	108	114	118	134
Japan	1.2	0.8	3.4	1.5	163	131	346	207
Sweden	1.0	1.1	1.2	1.4	105	103	154	144
UK	1.3	1.0	2.0	1.2	133	130	195	93
USA	1.0	0.8	1.5	1.3	126	113	176	190
West Germany[d]	...	0.4	...	0.5	114	...	...	154
Average (unweighted)	0.9	0.8	1.4	1.2	124	128	185	175
LDCs								
Chile	0.5	0.2	0.5	0.9	147	96	90	482
Colombia	0.2	0.5	0.4	1.5	173	152	190	330
Indonesia	0.0	0.0	0.1	0.0	88	96	610	112
South Korea	1.2	0.7	2.4	1.7	154	149	219	297
Average (unweighted)	0.5	0.4	0.9	1.0	141	123	277	305

Sources: For West Germany, OECD (1984). For all other data, United Nations, *Yearbook of Industrial Statistics*, Vol. 1 (various issues).

[a] Relative skill intensity is represented by wages and salaries per employee in the industry divided by the corresponding ratio for the manufacturing sector.

[b] Relative capital intensity is defined as non-wage value added per employee divided by the corresponding expression for the manufacturing sector.

[c] Includes organic and inorganic chemicals (e.g. dyes, solvents, processing chemicals, urea, etc.), acids, nitrates and related products.

[d] Data refer to 1980.

[e] Includes synthetic resins in the form of molding and extrusion compounds; plastic sheets, rods, tubes and granules; cellulosic and other man-made fibres, except glass in the form of mono-filament, multi-filament, staple and tow.

problematic. Only the more difficult molecular chains were left to develop and the prospect of high returns on R and D expenditures faded.

At the same time, the boundaries between chemicals and petrochemicals had become indistinguishable. Over 90 per cent of the basic organic chemicals were being produced from oil and gas feedstocks, while 95 per cent of the ammonia (one of the most important organic chemicals) was derived from these sources. Moreover, petrochemicals often accounted for a significant portion of the material costs. For instance, they amounted to 40 per cent of the cost of inputs used to produce inorganic chloride and for many bulk chemicals the share for oil-derived feedstocks was even higher.

The heavy usage of petrochemicals meant that chemical firms were particularly hard hit by the recurrent energy crises in the 1970s. The impact of the rise in the relative price of energy was twofold, operating directly through higher energy prices and indirectly by raising the prices of materials and intermediates. For instance, during the first energy crisis in 1973–74 the prices of raw materials (for example, naphtha) rose 300–400 per cent; the cost of intermediates such as ethylene and propylene increased 100–200 per cent; and finished products (bags, film, moldings, etc.) rose 35–50 per cent in price (ECE, 1974, p. 2).

Once the era of cheaply priced feedstocks ended many of the conventional rules governing plant economies were no longer applicable. By the 1980s the input requirements of most of the world's chemical producers could be described as 'feedstock-intensive' as well as capital-intensive. The new significance of feedstocks had several implications. First, the economies of scale to be realized by building large plants no longer brought significant cost savings. This development led firms to reorient their research programmes to search for ways to reduce the costs of raw materials and feedstocks. Second, variable costs (including labour costs) had previously accounted for only a small portion of total production costs. Under these circumstances the savings offered by cutting back on production were not very obvious in the short run. Traditionally, chemical plants had been run at close to full capacity, in the hope that a larger market share could be captured by selling the extra production at reduced prices. That alternative became less attractive when the rise in feedstock prices made variable costs a significant part of total costs.

Chemical producers experienced a second price shock in the late 1970s when oil prices again rose significantly. For instance, the spot market price of one of the most basic chemical inputs, naphtha, rose by 250 per cent during the first quarter of 1978 (ECE, 1982, pp. 3–4). Because of greater competition between producers, many were unable to pass on all the rise in costs to their customers. The experiences of chemical firms in the 1970s helped to launch a new research drive for alternatives to oil and gas. Chemists began to search for new ways to use coal as the basic raw material and to produce chemicals from vegetable matter, that is, biomass. But the search for alternative inputs again slackened when the price of oil plummeted in the mid–1980s.

In conclusion, it is obvious from Table 6.3 that international differences in labour costs and the related issue of labour-intensity are of little importance in determining the competitive abilities of chemical firms. During the 1970s much of the conventional wisdom was that feedstocks were the major determinant of competitiveness and would govern the location of new chemical-producing centres. In periods when oil prices have slumped, however, that view has given way to arguments which stress the proximity to markets and buyers as the predominant criterion for success.

Further analysis of other industries can only add to the diversity and variation of experiences noted here. The discussion, however, is sufficient to demonstrate some of the problems encountered in carrying out an industry-wide assessment of relative factor intensities. In addition to the conceptual and theoretical issues which have to be addressed, the cluster of products involved will often have a fairly diverse range of input requirements. Despite these difficulties the material which has been assembled provides the basis for at least a few tentative conclusions. First, it is clear that the relative significance of various factors will vary between industries and in some cases the cost of labour can be of minor importance in comparison with other factors. Second, the impression that technological change often entails a consistent sequence of innovations singularly intended to erase a specific cost differential is overdrawn. Large segments of an industry may seek to blunt the threat of more efficient competitors through other means, such as moving up-market or by specialising in products which offer them a built-in advantage not directly related to cost. The relative prices of various factors can also change (as illustrated by the effects of the energy price rise for chemical firms) and will alter patterns of factor intensity. Because an industry's technological objectives will be subject to all these considerations, they are likely to be diverse and to change over time. Finally, theoretical discussions of relative factor intensity can be carried out in isolation from other industry characteristics, but once the concept is applied all sorts of interrelationships can enter the picture and complicate the analysis.

Supplementary Reading

Bhalla (1975) surveys the limitations of various measures of labour intensity. With regard to the elasticity of substitution, Morawetz (1976) summarizes the results of econometric studies carried out in the 1960s and early 1970s. A more recent discussion of these aspects can be found in Krueger (1982). Hirsch (1974) provides an example of an applied study relating to technological change, factor intensities and factor endowments. Hamilton and Svensson (1983) examine the issues arising from the choice between direct and total factor intensities. The same two authors have carried out a study of factor intensities (1984) using a flow measure.

Among the industries discussed in this chapter, an introduction and overview of the textile industry is found in Toyne *et al.* (1984). The analysis by GATT (1984) provides an overview of structural change and trade policy in textiles, as well as a useful discussion of how various industry characteristics will affect the estimates of capital stock, productivity, import penetration and other features. For a discussion of the restrictions imposed on trade in textiles and the underlying issues, see Keesing and Wolf (1980). Choi, Chung and Marian (1985) also examine the MFA but also consider several of the circumstances governing trends in production and employment. Pelzman (1983) surveys the methods for measuring the costs of protection in this industry and the results obtained. From his study of the US textile industry, Williams (1984) concludes that capital is not readily substituted for labour. Balassa (1983) emphasizes the importance of product specialization by American producers as a response to competition from LDCs, while Yamazawa (1980) has studied the Japanese textile industry and its responses to greater competition from LDCs.

In the field of chemicals, the ECE publishes a survey of market trends and prospects every five years and conducts an annual review of the chemical industry in Western Europe. A detailed account of the behaviour of major chemical firms during the 1970s has been compiled by UNCTAD (1979). Freeman, Clark and Soete (1982, pp. 82–100) have studied the long-term process of innovation in the chemical industry, as well as other industries discussed in later chapters of this book. Turner's account of the petrochemical industry (1982b, pp. 118–29) stresses the fact that leading firms have remained adaptable, although the industry itself is rapidly maturing. Worldwide studies of the industry are periodically carried out by UNIDO. Additional material on other industries discussed in Chapter 6 are given elsewhere in this book.

CHAPTER SEVEN

Industrial Processing of Natural Resources

Industrial processing of natural resources is a comparatively distinctive phase of manufacturing, owing to factors such as the capricious distribution of resource deposits, the emotive issues of ownership and national sovereignty, the large capital requirements involved and the oligopolistic structure of firms engaged in these operations.

The political history of the mineral processing industry dates back to the nineteenth century when demand first began to expand rapidly. In addition to increasing their capacity to extract domestic minerals, firms in Western countries began to seek supplies abroad, notably in areas of new settlements and colonies. The resultant growth in international trade in minerals was matched by a dramatic enlargement in optimal size of operation. Greater economies of scale and associated increases in capital requirements eventually led to extensive vertical integration of extraction and processing activities. As early as the 1920s, the mineral processing industry had become oligopolistic in structure. By that time, many of the operations based in LDCs were foreign-owned and their production marked for Western countries. Thus, the current global configuration of extraction and industrial processing activities is the result of a complex set of determinants. Some of these involve purely economic considerations, such as resource endowments and relative costs of other inputs. Others relate to techno-logical considerations, the operating practices of multinationals and the outcome of a long history of confrontation and negotiation between multinationals and governments – involving both LDCs and Western countries. The following section provides a survey of these determinants.

Political Motives and Economic Determinants

The reasons why governments of LDCs have sought to extend the degree of resource processing as an alternative to exporting the raw material are varied. Both economic and political considerations are involved. Initially, attention was focused on the extraction, rather than the processing, of natural resources. Governments were mainly concerned with ways to wrest a larger share of the revenues away from the multinationals involved in resource extraction. This desire was encapsulated in the notion of 'returned value', which referred to the proportion of the value of final output retained in the host country. Early studies suggested that returned value could be increased considerably through appropriate government policies. For instance, an investigation of Chilean copper operations found that the proportion of the total value of output returned to the country rose from 30–35 per cent in the 1920s to around 60 per cent in the late 1950s. The redistribution partly resulted from government-sponsored increases in wage levels. But direct and indirect government levies on foreign-owned mining companies were found to be even more important (Reynolds and Mamalakis, 1965).

Gradually, the ambitions of LDCs extended from the extraction phase to include domestic processing of natural resources. Greater involvement in local processing would mean enlarged capital imports to erect domestic facilities. Supporters argued, however, that the long-term gains – achieved through increased export earnings, a reduction in the volatility of export prices and other reasons discussed below – would outweigh the costs. While the tone of the political rhetoric was sometimes flamboyant, involving multinationals as well as governments of both LDCs and Western countries, there were several tangible reasons for the drive to extend domestic control over resources. One was the desire, observed in LDCs of all political persuasions, to sever ties with Western countries which savoured of colonial relationships. The continuation of such links were regarded as a blot on their integrity and commitment to nationalism to governments of LDCs. A second common motive was the wish to ensure that uses of the countries natural resources, in terms of revenues generated and impetus provided to domestic growth, were consistent with intentions set out in development plans. Third, government officials and industrialists in LDCs – like their counterparts elsewhere – recognized that their countries' natural resources were capable of generating substantial revenues which offered powerful sources of patronage. The ability to control (and disperse) large sums of money and to allocate prestigious jobs should not be underestimated in any country. Fourth, governments of LDCs aspired to arrogate more control as a means to achieve political goals, both domestic and foreign.

The political motives for enlarging the domestic processing capabilities of LDCs are perhaps the most obvious ones. Economic considerations are equally relevant, but are less easily explored. When viewed in economic terms, a decision to establish domestic processing capacity can be approached in one of two ways. First, activities such as refining or fabricating can be evaluated in terms of their input requirements, the possibilities for weight reduction through processing, transport needs and other associated costs. Alternatively, all relevant factors can be lumped together and weighted (or scaled) in an appropriate way to yield a one-dimensional indicator of efficiency (for example, an internal rate of return from a cash flow analysis or an estimate of domestic resource costs). Most investigations opt for the former approach and this is adopted in the following section.

Comparative Advantage and the Cost of Major Inputs

The concept of comparative advantage provides a convenient framework for examining the locational determinants of any economic activity but is nevertheless subject to various qualifications. In the neoclassical (Heckscher-Ohlin) tradition, only two factors of production, usually labour and capital, are considered. In the present case several inputs, including labour, capital, energy and raw materials, are relevant to a discussion of international competitiveness and its implications for the location of processing facilities.

Other assumptions common to the simplified version of comparative advantage pose more difficult problems. First, the theory often treats levels of production as divisible, in the sense that economies of scale are minimal, or not appropriate (Johnson, 1975, p. 33). But the question of economies of scale has already been singled out as a prominent characteristic of many processing enterprises and later discussion will show that it has important implications for the siting and marketing of processed commodities. Second, production technologies are usually assumed to be identical, or homogeneous, in different countries. The extent to which the multinational dominates mineral processing activities would suggest that, in comparison with other areas of manufacturing, technologies in use may be similar regardless of location. However, multinationals are no longer the only operatives in the field. And the heavy capital outlays needed to erect modern processing facilities mean that even the largest firms (including state-owned ones) may be reluctant to modernize their operations as soon as new technologies become available – particularly when new advances emerge shortly after the original plants have come onstream.

Despite these qualifications, the theory of comparative advantage can still tell us something about both the interrelationships between relative costs and factor abundance and the locational implications for the processing and fabrication of minerals. This requires information about production costs. Table 7.1 summarizes some of the available evidence, showing the approximate shares of four inputs in total costs. Several generalizations can be made on the basis of this evidence.

First, labour accounts for a comparatively small proportion of the total. The low shares reported for aluminium,

Table 7.1 Approximate Cost Structure for Selected Inputs (percentage)

Industry	Country of location	Materials	Labour	Capital charges	Energy
Refined copper (ore input)	LDC	60	...	...	...
Aluminium					
Alumina (bauxite input)	LDC	27	5	37	15
Aluminium (alumina input)	LDC	30–33	3–4	23	16
Aluminium (alumina input)	Western	28–30	4–5	16–18	30
Semi-fabricated products	Western	43	21	15	...
Ammonia (natural gas)	Western	22–43	2–6	41–46	...
Steel					
Crude	LDC	24–43	15–33	18–24	17
Crude	Western	22	35	8	...
Specialty	Western	28	27	34	11
Wood					
Plywood	LDC	31	10–16	12–23	...
Veneer	LDC	55	8	10	8
Pulp/paper	LDC	26	4–6	30–34	...
Petrochemicals					
Styrene	a	60	4	13	20
Polyvinyl chloride	a	70	2	18	4

Sources: For copper, aluminium, ammonia, plywood and pulp/paper: UNIDO, 1979a, p. 180; for alumina, ESCAP, 1983, p. 68; for steel: Ballance and Sinclair, 1983, p. 111; Fong et al., 1981, p. 104; Taniura, 1981, p. 89; for veneer: Velasco et al., 1981, p. 51; for petrochemicals: UNIDO, 1981d, p. 90.

ammonia, wood pulp or petrochemicals would suggest that there may be little advantage in locating these processing facilities in LDCs simply because of cheap labour. The situation is more ambiguous when labour accounts for a moderate share of total costs – for example, in the case of crude steel, wood products and, surprisingly, semi-fabricated aluminium products. The latter may be largely owing to the source of the data (the USA) and illustrates one difficulty with this type of comparison. A small share of labour costs for industries in low-wage countries may simply reflect their competitive advantage in this factor. There is often a large wage differential between rich and poor countries – a multiple of five or more in some cases. Thus, even if producers in high-wage countries are willing to replace their expensive labour with capital, their ability to do so may be limited by the nature of the production process. This could mean that labour's share in total costs would still exceed the corresponding proportion in low-wage countries. Cost advantages based on cheap labour can be dismissed as insignificant only if the wage share is low in both rich and poor countries, as appears to be true for the production of aluminium or petrochemicals.

Table 7.1 shows that capital charges account for a moderate to significant proportion of the total for most mineral processing activities. Because capital is likely to have much smaller unit cost differences among countries than labour, a comparison of capital shares is not subject to the same qualifications. However, when capital accounts for a high proportion of total costs, savings in capital charges will influence decisions on the location of processing sites. Governments in many LDCs have given a high priority to the development of mineral processing industries and have frequently attempted to tip the balance in their favour by subsidizing some capital costs. Institutions in Western countries also make loans available to LDCs for extraction for material processing activities. These practices are widespread and, coupled with the growing distaste for 'polluting' industries in Western countries, have speeded the development of processing facilities in LDCs. Another aspect, however, may favour a decision to locate in a

Western country. As producers of capital equipment, Western countries have an inherent cost advantage in the price of capital goods, one that is enhanced by the often poor conditions under which plant construction takes place in LDCs. These considerations can be significant as suggested by the fact that, in 1979, construction costs for chemical plants in the Middle East were 60 per cent greater than those for similar plants in Western Europe (UNIDO, 1981a, p. 119).

Third, the share of raw materials varies widely among industries but is almost always an important, if not the predominant, cost consideration. While the quality, quantity and accessibility of natural resources will determine which deposits can be most profitably extracted, the implications for locations of downstream processing facilities are somewhat different. The theory of comparative advantage emphasizes the importance of the relative prices of inputs. Countries having an abundance of a particular raw material would presumably enjoy some competitive superiority in processing over other countries where the resource is scarce. However, little or no information of a comparable nature is available on relative prices for use in international studies.

Fourth, the amount of data which can be compiled on the proportion of total costs accounted for by energy is limited and not reliable. Energy charges vary widely owing to differences in available supplies and energy sources (even within a particular country), price control, subsidies, taxes, etc. Thus, meaningful statements are difficult to make unless the investigation is conducted at the level of individual projects or firms. One generalization that can be made without undue qualification is that energy often accounts for a smaller share of total costs in LDCs than in Western countries. This is largely attributable to the different energy sources in the two groups of countries. For example, many steel-makers in LDCs practice charcoal iron-making, using local wood rather than importing coal for later use as coke. Until recently, Latin America's leading producer of iron, Brazil, obtained about one-third of its iron through this process and the present figure is expected to rise. Because the method is relatively labour-intensive and yields a high quality iron, it is common in many LDCs.

Transport Costs

It is generally believed that, since processing both reduces the weight and increases the value of the commodity, transport costs would favour producers of the mineral who wish to process locally before exporting. The situation, however, is complex and depends on the commodity concerned. For copper, which is typical of many non-ferrous metals, tonnage is reduced by smelting near the mine since more than half the ore concentrates are waste material. But there is negligible weight saving by refining blister into copper, and no transport advantage would result from establishing a refinery in a LDC. Moreover, shipping charges can be lower for bulk cargo (for instance, alumina which is a powder), than for ingots. The latter are costly to handle and may cancel any weight saving obtained through smelting. Shipping rates are also higher per tonne for fabricated metal than for ingots, a consideration which could limit the efforts of producers in LDCs to move into semi-fabricating. In the case of timber processing, for instance, nearly one-half of the wood is waste and logs take up more volume than sawnwood or boards. However, shipping charges are higher for processed wood than logs and cancel a part of the advantage.

In at least two instances transport costs may deter processing in LDCs. Rubber gains in weight and (especially) volume in the shape of tyres and this fact contributes to the location of tyre manufacturing in consuming markets. Problems of shipping or handling can also deter local manufacture of intermediate chemicals (for example, ethylene and sulphuric acid) from their raw materials. Although transport costs have generally declined over the last two decades, their significance in determining the location of processing facilities should not be underestimated. Even when they amount to only a small proportion of production costs, variations may still be important. They are particularly important when technologies and other input costs are similar at different locations.

Economies of Scale

Almost all processing activities are subject to economies of scale. Countries which are leading suppliers can usually produce volumes well in excess of those required to achieve scale economies. Problems can arise, however, from the exporter's inability to market the large volume of output associated with a plant of optimum size. In addition, small producers (for example, Nigerian tin or Bolivian copper) are sometimes not able to generate the volume necessary to justify local processing.

The figures in Table 7.2 provide rough estimates of the minimum volume of output necessary to obtain an economic level of operation. Only countries with big domestic markets could absorb the outputs from those operations having the largest minimum scale of efficient operation; levels of domestic demand in small and/or poor countries would be insufficient. The latter countries may be forced to choose between four difficult options. First, in recognition of the need to achieve a minimum efficient scale of operation, they can forego local processing and export unprocessed commodities or minerals. This decision, however, could require them to import manufactured versions of the same commodity from other countries. Second, they may undertake local processing and then attempt to export that portion which cannot be absorbed domestically. Here, the problems to be faced may involve transport costs, trade barriers and the difficulty of breaking into marketing systems operated by the dominant firms in the industry. Third, processing facilities of an economic size can be erected but, whenever necessary, operated at less than the minimum efficient scale of output. This option would avoid the difficulties encountered in exporting a large proportion of output and, possibly, importing additional inputs. But it will seldom make sense to cut back significantly on the level of operations because marginal costs of production (mainly labour) are low compared with capital costs. Finally,

Table 7.2 Indicative Minimum Plant Sizes

Type of plant	Minimum economic capacity (thousands of tonnes per annum)
Alumina	200
Aluminium	60–80
Copper smelter	100
Copper refinery (primary)	60
Steel mill (integrated)	1,000
Steel mill (DR/EF)[a]	100
Tin smelter	15
Lead smelter, refinery	30
Zinc smelter	30
Nickel smelter (sulphide)	25
Nickel refinery	25
Ferro-nickel plant (oxide)	10–15

Sources: UNIDO, 1981b, p. 25; UNCTC, 1981, p. 18.

[a] DR = direct reduction; EF = electric furnace.
Note: Considerable economies of scale (up to 20 per cent per unit of product) can still be achieved at larger capacities (for example, up to 5 million tonnes per annum for integrated steel mills, and up to 2 million tonnes per annum for alumina refineries).

processing installations of less than optimum size may be installed. Again, however, the failure to attain an efficient scale of operations can impose significant costs. Alumina refineries experience significant economies of scale in plants exceeding one million tonnes of output per year. At this level of operation, investment costs per unit can be 15–20 per cent less than for a plant of 350 tonnes (UNCTC, 1981, pp. 17–18). And yet the lower volume of output still exceeds minimum economic size; smaller plants would incur even higher unit costs! Similarly, during the early 1970s petro-chemical plants could realize a 20–30 per cent saving in investment costs by doubling capacity. In Colombia, for instance, plants were one-fifth the average size found in the USA and unit investment was six times higher (UNIDO, 1979a, p. 184).

The rise in energy costs during the early 1980s reduced, to some extent, the relative importance of scale economies. For instance, a doubling of capacity of an ethylene steam-cracking plant from 150,000 to 300,000 tonnes per year was thought to lead to a 20 per cent reduction in olefin production costs under pricing conditions prevailing in 1972. Based on the structure of prices of inputs which has emerged by 1979, however, the same expansion would lead to only a 6 per cent reduction in production costs. The impact of higher oil prices was probably greatest for the chemical and petrochemical industries, with results which have already been noted in Chapter 6. In other fields of mineral processing, however, new energy-saving technologies were developed (some of which are described in this section), which gradually reduced the share of this input in production costs. The significance of these adjustments was later undercut by the drastic fall in oil prices in the mid–1980s.

The actual capital required for investment in processing facilities can be significant and, thus, the proportionate savings made by attaining a minimum efficient plant size are considerable. Table 7.3 indicates approximate capital outlays per tonne of output. Annual capital charges often exceed operating costs and, together, the two can be equivalent to one-quarter of the initial capital investment. And for plants of somewhat smaller size, capital charges per unit of output would be even higher. More generally, the amounts of capital involved in most investments point to the need to ensure steady rates of return. The substantial sums committed to processing plants are a major reason for the extensive degree of vertical integration which characterizes many commodity processing activities.

Complementary Inputs

For some forms of processing, the need for inputs other than natural resources may determine location. One dramatic example occurs in aluminum smelting; 14–16 megawatt hours of electricity are required to produce one tonne of aluminium (UNCTC, 1981, p. 27). As a result, electricity consumption can account for 14–18 per cent of the cost of ingots at average power rates. However, variations in

Table 7.3 Investment Requirements and Costs of Running Mineral Processing Operations[a] (dollars per tonne)

Process	Capital investment in annual capacity	Annual capital charge	Operating costs	Total costs
Alumina refining	650	105	54	159
Aluminium smelting	2,700	440	518	958
Copper smelting	2,000	325	220	545
Copper refining	500	81	132	213
Steel-making[b]				
DR/EF	370	60	110	170
BF-BOF	820	133	110	243
Lead				
Smelting and refining	700	113	132	245
Nickel processing				
Sulphides	8,200	1,340	860	2,200
Laterites	12,000	1,960	1,370	3,300
Tin smelting	8,000	1,300	410	1,710
Zinc smelting	1,600	260	150	410

Source: UNIDO, 1979b, p. 81.

[a] All values are averages of 1977 conditions for new projects, expressed in 1978 dollars. Figures are approximate values. Different sources and different operating circumstances (e.g. the quality of the inputs used, available infrastructure and technology) would alter the results. For further discussion see the statistical appendix.

[b] DR/EF = direct reduction/electric furnace; BF/BOF = blast furnace/basic oxygen facility.

energy charges may reduce the average cost of ingot production by as much as 6 per cent or raise it by 18 per cent. The importance and potential variation in power costs is a major reason why alumina is often moved long distances to smelters situated near cheap power and why many aluminium-exporting countries do not have smelters. To make use of their ample domestic supplies of energy petroleum producing countries, such as Qatar and the United Arab Emirates, face the opposite problem: they must import alumina for smelting or iron ore for reduction.

In the case of tin the problems concern complementary

metals. Nearly all the tin produced is used in the manufacture of tinplate for cans, but only a small proportion of the product actually consists of tin (currently about 0.5 per cent of the total weight and around 10 per cent of the cost). Instead, the location of other metals is the crucial factor. In the case of steel the growing importance of mini-mills is partly explained by the fact that they rely on scrap as a source of cheap inputs. Such operations are limited to the larger Western countries where scrap is abundant and domestic transport costs provide a natural form of protection which contributes to the existence of regional markets. Steel producers in LDCs have no similar option.

External Economies

External economies are usually thought to favour location in a Western country. For example, it has been suggested that one reason why the huge Bougainville copper mine in Papua New Guinea did not include a smelter was that there would be no local market for the acid by-products (Mikesell, 1975, p. 121). And in the 1950s, aluminum companies built alumina plants in Louisiana, despite the cost advantages of locating near the Jamaican bauxite mines. This decision was based partly on the desire to attain greater economies of scale in producing chemical inputs such as aluminum fluoride. Production of basic chemicals from salts, sulphur and hydrocarbons can also benefit from siting near user industries. Since each chemical has many end-uses and most of the operations are subject to considerable economies of scale, location near consumer markets was preferred. Similarly, a reason for the low productivity in wood processing operations in LDCs is the inability of the producers to utilize residues from sawmilling and board manufacture. Residues are cheap inputs for production of pulp or particle board but either large plants or agglomerations of small units are essential to produce sufficient inputs.

The argument for external economies can be turned around and, in its familiar guise of industrial linkages, be used to justify local processing within the commodity-producing country to stimulate related industries. Thus, it becomes one of the most powerful and often cited arguments for establishing processing facilities in LDCs. The linkages from ore mining through smelting and refining to the fabrication of metal products and finally to the manufacture of capital goods are central strands running through the literature on industrial processing of raw materials. The strategic role of steel in the growth process of the developed countries is frequently cited as evidence of the importance of industrial linkages. More recently, linkages based on local (and comparatively cheap) energy supplies, such as natural gas, are seen as a basis for industrialization in LDCs with few other resources. This version of the argument, based on an abundance of natural gas and which runs through basic chemical operations to the production of ethylene glycol, ethanol, styrene, urea and other simple products, is closely identified with OPEC countries. By 1990, petrochemical capacity in Saudi Arabia alone, for instance, could be sufficient to meet 10 per cent of Europe's needs for basic chemicals (UNIDO, 1983, p. 322).

Technological Change

For several resource-based industries, especially metals, technological change can alter a producer's cost structure significantly. Some observers maintain that innovations by multinationals will generally tend to favour the location of processing facilities in the Western countries, thereby reducing the risk of further exposure of investment in LDCs. Not all innovations have worked in this fashion, however. One of the most important technological advances has been the development of continuous casting in the metals industry. The process converts the molten metal from the final reduction stage (smelter in the case of aluminum, refinery in copper or furnace in steel) into semi-finished forms with an unbroken flow in the operation. This eliminates the need to strip ingots from moulds, to re-heat them and, only then, to form the semi-finished products. Continuous casting saves on energy costs, labour time and improves input utilization. Because of the significant reductions in cost which can be obtained, any producer willing and financially able to install casting facilities will benefit relative to competitors using older technologies. New entrants into metal processing (for instance, in LDCs) will also have some advantage over established producers. They can erect entirely new, or 'greenfield' plants and do not have to deal with the problem of amortizing the costs of previous investments which embodied older technologies.

Another very new technology, with potentially important implications for the structure of part of the world's metal processing industry, is the advent of thin-slab casting for steel. This would sharply reduce the need for today's high rolling mills which apply enormous pressure to squeeze metal slabs down to the necessary thickness. Currently, the continuous slabs that emerge from casting are flattened by a series of rolling mills that can stretch for almost one kilometre and cost up to $500 million. The new caster, which produces much thinner slabs, would require considerably less investment, reduce the optimal plant size and allow greater ease of entry. Among other consequences, these innovations could lead to a further reduction in the degree of oligopolistic control in the steel industries of many Western countries, while simultaneously spurring on the establishment of new capacity on LDCs.

A detailed discussion of technological change in mineral processing is too far removed from the main subject of this chapter. However, the two examples noted above should be sufficient to demonstrate that the significance of technological changes often goes far beyond the confines of the individual firm concerned. The impact of technology may alter the domestic structure of the industry, the international distribution of productive capacity, the extent of foreign competition and even the negotiating positions of major economic actors such as multinationals and host governments.

Multinational Corporations

The last factor to be considered in this section is the role of the multinational. Historically, many of the markets for mined, semi-processed and processed raw materials were controlled by multinationals operating in an oligopolistic manner. The multinationals' domination of these markets resulted from two factors: the desire for security of supplies which, in turn, gave rise to the creation of vertically integrated companies for mining and processing and the need to ensure adequate returns from steadily increasing amounts of capital investment.

Because of these factors, mining companies were among the first multinationals and flourished during the boom that followed the Second World War. Their domination of certain mineral markets was sometimes excessive. Amax, for instance, controlled 50 per cent of the non-socialist world's market for molybdenum (a metal used in everything from light bulbs to jet engines) and a Canadian-based firm, Inco, supplied 90 per cent of the world's nickel. The pre-eminence of the multinationals was reduced somewhat in later years through the nationalization efforts of the LDCs. However, the data in Table 7.4 show that in the mid–1970s multinationals still retained an important role in minerals and mineral processing. In bauxite, the largest corporation was

Table 7.4 Involvement of Multinational Corporations in Mineral Processing in the Mid–1970s (percentage)

Mineral	Share of mineral output		Share of semi-processed output	
	Of biggest company	Of five largest companies	Of biggest company	Of five largest companies
Bauxite	22.0	54.6	22.4	60.1[a]
Copper	11.1	43.1	9.9[b]	39.5
Lead	...	...	7.7	33.7[a]
Nickel	...	...	36.8	77.8[a]
Tin	...	...	29.6	77.0[b]
Zinc	6.8	27.5	12.2	31.7[c]

Source: UNIDO, 1981b, p. 30.

[a] Refining.
[b] Smelting.
[c] Reduction.

responsible for about one-fifth of world output and multi-nationals continued to be well established in other mineral markets shown in the table.

The example of copper can be cited to illustrate the varying degree of multinational involvement in successive stages of processing. The nationalization of mines and processing facilities, which began in the late 1960s, success-fully reduced multinational control over copper markets. In 1970, the eight largest copper firms accounted for over one-half of all copper production in Western countries and LDCs. Approximately 30 per cent of this output was government-owned or controlled, while the remainder was in the hands of multinationals. By 1975, however, the share of production capacity owned by multinationals had been reduced, through nationalization, to around 20 per cent (UNCTC, 1975, p. 5). There were two major reasons why governments of LDCs were able to chip away at the pre-eminent position of the multinationals. First, not all these firms were fully integrated forward into intermediate processing and, second, the technology for copper process-ing was widely known and easily acquired.

Ownership of refining capacity has tended to be more widely dispersed than that for production of copper ore. In 1974, the bulk of refining was carried out by approximately thirty firms, with the ten largest accounting for around 60 per cent of capacity in Western countries and LDCs (UNCTC, 1975, p. 6). And at later stages, such as semi-fabrication and fabrication, patterns of ownership are even more fragmented. In the case of semi-fabrication, the twenty-two largest firms account for about 50 per cent of total capacity outside the socialist countries (UNIDO, 1979b, p. 205). The degree of concentration falls dramatically in copper fabrication and manufacturing, where the number of buyers are dispersed among the electrical machinery, construction, automobile and transport industries. Even the largest fabricators have capacities far less than the output of refined copper by major producers and, for the most part, they are independent firms without forward links.

The desire of LDCs to extend their processing capabilities is complicated by a long-standing preference of many

170

integrated companies to process minerals in their home country. Among the major minerals, Western countries owned roughly one-half of the non-communist world's mining capacity in 1966, but at the same time controlled 60 per cent of smelting and 78 per cent of refining capacity. Ten years later, an even higher proportion of the world's processing capacity was located in Western countries; they owned only 47 per cent of mining capacity while the corresponding figures for smelting and refining were 63 and 79 per cent respectively (UNIDO, 1981b, p. 30). Ozawa (1980) argues that in Japan, a country where multinationals have been a less prominent part of the industrial landscape, the approach has been somewhat different. There, the government's efforts to secure supplies of raw materials meant that Japanese industrial groups were more willing to assist in the establishment of processing facilities in LDCs. Smelting activities for copper, aluminum, iron ore and other metals were gradually transferred to the source of ore supply.

Gradually, however, the multinationals' ability to ensure that their sources of raw material supplies were secure has been eroded. The expropriation of mines in Africa and South America was only one reason for this. Many new, government-sponsored projects in LDCs now exceed the scale of operations by multinationals. Chile, for instance, is now the capitalist world's biggest producer of copper and 80 per cent of the country's production is controlled by the state-owned mining house Codelco. Likewise, the state-owned Carajás mine in Brazil is the world's largest supplier of iron. The mine contains 20 billion tonnes of high quality iron ore and by 1988 annual output could reach 35 million tonnes – nearly as much as the entire US industry produced in 1983. More generally, access to a growing proportion of the world's mineral supplies is being determined by decision centres which are outside the multinationals. Some multinationals responded by attempting to ensure supplies by negotiating long-term contracts spanning periods of 5–20 years with exporters of concentrates. This shift has perhaps gone furthest in the field of oil refining where the actions of OPEC have hastened the transfer of ownership.

171

The multinationals' ability to achieve an adequate rate of return on investment has also been diminished. Responsibility for price-setting, once the sole province of Western oligopolies, has now shifted to the floors of commodity exchanges and LDCs. The result has been that a long tradition of price stability has given way to price volatility. Mineral prices, like those of other commodities, plummeted during the recession which began in the 1970s. The effects were accentuated by the fact that major mineral-consuming industries, such as steel, were particularly hard hit. By 1984, the real price of some minerals was lower than at any time this century – except for the worst years of the Great Depression. The profitability of multinationals has been further reduced by other factors. Most of the high-grade, easily accessible, deposits which were available in the multinationals' home markets have been exhausted, meaning that these operations are now the most expensive. In contrast, many of the new entrants from LDCs are blessed with abundant resources of a relatively high quality. Also, Western firms are now compelled to devote a growing portion of their funds to environmental controls and this, too, has raised their cost.

Multinationals specializing in minerals have been slow to adapt to their new operating environment. They have been hesitant to enter into joint ventures with foreign partners and often lack the marketing and financial expertise associated with multinationals in other fields. Despite their hesitancy, involvement of multinationals in the processing activities of an LDC can be attractive to both sides. These firms sometimes agree to a 'buy-back' clause which provides them with a portion of the output from the plant they are involved in establishing. Such clauses reduce the market risks faced by the LDC participants. In addition, processors in LDCs often encounter problems in marketing their output and these can be mitigated by the participation of multinationals with established distribution systems and a wide range of market contacts.

Evidence from the oil-refining industry suggests a pattern which non-oil firms may eventually adopt. Development of the huge Saudi Basic Industries Corporation (Sabic), for example, involved at least six joint-venture projects between the Saudi government and a host of multinationals – Dow Chemical, a Japanese consortium led by Mitsubishi, Shell, Exxon, Mobil and Taiwanese Fertilisers – among others. Plants now coming onstream will produce 4 per cent of the world's petrochemicals and by the end of the 1980s the total value of investment will be roughly $10 billion. An assured supply of oil was the attraction to Western companies; they were offered 500 barrels per day for every $1 million of investment. Complex cross-financing agreements were also negotiated. For example, Dow and Sabic share ownership of a large ethylene cracker and similar arrangements have been negotiated with the Japanese. Sabic itself is setting up marketing offices, but Western participants, too, may distribute some of the Saudi products. Japanese companies are cutting back their own capacity and hope to re-export the petrochemicals to the Asian markets.

In conclusion, the multinationals' desire for security of supplies and high rates of return can no longer be achieved through vertical integration and traditional price-setting practices. Patterns of ownership and control have changed significantly since the Second World War. However, one characteristic has not been altered. Today's markets for minerals are not any less oligopolistic than those in the past.

Many decision-making responsibilities are still concentrated in the hands of a very few. At the extraction stage most of the mineral exports of LDCs are handled by government-run marketing organizations, or by the government itself. And at later stages of processing, joint ventures between governments of LDCs and multinationals are the general rule. The following section provides an overview of global trends in the processing of natural resources during the last two decades.

International Patterns of Industrial Processing

Having examined the determinants for the location of industrial processing capacity, we now require some factual evidence regarding changes in the global pattern of industrial processing. In particular, is it possible to determine the extent to which the LDCs have succeeded in shifting their industrial base from extraction to downstream processing activities? Some impression of global trends can be gained from data concerning both industrial production and patterns of trade, but before doing so a framework for examining global trends in different fields of industrial processing is helpful.

Industrial development is conventionally pictured from what may be described as a 'horizontal perspective'. Attention is focused on the composition of manufacturing as it relates to production, employment, productivity and trade in the industries making up the manufacturing sector. An examination of manufacturing in terms of light and heavy industry, or with regard to consumer goods, intermediate and capital goods, are useful ways of depicting industrial progress. Nevertheless, these perspectives provide little information concerning the different activities carried out within a particular industry. By its nature, the present topic lends itself to a 'vertical perspective'. That is, activities are examined according to their stage of processing, for example, primary, semi-finished and finished goods, rather than according to the nature of the final product (for example, clothing, footwear or automobiles).

Differences in the industrial structure of Western countries and LDCs are only partially captured when attention is centered on the relative importance (however measured) of certain industries in the former countries and their unimportance – or non-existence – in the latter. Industrial activities are usually reported for a particular industry in both sets of countries. In addition, it is useful to ascertain the extent to which one set of processing activities is carried out in a Western country, while a distinct, and perhaps more rudimentary, set of activities is performed within the same industry in a LDC. Thus, the pattern of industrial processing is an essential feature that reflects the degree of industrial sophistication in a country. Investigation according to a vertical rather than a horizontal arrangement of industries is helpful in discerning the gap between countries at different levels of development.

Such an analysis necessarily depends on some systematic means of quantifying and measuring patterns of industrial processing. A gradation of manufactured commodities and goods according to level or stage of processing is needed. In general, the ensuing discussion distinguishes between degrees of processing, according to whether the good or raw material undergoes a physical transformation. Table 7.5 provides evidence compiled from production statistics on the global distribution of processing activities for seven different resource inputs. In line with the approach sketched above, the products related to each input have been arranged to approximate to a rough version of a 'processing chain', beginning with ores and going through crude metals to shaped metal forms and simple metal products.

At early stages in the processing chain, world production is seen to have frequently declined or to have expanded very slowly since 1976. This is true for several metal-bearing ores, including iron, lead, nickel, tin and zinc, as well as other lightly processed items such as pig iron and steel ingots. Several factors have contributed to this pattern. One is the general economic slowdown which has persisted since the mid–1970s and the related fact that prices of several minerals have been severely depressed throughout this period. Second, improvements in production processes have reduced input requirements in many industries. Third, new forms of materials – ceramics and heat-resistant glasses – have begun to supplant several metals in some of their traditional uses. Fourth, continuous casting techniques used in several industries not only economize on input require-ments but bypass the ingot stage and reduces figures on world tonnage at this stage. Finally, the increased usage of scrap (especially in mini-mills producing steel) has also been noted and this depresses the demand for output of metals at early stages of processing.

These facts provide us with some insights with regard to global trends, but we are primarily interested in the relative distribution of production between Western countries and the LDCs. A glance at the percentages in Table 7.5 shows that the LDCs tend to be major suppliers only at early stages

Table 7.5 World Production[a] of Selected Minerals and Related Products and the Share of the LDCs

Product	World production (thousand tonnes)			Share of the LDCs (percentage)		
	1967	1976	1981	1967	1976	1981
Iron and steel						
Iron-bearing ores	337,868	520,443	498,200	25.5	30.0	28.0
Spiegeleisen and ferro-manganese	5,020	4,073	3,311	4.0	8.4	12.9
Pig iron, foundry	23,052	22,406	18,752	3.8	12.0	13.4
Pig iron, steel	325,954	468,940	486,814	4.2	6.0	8.3
Other ferro-alloys	4,831	7,175	7,548	5.2	12.9	18.3
Crude steel for castings	10,758	15,944	19,078	1.3	2.2	2.2
Crude steel, ingots	482,791	661,499	672,976	3.7	4.9	6.2
Ingots for tubes	4,303	5,640	6,103	9.0	9.4	6.7
Semis for tubes	13,837	18,699	34,076	8.8	18.9	38.3
Wire rods	29,072	44,124	45,480	4.1	6.0	9.2
Angles, shapes and sections	102,180	131,230	135,853	1.5	2.3	3.0
Plates (heavy), over 4.75 mm.	44,767	66,140	73,091	3.3	6.2	9.6
Plates (medium) 3 to 4.75 mm.	9,080	14,603	17,172	4.4	6.0	7.4
Sheets, electrical	3,137	5,134	5,359	1.7	18.8	27.8
Sheets under 3 mm., cold-rolled, uncoated	52,078	79,286	80,095	1.0	1.5	2.3
Sheets under 3 mm., hot-rolled	75,046	115,610	86,940	2.1	2.6	4.9
Tinplate	11,801	14,315	13,416	5.1	6.8	8.9
Sheets, galvanized	10,255	18,155	21,422	3.2	2.9	3.9
Hoop and strip, cold-reduced	5,577	6,614	6.254	2.7	0.5	0.2

Hoop and strip, hot-rolled	23,618	30,988	31,172	0.4	0.8	1.2
Railway track material	7,808	10,627	9,931	3.6	2.1	2.3
Wire, plain	13,632	21,456	20,518	3.3	8.9	10.4
Tubes, seamless	15,135	19,986	26,816	3.2	6.3	9.2
Tubes, welded	22,719	34,405	41,458	2.3	5.3	6.1
Steel castings in the rough state	4,631	5,301	5,290	1.0	5.1	8.9
Steel forgings	5,984	7.722	8,638	0.1	1.7	2.8
Aluminium						
Bauxite	45,690	74,927	86,396	54.8	48.6	47.6
Unwrought	8,779	15,279	18,459	3.2	6.7	8.3
Alloys	245	819	1,022	0.0	1.0	1.0
Bars, rods, angles, shapes and sections	1,122	2,964	3,208	1.8	4.7	5.6
Wire	724	887	942	1.1	8.6	7.8
Plates, sheets, strips and foil	2,553	5,008	5,562	3.7	4.5	5.5
Tubes and pipes	264	459	357	15.6	31.7	21.0
Copper						
Ores	5,028	8,021	8,414	42.5	39.3	42.6
Blister and other unrefined	4,960	8,258	8,713	38.2	32.1	33.0
Unwrought, refined	6,128	9,073	9,803	21.1	22.1	21.8
Unwrought alloys	878	889	1,057	0.0	4.0	2.5
Bars, rods, angles, shapes and sections	765	882	415	0.3	11.7	0.7
Plates, sheets, strip, foil	825	1,061	771	1.4	12.6	8.6
Tubes and pipes	739	1,034	1,029	1.1	2.8	3.3
Wire	2,174	2,577	2,935	1.4	4.0	6.1

continued

Table 7.5 continued

Product	World production (thousand tonnes)			Share of the LDCs (percentage)		
	1967	1976	1981	1967	1976	1981
Lead						
Ores	2,907	3,276	3,200	22.4	21.2	22.9
Refined, unwrought	3,474	4,582	4,764	11.6	7.9	10.0
Alloys	175	135	106	0.9	1.4	2.9
Tubes and pipes	143	120	104	1.4	5.1	6.3
Nickel						
Ores	479	790	692	18.7	27.7	28.5
Tin						
Ores	207	214	226	77.6	73.9	75.5
Unwrought	233	236	247	52.0	60.8	67.9
Zinc						
Ores	4,919	5,680	5,733	18.9	23.8	22.6
Unwrought	4,346	5,522	5,858	6.2	8.8	11.1
Alloys	97	161	160	4.9	11.2	10.1
Plates, sheets, strip, foil	280	233	281	22.4	15.7	25.4

Source: United Nations, *Yearbook of Industrial Statistics, commodity production*, Vol. 2 (various issues).

[a] World totals include figures for China and the socialist countries of Asia. These countries are excluded, however, from the percentages referring to LDCs.

in the processing chain. Their importance is greatest in the production of ores, although their share of world production has usually declined or stagnated after 1976. In later stages, LDCs account for lower proportions of world output – typically 10 per cent or less. However, for a majority of the products shown the LDCs have increased their share of the world total, albeit modestly.

Closer inspection shows that, in isolated instances, the LDCs do supply at least a moderate share of global production. The original sources of information reveal these high proportions are due to production in one or two LDCs. Examples of such products (and the predominant LDCs) are semi-manufactured steel, or semis (South Korea), electrical sheets of steel (South Korea), aluminium tubes and pipes (Brazil) and zinc plates and sheets (Brazil and Chile). The pre-eminence of individual LDCs is not due to any inherent cost advantages but is explained by the need to realize maximum economies of scale, along with the disproportionate impact of large foreign investment in a few instances.

While the international data reviewed in Table 7.5 are sufficient to support the conclusion that LDCs have made modest headway in the establishment of domestic processing facilities, the data are subject to certain shortcomings and in any case provide only a partial picture. An equally important aspect of the issue relates to patterns of trade by stage of processing. When an analysis of processing patterns is carried out in these terms, the statistical difficulties encountered by the user are also reduced. Because data are compiled at a fairly detailed level of disaggregation, the discussion can be extended to finished goods and processing activities based on materials other than minerals. The demarcation point between processing stages can also be drawn more precisely, depending on whether the intermediate good or raw material undergoes a physical transformation. Goods that do not require any further transformation of significance before their final consumption are defined as processed goods. Pictured in this way, some processed goods, that is, finished goods that will not be transformed further before their final consumption, may still

179

be subject to further industrial operations such as the assembly of components. Examples include the assembly of automobiles, television sets or electrical appliances. In so far as possible, the following examination treats the relevant components (automobile tyres, television picture tubes or camera lens) as completed or processed goods, even though they are still to be assembled as part of the final product.

The results of this exercise are summarized in Table 7.6 which shows imports and exports of industrially processed goods arranged in four categories. When the composition of trade is pictured in this way, a clear distinction between the LDCs and Western countries emerges. The bulk of exports from Western countries are fully processed goods and ready for final use. Furthermore, that proportion has remained constant throughout the 1970s. Fully processed exports account for a significantly lesser share of total exports in the LDCs – between 25 and 40 per cent during the years 1970–80. But this percentage steadily increased during the 1970s, suggesting that the LDCs have been successful in extending their domestic processing activities. At the other end of the spectrum, unprocessed exports and products to be transformed further in the importing countries have accounted for the predominant share of exports by the LDCs in every year shown in Table 7.6. These two categories together amounted to 56 per cent of total exports in 1980, down from 67 per cent in 1970. Again, there is evidence of progress on the part of the LDCs, although the corresponding proportion of unprocessed and semi-processed exports from Western countries (almost 26 per cent in 1980) is considerably lower.

In the case of imports, the situation is somewhat different. Roughly three-fifths of the imports going to the LDCs were ready for final use in 1980 and this proportion had changed very little throughout the previous decade. These figures, however, are only slightly larger than those reported for Western countries; in 1980, 58 per cent of all LDC imports were ready for final use. The share of imports requiring additional processing was roughly equal in the two sets of countries, while the percentage of unprocessed imports edged upward in Western countries throughout the 1970s.

Table 7.6 Trade by Stage of Processing (Percentage and growth rates)

Economic grouping	Period	Unprocessed for processing		Processed for further processing		Unprocessed for final use		Processed for final use	
		Imports	Exports	Imports	Exports	Imports	Exports	Imports	Exports
LDCs	1970	14.2	52.5	17.9	14.4	3.4	7.7	64.5	25.4
	1972	14.2	46.4	17.7	14.9	3.3	8.8	64.8	29.9
	1974	21.7	49.2	18.5	14.5	2.5	4.8	57.3	31.6
	1976	21.8	46.2	15.8	13.0	2.9	5.5	59.5	35.3
	1978	19.5	40.7	15.0	13.8	3.2	6.3	62.3	39.1
	1980	23.9	43.0	14.6	13.1	2.9	5.0	58.6	38.9
Growth rate, 1970–80		28.7	19.8	19.7	21.1	20.1	17.1	21.0	27.6
Western economies	1970	21.0	9.3	18.0	17.2	5.8	3.9	55.3	69.9
	1972	19.9	9.1	16.3	16.0	6.1	4.1	57.7	70.8
	1974	27.5	10.0	17.1	18.2	4.8	3.6	50.7	68.2
	1976	27.4	9.2	14.6	15.7	5.8	4.3	52.2	70.8
	1978	24.7	8.7	14.0	15.0	6.0	4.1	55.3	72.2
	1980	28.2	9.7	13.9	15.9	6.1	4.5	51.8	69.9
Growth rate, 1970–80		23.4	19.3	16.7	17.9	20.3	20.5	19.0	18.9

Source: UNIDO, 1983, p. 211.

[a] Included are twenty-five Western countries and forty-seven LDCs for which data were available from 1970 to 1980.

Note: For a statistical definition of individual four- and five-digit SITC items assigned to each processing category, see UNIDO (1979a), chapter VI, appendix.

Table 7.7 Pattern of Industrial Processing in the Exports of LDCs (maximal coverage[a])

Year	Unprocessed for processing	Processed for further processing	(percentage) Unprocessed for final use	Processed for final use
1972	44.2	20.0	9.0	26.8
1978	43.9	15.0	6.8	34.2

Source: UNIDO, 1983, p. 213.

[a] Data refer to 72 LDCs, including all major exporters.

As data were available for only 47 LDCs for the years shown in Table 7.6, some of the trends may not be representative for the entire group. Wider country coverage was available for the LDCs in two years, 1972 and 1978, and the results are shown in Table 7.7. A comparison of the two sets of figures shows that for the enlarged sample of LDCs the share of exports which are unprocessed is increased somewhat, while the proportion of exports ready for final use is reduced (34 per cent with maximal country coverage compared to 39 per cent shown in Table 7.7). Clearly, many of the marginal exporters among the LDCs rely heavily on unprocessed, or only lightly processed, items in their trade with the rest of the world. In conclusion, there is unmistakable evidence that some LDCs have made real strides in reducing their dependence on the export of raw materials in favour of semi-processed and finished goods. Progress, however, is probably confined to the more advanced LDCs; the large majority of these countries still depend heavily on the export of raw materials and lightly processed items to earn foreign exchange.

Supplementary Reading

The United Nations Centre for Transnational Corporations (UNCTC) produces a number of industry-specific studies which not only document the operations of the multinationals but examine processing patterns and trends in investment technology, trade and prices. Garnaut and Clunies Ross (1983) consider many of the economic and political aspects of government policy and competition between multinationals. Stuckey (1983), in his study of vertical integration and joint ventures in the aluminium industry, examines and tests various facets of industrial organization theory. Amsalem (1984) examines possible strategies available to mineral-producing and consuming countries to improve their bargaining power.

CHAPTER EIGHT

Post-War Trends in Manufactured Exports

The growth of trade in manufactures has already been singled out as one of the prominent features of the post-war era. Most economists would agree that trade – or, more specifically, exports – can be a valuable adjunct to economic growth. Many would go further to argue that exports are a vital stimulus to growth. Intense interest in this issue has given rise to a huge body of literature, both theoretical and empirical, based on the premise that economic growth can be 'export-led'. However, there are a number of reasons why the interrelationship between economic growth and exports remains obscure. First, the hypothesis that growth is export-led is only one of several possible explanations; other interpretations stress the importance of technological progress and the accumulation of capital. Second, the expansion of markets for exports is merely part of a wider process of growth in demand. Domestic demand can also propel economic growth and its significance could overshadow the contribution of foreign demand. Third, the relationship between exports and economic growth appears to be one of mutual interdependence rather than unilateral causation. Fourth, the interaction between exports and economic growth can be affected by many underlying factors which influence either or both these variables. Nevertheless, whatever the precise nature of this relationship, the growth of manufactured exports has been a powerful force for structural change.

184

Although many of the issues debated within the context of export-led growth have a bearing on the following discussion, a systematic review of the literature is beyond the scope of this book. Instead, the purpose of this chapter is to provide a factual account of export performance in the manufacturing sector and the reader who wishes to explore the subject of export-led growth will find suggested sources cited as supplementary reading. The chapter begins by looking at the growth of trade in manufactures, along with accompanying changes in export patterns. Later the relationship between manufactured exports and manufactured output is examined. Changes in patterns of manufactured trade have been the source of international friction and adjustment pressure and the final section of this chapter describes some of the trade policies which have been introduced in response to these problems.

The Growth of Manufactured Exports

Trade in manufactures has always been subject to more violent swings and fluctuations than production of these goods. However, over long periods of time the relationship between the two rates of growth has been relatively stable, with exports tending to expand somewhat more rapidly than production. Stability broke down during the years between the First and Second World Wars. The growth of manufactured exports fell significantly below the rate implied by the traditional export-output relationship. A more conventional pattern re-emerged during the 1950s and early 1960s. In later years, however, the two sets of growth rates diverged from their long-term relationship for a second time: trade in manufactures accelerated rapidly, although output expanded at an unchanged rate. The new relationship was maintained until the mid–1970s when the effects of the world recession began to take its toll. Altogether, the years between 1950 and the mid–1970s were notable because they entailed a rate of growth in manufactured exports unparalleled during the last century. The world's per capita output of manufactures doubled during that period, but the volume of world trade in manufactures trebled (Batchelor, Major and Morgan, 1980, p. 16).

The foregoing description implies that foreign markets for manufactures have gradually assumed more importance. At the same time, the growth of trade in primary products was overshadowed by manufactures. Table 8.1 documents the latter trend, showing manufactures both as a percentage of total exports and as a percentage of non-oil exports, that is, excluding SITC 3. Manufactures have accounted for 50–60 per cent of world trade in all goods throughout the period since 1960. Roughly three-fourths of exports from Western countries are now in this form. Socialist countries, however, are less dependent on manufactured exports; their share began to decline in the late 1970s and currently accounts for slightly less than one-half of the total exports by these countries. The proportion of manufactures exported by the LDCs has steadily grown but is still far below the levels attained in other groups (only 25 per cent in 1983).

A better indication of the manufacturing sector's contribution to world trade is obtained when the special case of trade in crude oil and refined petroleum is excluded. Manufactures were 57 per cent of the world's non-oil exports in 1960, but by the early 1980s they claimed nearly three-quarters of the total. The composition of exports from the LDCs is most sensitive to trade in crude oil. By 1982, the share of manufactures in the non-oil exports of LDCs was approaching that of industrialized countries. This result would seem to dispel the notion that LDCs are especially dependent on exports of agricultural products. Furthermore, the rise in the share of fuel exports in the 1970s was largely due to price effects and did not reflect any shift in the underlying composition of the commodities being exported by LDCs. The same observation would not apply, however, in the case of manufactures. The rising share of manufactures in the exports of LDCs was not due to any price effects but was the result of an accumulation of costly, and sometimes painful, efforts to industrialize. Together, these trends meant that manufactured exports claimed an increasing share of that sector's production and assumed a greater importance relative to trade in non-manufactures.

Table 8.1 Share of Manufactures[a] in Total Exports, by Economic Grouping, 1960–1983

Economic grouping	Basis[b]	1960	1970	1975	1976	1977	1978	1979	1980	1981	1982	1983[c]
World	A	51.5	60.9	57.4	57.0	57.5	60.4	57.5	54.7	55.3	56.8	58.2
	B	57.1	67.1	71.1	71.5	71.7	72.9	72.2	72.0	73.1	74.2	…
Western countries	A	64.6	71.9	73.1	73.5	74.1	74.8	72.8	71.6	71.7	72.3	73.0
	B	67.2	74.4	77.0	77.4	78.0	78.4	77.3	76.9	77.7	78.8	…
Socialist countries	A	54.1	58.2	55.2	54.5	53.9	54.9	52.5	50.6	48.6	47.9	47.3
	B	60.7	63.9	66.8	67.1	66.7	67.9	68.0	68.2	67.2	68.1	…
LDCs	A	9.2	17.3	15.1	16.6	17.3	21.0	19.8	17.8	20.8	22.9	25.2
	B	12.8	25.9	37.0	40.3	40.3	44.5	46.1	47.1	52.4	53.3	…

Source: United Nations, *Monthly Bulletin of Statistics*, various issues.
[a] SITC 5 to 8 less 67 and 68.
[b] A = manufactures as percentage of total exports; B = manufactures as percentage of total exports excluding SITC 3, mineral fuels and related materials. All figures are calculated from data expressed in current prices.
[c] Estimate.

Despite rapid growth and structural change, several features of the pattern of world trade in manufactures have proved to be of a lasting nature. Notable among these is the predominance of Western countries in world trade in manufactures. Table 8.2 shows that throughout the post-war era these countries have consistently accounted for over 80 per cent of world trade. At the same time, the contribution of socialist countries has steadily declined. By the early 1980s, the value of the manufactured exports of socialist countries was less than that of the LDCs. Curiously, the involvement of the industrialized countries in world trade has proceeded according to a pattern markedly different from the post-war redistribution of world MVA. In the latter case, socialist countries have claimed a steadily growing proportion of world MVA, while the dominance of Western countries has waned (see Table 2.1).

A related feature of world trade is the prevalence of 'bloc trading' which has persisted among industrialized countries since the Second World War. As recently as 1982, almost 60 per cent of the manufactured exports of socialist countries remained within a 'bloc trading' group, while the figure for Western countries was even higher – 68 per cent. But the same pattern is not found in the LDCs: in 1982, 59 per cent of their manufactures went to Western countries (UNIDO, 1985b, pp. 40). The fact that such a large proportion of world trade in manufactures takes place between countries in the same group casts some doubt on the Heckscher-Ohlin version of the trade theory which stresses international differences in factor availability. Although factor intensities can obviously vary between countries, factor endowments, at least in Western countries, are known to have converged during the post-war period (see Chapter 2). In this sense at least, existing patterns seem compatible with the interpretation offered by Linder (1961) who suggested that trade in manufactures results primarily from similarities in demand rather than from differences in the supply side. Empirical tests, however, have yielded little support for the Linder hypothesis (Deardorff, 1984, pp. 505–6).

Table 8.3 provides information on another aspect of structural change – the share of manufactures in total

Table 8.2 Share of Economic Groups in World
Manufactures[a] (percentage)

Year	LDCs	Socialist countries	Western countries
1963	4.2	13.3	82.5
1964	4.3	12.8	82.9
1965	4.4	12.3	83.3
1966	4.5	11.6	83.9
1967	4.6	11.7	83.7
1968	4.5	11.0	84.6
1969	4.6	10.4	85.0
1970	5.0	10.0	85.0
1971	5.2	9.6	85.2
1972	5.7	9.9	84.4
1973	6.7	9.4	83.9
1974	6.8	8.5	84.7
1975	6.3	9.3	84.4
1976	7.5	8.9	83.6
1977	7.8	8.9	83.3
1978	8.1	8.7	83.2
1979	8.7	8.4	82.9
1980	9.1	8.1	82.8
1981	10.5	8.0	81.5
1982	10.7	8.7	80.6
1983[b]	10.9	8.8	80.3

Source: UNIDO, 1985a, p. 6.

[a] SITC 5 to 8, less 67 and 68.
[b] Estimates.

exports. All the countries shown in the table are leading
exporters of manufactures in their respective groups.
Although the aggregate value of manufactured exports from
Western countries has soared since 1965, only Japan shows a
sizeable increase in the share of manufactures in total
exports. A moderate rise occurred in several other countries,
while in the UK the proportion of manufactures in total
exports has declined since 1965.

The situation is strikingly different in LDCs. As a group,
the LDCs have yet to reach a level where their reliance on

Table 8.3 Share of Manufactures[a] in Total Exports
in Selected Countries (percentage)

	1965	1970	1975	1980	1982
Western countries					
France	60.9	64.9	67.7	66.7	67.8
Italy	71.4	79.4	75.4	79.0	77.7
Japan	75.3	77.8	76.2	82.8	84.6
UK	76.0	75.8	77.1	69.5	62.8
USA	59.7	63.7	63.3	64.1	65.9
West Germany	78.8	80.1	77.9	78.5	79.6
LDCs					
Brazil	5.0	9.7	23.3	32.8	33.3
Hong Kong	92.4	95.3	96.7	95.6	96.3
India	46.7	45.1	42.2	57.5	...
Malaysia	5.6[b]	6.3	17.1	18.6	22.8
Pakistan	36.0	57.2	54.3	48.2	57.5
Singapore	28.9	26.7	39.9	45.6	46.9
South Korea	52.0	74.9	76.8	80.1	81.3[c]
Thailand	2.0	4.4	14.4	24.4	26.0

Sources: UNCTAD, *Handbook of International Trade and Development Statistics*
1983 and 1984; United Nations, *Monthly Bulletin of Statistics*, various issues.

[a] SITC 5 to 8 less 67 and 68.
[b] 1968.
[c] 1981.

manufactured exports matches that of Western countries. By
the early 1980s, manufactures still accounted for no more
than one-quarter of export earnings (see Table 8.1 on
p. 187). However, shifts of a much greater magnitude took
place in certain Asian LDCs. Hong Kong has long been
excessively dependent on manufactured exports and the
share has risen dramatically in Brazil, Malaysia, Singapore,
South Korea and Thailand. These trends are quite different
from the experience of some large LDCs, particularly those
in Latin America. For example, in the early 1980s the share
of manufactures in total exports was less than 20 per cent in
Argentina, Chile, Colombia and Mexico (UNCTAD, 1984,
Table 4.1). Obviously, if the export composition in many

LDCs were to reach the proportions attained in Western countries the problems, dislocations and adjustment pressures which could result would be significantly greater than those experienced today.

Table 8.4 provides more detailed evidence on the relative distribution of manufactured exports among Western countries. In Chapter 2, the discussion stressed the fact that realignment in production capabilities among these countries had important policy implications. Western countries entered the post-war era with the USA as the dominant producer of manufacturing (see Table 2.2) and the subsequent erosion of that country's leadership contributed to the form of competitive coexistence which prevails today. No changes of an equivalent magnitude occurred in the case of trade. Japan's share in Western exports of manufactures has risen significantly since 1965, but the effects of the redistribution were borne by several countries. Subsequent discussion shows that Western trade policies have undergone considerable change since the early 1960s. However, this transition was not accompanied by a fundamental realignment in the trading role of various countries. The following section looks at empirical evidence relating trends in

Table 8.4 Distribution of Manufactured Exports[a] among Major Western Countries (as a percentage of manufactured exports of all Western countries)

Country	1965	1970	1975	1980	1982
France	7.8	7.8	9.1	8.8	7.9
Italy	6.6	7.1	6.9	7.3	7.2
West Germany	18.1	18.6	18.4	18.0	17.7
Japan	8.2	10.2	11.1	12.8	14.9
USA	20.7	18.4	17.6	16.3	17.2
UK	12.9	10.0	8.8	9.5	7.7
Total of the above	74.3	72.1	71.9	72.7	72.7

Sources: UNCTAD, *Handbook of International Trade and Development Statistics*, 1983 and 1984; United Nations, *Monthly Bulletin of Statistics*, various issues.

[a] SITC 5 to 8, less 67 and 68.

191

manufactured exports to the growth of manufacturing production.

The Relationship between Exports and Manufacturing Production

Up to this point the growth of manufactured exports has been described without reference to the production of manufactures. However, links between the two fields are important, not only for their theoretical implications but also because they help to determine patterns of structural change and policy choices. This section of Chapter 8 provides additional information on these interrelationships by examining data on the share of manufactured exports in domestic production.

Similar measures have been employed by other economists, particularly those concerned with the hypothesis of export-led growth. Some analysts have wanted to determine whether a declining trade ratio is a normal accompaniment of economic growth. In other cases, such measures have been suggested as a means of gauging the extent to which foreign demand may contribute to economic growth (Kravis, 1970, p. 853). Because most of these investigations were conducted on an economy-wide basis, attention has focused on the share of total exports in GDP. A smaller number of studies have been specifically concerned with the manufacturing sector and fewer still (e.g. Balassa, 1978b) have considered the share of manufactured exports in manufacturing output.

Comparatively little information is available regarding the behaviour of the export-output ratio for manufacturing. Thus, the primary purpose of the present exercise is to gain some idea of the relative importance of foreign markets in total demand. In addition, previous assessments were carried out during a period when growth in world income and trade was high and it is not clear that the same conclusions would apply during the present era. In line with these objectives, the investigation focuses on events in the 1970s and early 1980s and draws on the experience of both

192

Western countries and LDCs. The present period is certainly a unique part of the post-war era because of the global slowdown in economic growth. It has also been exceptional in comparison with earlier long-term cycles; the downswing was marked by a decline in the rate of growth of incomes, but did not entail an absolute fall in income levels.

With regard to the empirical measure used here, that is, the share of exports in gross output of manufactures, a decline would seem to be the most likely result when growth rates of income are falling. In fact, in the downward phases of previous cycles the ratio of exports to income has tended to fall. Michaely (1983, p. 399) identifies two sets of forces which would explain this result. One is an automatic response attributed to the fact that the demand for foreign goods is likely to be particularly sensitive to the business cycle and to changes in income. When incomes rise (as they did in most countries between 1950 and 1974), the demand for foreign-made goods can grow disproportionately, leading to an increase in the export share of income. But when levels of income fall or the pace of growth slows, exports markets would be the first to suffer. Michaely goes on to argue that manufactures rather than primary products will bear the major burden in the downward phase of the business cycle, because demand for the former goods is more sensitive to a fall or slowdown in the growth of income. A second possibility is that governments will adopt more restrictive trade policies during the course of a prolonged slowdown. As the growth in demand slackens, there would be pressure to assist local producers and to preserve employment by imposing tariffs and other trade barriers. Because trade in primary products is already widely restricted, any new barriers tend to fall most heavily on manufactures.

In compiling data for this exercise, sufficient information was available for the period 1970–80 to include thirty-three countries in the analysis. Twenty-two of these are LDCs, while the remainder are Western countries. The Western countries included here account for an overwhelming share of manufactured exports by all non-socialist countries and for a large proportion of world MVA. Similarly, the twenty-two LDCs dominate manufactured exports and production of all LDCs.

Estimates of export/output ratios are shown in Table 8.5. Contrary to expectations, the proportion of exports in gross output has not declined during the present slowdown. The weighted averages for both groups of countries rose throughout the 1970s. A comparison of the data for individual countries provides further information. Between the first and last biennia, the export/output ratio fell in eight LDCs, although no similar drop occurred in any Western country. The consequences of the slowdown are more apparent when the same comparison is made for 1974–75 and 1979–80. Among the LDCs, the export/output ratio declined in thirteen cases. Moreover, several of these countries were relatively important exporters and, together, they accounted for 58 per cent of manufactured exports in 1980. In contrast, only one Western country, West Germany, experienced a drop in the export/output share between 1974–75 and 1979–80. The net effects of these shifts are reflected in movements of the weighted averages for the two groups of countries. At the beginning of the decade, the averages were almost identical. However, the values for later years diverge; in 1979–80 the LDCs were exporting, on average 15.5 per cent of gross output, while the proportion was 18.0 per cent in Western countries. Thus, the figures in Table 8.5 indicate that the slowdown affected the behaviour of exporters in the two groups of countries in different ways.

The table provides related evidence on two other features of the export-output relationship. First, there are very few instances where exports account for more than one-third of gross output. The comparatively small proportion of manufacturing production exported underlines the role of domestic demand and the importance of an expanding domestic market. Second, the degree of export dependence appears to vary inversely with the size of the domestic market. Countries having a small domestic market – for example, Belgium, Hong Kong, Luxembourg, Netherlands and Singapore – export a comparatively large proportion of their gross manufacturing output. Conversely, many large countries, such as Brazil, Mexico, India, the USA and even

Japan, tend to export only a modest proportion of their total production. The fact that exports generally claim only a small share of production in large countries is well known to structuralists and others who have examined the data. Curiously, the major strand of trade theory, the Heckscher-Ohlin model, appears to suggest the contrary; countries of a different size would still be expected to trade an identical proportion of their production (Arad and Hirsch, 1981).

A more complete picture of the export/output relationship can be obtained when rates of change are considered. Table 8.6 provides such a comparison for 1970–74 and 1974–80, indicating the growth of exports (x), gross output (o), growth rate differences and changes in the export/ output share. An examination of the data shows that the effects of the global recession are evident for all countries. Moreover, during the downward phase in the present cycle, the fall in growth of exports in most countries was more precipitous than the corresponding decline in gross output. Apart from these broad similarities, however, there are marked differences in results for the LDCs and those for Western countries.

Among the LDCs the average differential between the two rates (x-o) was reduced from 7.5 per cent in the early 1970s to 1.8 per cent in 1974–80. In fact, after 1974 the growth of domestic production in a majority of the LDCs (thirteen), actually exceeded the growth of exports. Several relatively important exporters – Hong Kong, India, the Philippines, South Korea and Venezuela – are included in this list. Similar evidence can be found in the growth rates for the share of exports in gross output. By this standard, only four LDCs managed to improve on their performance after 1974. And in each case, these countries had recorded a negative rate of growth for the share in 1970–74. The results for Western countries give a different picture. Although the average growth rate differential (x-o) was reduced, the relative dynamism of exporting was maintained. More specifically, the traditional relationship between the two rates of growth was preserved; with the exception of West Germany, exports of manufactures continued to expand at rates significantly higher than those for gross output.

Table 8.5 Manufactured Exports (ISIC 300)[a] as a Share of Gross Output (percentage)

| Country[b] | Share of exports in gross output | | | | Share of exports in group total | |
	1970–71	1974–75	1979–80		1970	1980
LDCs						
Singapore	58.9	64.6	72.7		5.8	10.4
Hong Kong	58.5	67.0	60.8		13.6	12.1
Malaysia	48.0	46.0	46.1		4.8	5.5
Pakistan	19.5	33.9	35.3		3.5	2.1
Indonesia	17.8	30.3	29.1		0.9	2.7
Chile	21.1	30.8	26.3		7.3	3.3
South Korea	17.1	27.6	26.1		4.5	15.0
Venezuela	17.9	27.2	21.5		6.6	5.9
Egypt	25.3	25.0	20.3		4.6	1.0
Philippines	16.4	19.9	18.9		3.1	2.9
Kenya	21.5	17.7	18.6		0.7	0.8
Ecuador	5.1	9.8	18.3		0.1	0.6
Thailand	14.2	14.9	17.4		1.9	3.4
Peru	19.1	12.8	17.3		5.3	1.7
Ghana	17.9	15.5	10.7		0.6	0.2
Yugoslavia	14.8	12.0	10.3		10.0	7.6
India	7.5	9.2	7.8		9.2	4.5
Brazil	4.9	5.7	7.5		7.7	12.9

Colombia	4.8	10.0	7.0	1.0	1.1
Mexico	4.7	5.3	5.7	5.5	4.5
Turkey	6.8	5.4	4.8	2.1	1.4
Nigeria	11.7	6.1	3.3	1.2	0.4
Group average[c]/total	12.7	14.1	15.5	100.0	100.0
Western countries					
Belgium-Luxembourg	49.9	54.1	63.5	6.1	5.9
Netherlands	40.0	47.6	57.1	5.9	6.6
Sweden	32.0	36.6	40.1	3.7	3.1
Italy	24.9	25.7	30.9	7.4	8.0
West Germany	23.1	29.6	28.2	19.1	19.4
Canada	23.0	21.0	26.1	7.1	4.8
France	17.0	20.7	23.7	9.3	10.9
UK	16.7	18.4	20.8	10.3	9.7
Japan	10.5	12.2	12.4	11.2	13.8
USA	5.2	7.4	8.2	19.9	17.8
Group average[c]/total	12.9	16.4	18.0	100.0	100.0

Sources: United Nations, *Yearbook of Industrial Statistics, Vol. 1* (various issues); *Yearbook of National Accounts* (various issues) and *Yearbook of International Trade Statistics* (various issues). Exchange rates were taken from IMF, *International Financial Statistics* (various issues).

[a] The definition of manufactured exports differs from that used elsewhere in this book. For further discussion, see the statistical appendix.

[b] Countries are listed according to their average (unweighted) share of exports in gross output in the period 1979–80.

[c] After conversion into US dollars, exports of the group for each two-year period were obtained and then divided by the corresponding total for gross output.

Table 8.6 Growth Rates for Manufactured Exports[a] (x) and Gross Output (o), 1970–80

	Growth of exports (x)		Growth of gross output (o)		Growth rate differences (x-o)		Growth of the share of exports in gross output	
	1970–74	1974–80	1970–74	1974–80	1970–74	1974–80	1970–74	1974–80
LDCs								
Singapore	44.8	21.5	40.9	18.5	3.9	3.0	2.7	2.5
Hong Kong	23.3	20.9	16.4	23.5	6.9	-2.6	5.9	-2.1
Malaysia	32.9	21.0	36.9	20.8	-4.0	0.2	-2.9	0.2
Pakistan	20.4	16.0	-2.7	15.6	23.1	0.4	23.7	0.3
Indonesia	70.5	20.4	37.3	21.5	33.2	-1.1	24.2	-0.9
Chile	18.0	13.1	7.9	18.6	10.1	-5.5	9.3	-4.6
South Korea	61.7	27.9	36.1	29.6	25.6	-1.7	18.8	-1.3
Venezuela	39.9	11.2	20.0	17.1	19.9	-5.9	16.6	-5.0
Egypt	17.9	-3.2	16.7	1.8	1.2	-5.0	1.0	-4.8
Philippines	33.3	14.5	25.7	16.2	7.6	-1.7	6.0	-1.5
Kenya	20.7	22.8	27.6	22.7	-6.9	0.1	-5.4	0.1
Ecuador	47.9	42.9	20.1	25.5	27.8	17.4	23.1	13.8
Thailand	46.5	21.2	47.1	18.3	-0.6	2.9	-0.4	2.5
Peru	8.2	12.8	20.1	6.7	-11.9	6.1	-9.9	5.7
Ghana	18.7	6.2	19.7	15.0	-1.0	-8.8	-0.8	-7.7
Yugoslavia	25.0	14.5	28.1	18.5	-3.0	-1.0	-2.4	-3.4
India	19.4	9.6	14.2	14.3	5.2	-4.7	4.6	-4.1
Brazil	46.5	20.5	34.1	13.6	12.4	6.9	9.3	6.1

Colombia	46.9	10.6	18.9	18.2	28.0	-7.6	23.6	-6.4
Mexico	31.1	15.1	17.9	12.3	13.2	2.8	11.2	2.5
Turkey	34.5	9.3	30.7	12.9	3.8	-3.6	2.9	-3.2
Nigeria	7.8	9.8	19.5	24.5	-11.7	-14.7	-9.8	-11.8
Group average[b]	32.1	17.9	24.6	16.1	7.5	1.8	6.0	1.6
Western countries								
Belgium-Luxembourg	27.0	14.5	24.0	11.0	3.0	3.5	2.4	3.2
Netherlands	30.0	14.0	23.7	10.2	6.3	3.8	5.1	3.4
Sweden	24.8	11.8	19.1	9.7	5.7	2.1	4.8	1.9
Italy	23.1	18.4	24.1	13.8	-1.0	4.6	-0.8	4.0
West Germany	28.2	14.9	20.1	16.2	8.1	-1.3	6.7	-1.1
Canada	16.0	14.1	17.9	9.4	-1.9	4.7	-1.7	4.3
France	27.2	17.1	21.0	13.9	6.2	3.2	5.1	2.8
UK	17.9	17.5	15.3	14.4	2.6	3.1	2.2	2.7
Japan	28.9	16.0	26.0	15.8	2.9	0.2	2.4	0.2
USA	21.5	14.0	13.2	11.5	8.2	2.5	7.3	2.2
Group average[b]	24.7	15.4	17.8	13.3	6.9	2.1	5.8	1.9

Sources: United Nations, *Yearbook of Industrial Statistics, Vol. 1* (various issues); *Yearbook of National Accounts* (various issues); *Yearbook of International Trade Statistics* (various issues). Exchange rates were taken from IMF, *International Financial Statistics* (various issues).

[a] The definition of manufactured exports differs from that used elsewhere in this book. For further discussion, see the statistical appendix.

[b] Group averages were calculated by first converting all data into US dollars. Country data were then aggregated to obtain group totals for exports and output throughout the period 1970–80. Finally, growth rates for each group were estimated by least squares.

The evidence presented here suggests that the degree to which external demand influences export performance may vary depending on the country's level of development. This would apply when the contractions in domestic and overseas markets are synchronized, as they have been during the downward phase of the current cycle. Furthermore, the distinction between LDCs and Western countries is a broad one, suggesting that some of the underlying explanations are of a general nature. Three possible explanations can be offered. The first is systematic differences in the way firms in LDCs and Western countries have responded to a fall in the demand for their products; the second, basic differences in application of export-oriented policies in the two groups of countries during the 1970s and the third is new trade restrictions which have been particularly burdensome to exporters in LDCs.

The behaviour of firms can be described in terms of their prevailing market orientation, whether for export or home demand. Firms that are experienced exporters are sure to contemplate alternative outlets when demand for their product weakens. They may not necessarily choose to pull back to their home market, but that possibility would be considered. Such a move might appear most attractive to LDC-owned firms bcause the contraction in domestic demand in these countries has not usually been so abrupt as the slump in exports. The relevant market conditions faced by comparable firms in Western countries, however, has been different; the growth of exports has continued to exceed the growth of the domestic market, albeit at a reduced level. Furthermore, a decision to disengage from export markets can be encumbered if the firm has a variety of international commitments. This is typical of many export-oriented firms (for example, multinationals) operating from Western countries. They often have far-flung organizations to produce, assemble and market their products and their overseas commitments, in the form of joint ventures, licensing agreements, or other collaborative arrangements, can be extensive. Such international links would make it relatively difficult for multinationals significantly to alter their prevailing market orientation but, at the same time, could serve to cushion the effects of contracting demand.

Different considerations would apply among firms which have traditionally been geared to meet domestic demand. Most important is the fact that exporting is an expensive and difficult task. Many home-bound firms would be reluctant to initiate a serious export drive unless a combination of market shifts, for example a contraction in domestic demand coupled with a boom in overseas markets, required them to do so. Fewer still would relish this prospect if the slowdown in demand were a feature shared by many countries. Again, however, Western firms may be more likely to choose this option than their counterparts in LDCs. The former frequently have larger plants and less flexibility in adjusting their work forces to a fall in demand. In fact, as the slowdown has persisted, several industries have exhibited a new-found interest in exporting. The behaviour of various steel producers in the EC provides a ready example. Plagued by excess capacity and rising unemployment, these firms initiated zealous export drives which were new to the industry. Between 1973 and 1979, steel production in the EC declined but exports rose by more than seven million metric tons – an eight per cent increase in the industry's export/output share (IISI, 1982, p. 19). In more general terms, the growing number of trade disputes between Western countries involving charges of price dumping, unfair subsidies or violations of GATT rules are usually regarded as evidence of renewed protectionist efforts to preserve shrinking domestic markets. while this interpretation is certainly accurate, the phenomenon may also be a reflection of a new-found interest in exports.

Systematic differences in the way policy-makers in LDCs and Western countries have responded to the slowdown have probably re-enforced the behaviour patterns of firms. During the 1960s many LDCs abandoned an inward-looking strategy and introduced new policies to foster exports (Donges and Riedel, 1977; Balassa, 1978c). But these programmes were not long established before the onset of the current downswing. All too frequently such programmes were among the first to be cut as financial problems associated with the downturn grew more intense. Policy-makers in Western countries reacted to the downturn in a different fashion. While trade barriers were being tightened in industries such as steel, textiles, automobiles, consumer electronics and chemicals, incentives offered in the way of export credits and similar forms of public support were maintained, if not extended. Significantly, the generous volume of export credits proffered by many Western governments has been a source of friction between these countries.

The resurgence in trade protection in Western countries may have further restricted the major export markets available to firms in LDCs. Since the mid–1970s, non-tariff barriers have come to be a common means of undercutting previous tariff reductions or supplementing existing tariffs. New restrictions have focused on imports of consumer goods, agro-processed manufactures and textiles (Ray and Marvel, 1984, p. 452) – all fields in which the LDCs have excelled as exporters.

Despite the relatively hostile trading environment since 1974, exports of manufactures have generally continued to claim a growing share of production in many countries. Nevertheless, recent export performance – particularly in the LDCs – has not been impressive. One reason for the poor showing can be traced to the growth in domestic markets *relative to* those in export markets. Another is that several major determinants of export performance are likely to be factors internal to the country concerned. The difficulties faced by fledgling exporters everywhere, however, have also been compounded by a gradual change in trade policy approaches of Western countries. This aspect is examined in the following section of this chapter.

Protectionist Policies in an Interdependent World

Based on post-war performance, the institutional arrangements and policy framework developed by Western countries for operation of the trading system were eminently successful. The original approach owed much to the

American practice of distinguishing between 'high foreign policy' and 'low foreign policy'. The former set of issues generally concerned national security, transatlantic relations and similar matters. In order not to impinge on high policy, problems relating to foreign trade and a host of other international economic issues were relegated to the lower track. Cases in this track were 'determined' rather than 'decided', according to criteria established by law, administrative regulations or precedents. Proper functioning of the agreements and institutions on which the international trading system was founded meant that most trade-related issues could be resolved in this domain. Economic matters were not completely depoliticized, but generally did not intrude into the realm of higher policy. However, as the discussion in Chapters 1 and 2 has shown, high policy did intrude, often in important ways, on lower-track decisions.

During the 1960s the demarcation between high and low policy began to be eroded. The real danger of this breakdown was foreseen by Cooper (1973, p. 55) who noted that once 'the rules break down or cease to be regarded as fair, they cannot be used effectively by governments to block particularistic pressures within their own countries'. From the American point of view, major sources of friction were the import restraints imposed by the Japanese, the Common Agricultural Policy (CAP) of the EC and other preferential trading agreements. The EC subsequently extended existing trade preferences offered to former colonies in Africa, the Caribbean and the Pacific (ACP countries) and established new trade arrangements and bilateral trade agreements with selected Mediterranean countries. In turn, the USA reached a preferential automobile agreement with Canada, used its economic power to persuade other countries to 'voluntarily' restrict their exports of specific products and recently concluded a bilateral trade agreement with Israel. When it became apparent that international trading rules could be violated on a large scale with impunity the coalition of American interests supporting free trade was weakened.

The distinction between high and low policy was breached with increasing frequency and had significant consequences for trade policy. Protectionist measures became more sophisticated in their design, while their objectives were extended beyond a simple attempt to control trade through the application of import barriers or export subsidies. The change in approach was a fundamental one, leading many analysts to distinguish between the present form of protectionist policies and earlier versions. 'Old' protection was pictured as concerned with trade-restricting or trade-expanding devices. What was new was the realization that virtually all forms of government activity could be used to affect international economic relations (Krauss, 1979, p. 36). New protectionist measures were no longer solely, or even predominantly, concerned with trade; instead, they became a tool for structural policy.

The forms of protectionism which have become common since the early 1970s can be placed in two broad categories, depending upon their motives. The first involves 'defensive policies' intended to slow the rate of contraction in specific industries, while the second consists of policies designed to support new or expanding areas of manufacturing. In the former case, governments may justify their interventions by the contention that the rapid growth of imports leads to politically unacceptable economic and social costs to the domestic firms and labour forces affected. Supporters emphasize the need to forestall rapid adjustment or change, implying that these trends are more costly and disruptive than gradual adjustments. When intervening in favour of new industries, however, governments are motivated by other reasons. Attempts to postpone the decline of ailing industries, that is, defensive policies, can delay growth in others. Policy-makers have found it necessary to compensate industries with viable growth prospects if their ability to expand is not to be handicapped when resources are diverted to contracting industries. The growth of international trade has also forced many countries to place a higher priority on their competitive position relative to their main trading partners. This trend coincided with declining rates of productivity growth and return on capital in Western countries. Accordingly, firms in many industries (often with the support of their governments) began to look for new systems of capital goods to boost productivity.

The beneficiaries of defensive policies are usually industries which are relatively important in terms of capital investment, domestic output and/or employment. Among Western countries, typical beneficiaries often include textiles, steel, automobiles, bulk chemicals or machine tools. Reasons for contractive pressure include over-capacity (often resulting from previous misjudgements about expected levels of demand), the establishment of new, competitive capacity – for example, petroleum refining in the Middle East and Mexico and new steel mills in many LDCs – or a surge in import penetration. Related explanations are widespread obsolescence (as in the American steel industry) or poorly timed expansion programmes abruptly undercut by new technological advances. Here, the major issue confronting policy-makers is how to accommodate a contraction in industry size. A secondary concern can be to find the means to rejuvenate the industry and to restore some measure of international competitiveness.

Highly specialized industries, often regarded as technology-intensive, are the usual targets of expansionary protectionist policies. In the opinion of some policy-makers, international leadership depends on 'who gets there first'. The importance which policy-makers attach to the second cluster of industries apparently derives from their belief that comparative advantage may be achieved artificially. Through various forms of government intervention, a country may aspire to technological leadership in some phase of manufacturing. Moreover, technological pre-eminence in a particular phase (for example, semiconductors and integrated circuits) can help to confer leadership in related industries such as computers or automated machine tools and their applications (computer-aided design and computer-aided manufacture). Policies to foster these types of activities are regarded warily by foreign competitors since the establishment of a pre-eminent position can affect a wide range of industries on an international scale.

In many cases the types of policies actually employed will be the same, whether intended to serve defensive purposes or to foster the growth of new industries. The most common examples are 'voluntary' exports restraints, orderly marketing agreements and other forms of non-tariff barriers (NTBs). Such policies, however, are not restricted to those with explicit trade-related consequences. Other notable efforts to support contracting industries include state aids and subsidies, government procurement policies, investment incentives, assistance to industry in depressed areas and temporary employment subsidy schemes.

An assessment of the significance of these measures, whether intended to delay contraction or to accelerate expansion of an industry, is difficult. The selective use of government procurement practices can be used to restrain imports (and thus support troubled industries) or to provide an assured market for new and expanding industries. In the first instance governments have long been regarded as much more restrictive than private purchasers. During the late 1950s and early 1960s, procurement procedures in France and the USA were estimated to be equivalent to a tariff of more than 40 per cent (Baldwin, 1970, p. 77). In the case of emerging industries the provision of assured markets through government procurement is a less obvious (and probably less expensive) method of support than government subsidies. The vital role of government purchases in establishing the American semiconductor industry and the computer and industrial robot industries in Japan were noted in Chapter 1. A common policy on public procurement emerged as one of the cornerstones of the EC's overall plan to support industries such as microelectronics, computers and telecommunications industries.

Much of the government support for expanding industries has been intended to stimulate R and D. Until well into the twentieth century, government funding and support for R and D was rare. By the end of the 1970s, however, worldwide government funding, whether direct or indirect, supported about 50 per cent of all R and D (UNIDO, 1983, p. 157). Here, again, evidence from the computer industry provides a ready example. The provision of public funds for R and D was one of the main elements in Western governments' programmes to spur the take-off of computer firms in the late 1960s and 1970s. And, as international competition has mounted, governments have become more

206

generous. In 1984 and 1985, the governments of France, the UK and West Germany all announced new spending programmes, totalling several billion dollars, to aid the producers of microelectronics, communications and computers.

With regard to government subsidies, direct subsidies to industry rose steeply in many Western countries in the 1970s. The preferred form was the provision of capital by the government at favourable rates, whether by grant, loan, loan guarantee or equity participation. In addition, governments provide indirect subsidies through favourable tax treatment for certain expenditures and the provision of risk capital at preferential terms. Such practices discriminate in favour of the recipient industries and firms and the amount of the subsidies can be large. Tax subsidies alone were equivalent to 10–12 per cent of all fixed investments in manufacturing in the UK and the USA in 1981 (*The Economist*, 25 December 1982).

The most common types of NTBs, voluntary export restraints and orderly marketing agreements, were described in Chapter 1 and are usually (but not necessarily) employed for defensive purposes. Again, their impact on international trade is difficult to determine, not only due to problems of measurement but also because some of these restrictions are negotiated by non-governmental bodies and so are not officially recorded. US authorities, for example, treat voluntary export restraints as trade barriers imposed by the exporting country and apparently maintain no comprehensive inventory. An indirect indication of the significance of these two policies is suggested by the fact that, in 1976, approximately 16 per cent of the total imports of Western countries were subject to one form or the other (Murray, Schmidt and Walter, 1978, p. 627). Around the same time, NTBs of all types were applied to at least one-fifth of the manufactures imported by the USA and EC (Olechowski and Sampson, 1980, p. 231). Between 1974 and 1980, the proportion of world trade in manufactures subject to some form of NTB rose from 13 per cent to 23 per cent (Page, 1982). New barriers, particularly in the motor vehicle industry, have subsequently been introduced and the corresponding figures today would be even higher.

Despite an inability to be precise about the general impact of these policies, it is possible to identify several important characteristics. In the case of VERs and OMAs both forms of trade restrictions are discriminatory or non-universal, that is, they are negotiated between the importing country and one major supplier. The measures are also highly 'communicable' from one supplier to others. Agreements may isolate the original supplier but the source of disruption is then refocused. Relief from foreign competitors will be effective only for the period of time required for other suppliers to cash in on the premium price established in the restrained market. At the same time the exporters which were the original target of the restraint will often shift into related products in order to bypass the agreement. The danger of communicability is that discriminatory agreements will eventually have to be generalized to cover entire industries such as steel, chemicals or semiconductors and will involve all major suppliers.

Non-tariff measures also have a remarkable tendency to become lasting features of the policy landscape. They have usually been granted as a form of short-term aid to contracting industries, but have frequently become long-term forms of protection. A prominent example is the MFA described in Chapter 6. Its forerunner, the Short Term Arrangement on Cotton Textiles, was drawn up in 1961. Subsequent negotiations converted this into a Long-Term Arrangement which was repeatedly renewed while its scope and protectionist content was broadened and strengthened. Currently, some version of the MFA has been in force for twenty-five years.

Because the measures evolve into long-term trade restraints they can distort patterns of investment. The agreements usually divide the restrained markets between producers in Western markets and established exporters in the more advanced LDCs. But they make no provision to re-allocate portions of the restricted markets to new producers. By 'freezing' market shares, restraint agreements prevent underlying changes in international competitive ability from being realized by corresponding shifts in trade patterns. Once the original suppliers find their prospects for export expansion are limited they often respond by investing in the protected market itself. Alternatively, these firms may move into the production of related items which either are not covered by existing trade agreements or are covered but yield a higher per unit return of export. The danger is that investments undertaken for reasons such as this cannot be justified on the grounds of efficiency or comparative advantage.

The benefits of government-supported R and D are obvious in fields such as computers, electronic componentry, industrial robots and aerospace. However, there are also dangers. Extensive government support can further centralize the responsibility for initiative and innovation. As a result, technological priorities may coincide with national priorities but not reflect the needs of individual firms and industries or even market conditions. The transfer of new technologies – whether to other industrialized countries or to LDCs – may be actively discouraged under such circumstances. Countries which have singled out certain research-intensive activities as a national priority are prone to protect their lead by jealously guarding against technological transfers.

In conclusion, the reader should note that this profile of new protectionist policies has not mentioned tariffs – the most common and traditional form of trade restriction. Tariff levels have declined steadily in Western countries (although not in many LDCs) since the end of the Second World War, but they still exert a significant restraint on trade. Post-war tariff negotiations, however, have limited the ability of Western governments to use these policies to provide additional protection. New forms of protection provide a better basis for judging current policy goals. Indeed, it is probably wrong to regard today's protectionist policies – even those with the most explicit consequences for trade – as being nothing more than trade barriers. In an era of competitive coexistence the battleground between competitors extends beyond trade-related issues. Modern protectionist policies are frequently intended to influence patterns of investment and technological development (both domestic and foreign) as well as to restrict foreign suppliers. The fact that these objectives have, to date, taken the form of trade agreements merely reflects the lack of alternative policy tools and the pressure on governments to take immediate action. The following chapter, which examines the links between industrial policy and the tactics of firms in major industries, elaborates on many of the policies mentioned above.

Supplementary Reading

With regard to export performance in the field of manufactures, Batchelor, Major and Morgan (1980) combine a discussion of economic theory with empirical evidence. The view that external demand is the major determinant of export growth is represented by Lewis (1980) who argues that the export performance of LDCs is dependent on the rate of economic growth in Western countries. Empirical grounds for these arguments are found in Lewis (1981). Kravis (1970) concludes that successful export performance is largely due to internal factors rather than to the buoyancy of external demand, while Riedel (1984) argues that the exports of LDCs are not particularly dependent on the growth of income and demand in Western countries.

The literature on export-led growth is succinctly reviewed by Choi (1983, pp. 120–47). The theory of trade policy and the role of government intervention is set out by Corden (1971, 1974). The World Bank has carried out a series of empirical studies on the political economy of protection in Western countries which are cited in Verreydt and Waelbroeck (1980). Finger, Hall and Nelson (1982) analyze the application of NTBs under the American two-track method, arguing that there is a built-in bias in the system in favour of domestic producers rather than consumers. Pugel and Walter (1985) survey patterns of corporate behaviour in relation to national trade policy and test alternative hypothesis offered to explain the tactics of individual firms. Brock and Magee (1978) examine the way special interest groups may influence tariff setting practices. Jones (1984) provides a thorough analysis of the trade-creating and trade-diverting effects of voluntary export restraints, while Greenaway and Hindley (1985) estimate the costs of these policies for industries in the UK.

CHAPTER NINE

Defensive Strategies in International Markets

The links between structural change, industrial policy and interest group behaviour have been a recurrent theme of previous chapters. The following chapters draw upon elements from each of these three fields to describe a number of industry strategies. Given the range of circumstances and options available to firms in a particular industry, any description must necessarily resort to simplification. At the same time, several features which give rise to at least some measure of commonality between firms, interest groups and policy-makers can be identified.

One justification for an industry-wide frame of reference is the expectation that a certain measure of commonality can be found among the firms that dominate a particular industry. For instance, a few large firms in each industry will usually determine national patterns of investment, employment or development of products and technologies. These firms seldom arrive at major decisions without at least attempting an appraisal of their competitors' tactics and responses. And in many instances decisions may be taken in collaboration with other firms, including foreign ones. The proliferation of joint ventures, co-operative programmes for R and D, capacity-sharing agreements, licensing arrangements and similar practices are only some of the more obvious forms of co-ordination and collaboration.

Producers may also attempt to fix prices or to divide up the market (either covertly or with government approval).

Unions, too, often play a role in fashioning an industry-wide approach to various issues. They may influence a wide range of decisions which go beyond employment practices or wage rates, involving automation, foreign investment or other aspects. In a similar fashion, the circumstances faced by foreign subsidiaries of the industry's major firms, the policies of the host governments and the role of foreign competitors will be taken into account. To the extent that these groups succeed in their collaborative endeavours, an industry-wide interpretation of various strategies will be useful.

The growing involvement of government in the manufacturing sector helps to re-enforce an industry-specific focus. In attempting to 'guide' or alter patterns of structural change policy-makers do not usually seek to address sector-wide issues. And, with few exceptions, government policies are not aimed at individual firms. The result is a 'halfway house', where many structural policies are specified in terms of clusters of firms or products. A related reason for the appeal of an industry-specific approach concerns the growing vulnerability of governments to pressure from interest groups operating on behalf of particular industries. The formulation of industrial policies and industry tactics are increasingly the result of protracted negotiations and compromises between a diverse set of interests. In addition to public officials, participants can include representatives of private corporations and state-controlled firms, trade unions, associations representing various parts of the industry and even foreign competitors. By using their growing ability to influence public policy, these groups have injected another dimension into the normal range of economic and corporate issues that make up a firm's decision-making responsibilities. They help to fashion decisions which become part of the government's structural policies for a given industry. A direct consequence of the amalgamation of decision-making authority is that some industrial policies are no longer devised solely by public officials. Nor are the tactics of major firms necessarily the exclusive responsibility of corporate officials. The boundary between the two fields has been blurred. With the widening base for policy-making authority, the tendency to consider issues in terms of industries has been re-enforced.

While these characteristics provide the basis for a stylized description of industry strategies, this interpretation differs in certain respects from the approach found in the literature on business policy. Studies of the latter type stress the role of the firm, rather than the industry, in the context of strategic choices. Analysts may attempt to identify key groups of firms, assuming that a commonality of strategies can be related to a firm's size, its product mix, the extent of vertical integration, or other features. However, a singular preference to focus on the firm can also lead to an incomplete picture. The need to incorporate the international dimensions of an industry and to relate business policy to public policy may be better served by an industry-wide approach.

A related issue is that much of the literature on business policy or industrial organization leads to the impression that no more than one strategy may prevail for a chosen group of firms. Nevertheless, in the present case, the importance attached to the role of public policy suggests that the environment in which firms operate is not so hostile as to preclude the use of more than one strategy. Individual firms or groups of firms (even in the same country) may pursue quite different strategies. Similarly, the choice of one strategy will not necessarily prevent the adoption of others; the versions sketched in this chapter are neither mutually exclusive nor contradictory. Several may be advantageously pursued at the same time.

Critics might suggest that the types of strategies described below are merely alternative sets of short-run tactics, all examined from slightly different perspectives. The effective lifespan for any set of strategies will certainly be limited by policy changes and events in the marketplace. Nevertheless, an examination of individual industries suggests that strategies, once adopted, cannot be quickly abandoned. There are barriers to mobility – often created by investment decisions and technological priorities associated with strategic choices. As a result, firms may lack the ability to shift easily from one strategy or strategy mix to another in a short period of time.

214

In conclusion, the identification of those firms and characteristics which give rise to a commonality of strategies becomes a judgemental process, whatever the preferred frame of reference. Ultimately, both perspectives – involving the industry as well as the firm – may need to be addressed and the analyst will have to move back and forth between the two. The following description adopts an industry-wide interpretation but makes no claim to be comprehensive in scope. The approach is illustrative, drawing upon evidence from several industries and markets. While the strategies discussed are frequently associated with contracting industries, they may also be found in other fields of manufacturing. Subsequent chapters will consider other versions based on the experience of additional industries.

Rationalization

Efforts to lower costs can take many forms but in large, mature industries the most substantial savings are usually realized by cutting back on existing capacity, shedding workers and limiting pay raises, or by reducing the range of products being supplied to the market. The following discussion is confined to these measures and draws upon evidence gathered from the steel, automobile, chemical and shipbuilding industries.

Steel

With hindsight, some of the reasons why major steel-makers were forced to undertake large-scale rationalization programmes are not difficult to identify. First, many firms seriously misjudged their demand prospects during the 1970s. Because steel needs are dependent on the demand for steel-using products (automobiles, ships, capital goods, etc.), structural changes internal to the manufacturing sector eventually altered the industry's long-run demand trajectory. Today's major growth areas in Western countries include telecommunications, energy, aerospace, computers and electronic components and, unlike the leading industries during the first two-thirds of this century, are not intensive users of steel.

Second, in LDCs the industry's development has been reminiscent of earlier experiences in Western countries. In a typical LDC, the construction sector itself may account for 50–60 per cent of steel consumption, while the demand for machinery and other capital goods generates additional markets for steel firms. During 1974–84 the amount of crude steel produced in LDCs rose by 126 per cent, although the level of production in Western countries fell by 19 per cent (IISI, 1985, Table 2). Western firms have not only lost some of their traditional export markets but also faced additional competition in their home markets from the more efficient LDCs.

Third, technical advances have reduced the steel requirements of many industries. Trends in West Germany during the 1970s are probably typical; figures for that country show that steel inputs per unit of output declined by 10–20 per cent in many industries (UNIDO, 1980, p. 18). The steel industry itself began to use less of its own inputs as it turned to production of lighter and more durable products and reduced the wastage of crude steel. The effects of these trends were re-enforced by other technological advances which hastened the substitution of aluminium, plastics and highly resistant glass for steel in many traditional uses. The cumulative impact of all technical changes was significant. In the USA, the amount of steel required to produce one dollar of GDP fell by an average of 3.7 per cent per year during 1973–84 (*The Economist*, 12 October 1985).

These were only a few of the reasons for the contraction in Western steel markets. Although the implications for the industry now appear to be self-evident, they were not anticipated by many Western firms. Massive investment programmes continued until the late 1970s. Surprisingly, the rate of growth in world steel-making capacity was still accelerating in 1975–7 although demand in major markets had already begun to contract. The effects of the industry's misjudgements were compounded by the 'tonnes mentality', common to many firms. Excess capacity in periods of shrinking demand was tolerated to protect the market share in periods of maximum demand. Steel capacity in Western countries was nearly 600 million tonnes in 1984, although consumption was only 440 million tonnes (*Financial Times*, 5 November 1984). Thus, the cumulative effects of earlier miscalculations will take some time to redress.

The legacy of over-investment is especially apparent in the EC and it is here that the most explicit attempts to rationalize the industry can be found. Beginning in 1968, a number of European firms embarked on programmes to enlarge their crude steel capacity. Measured in real terms, annual investment expenditures had risen nearly four-fold by 1975 (OECD, 1977, p. 45). As a result, European steel-makers were particularly vulnerable to the drop in demand in 1975. Their situation was worsened by a surge in the Community's steel imports – almost 2 million tonnes – in that year. Average rates of capacity utilization in the Community fell abruptly from 85 to 65 per cent, while average steel prices dropped 35 per cent (Jones, 1985, p. 33).

The predominant opinion at the time was that the slump in steel markets was only temporary. Thus, the response was a moderate one involving the establishment of a 'forward programme' by the European Commission to aid in planning investment and production decisions. When market conditions failed to improve, the plight of major firms reached alarming proportions and led to the establishment of Eurofer, a voluntary steel cartel, in late 1976. In return for greater market stability, producers were expected to rationalize plants with the help of cash payments from the Community.

The reaction of the Community's steel-makers to this programme was divided, depending on whether they were publicly or privately owned. Throughout the 1970s, state involvement had grown and, by 1979, one-half of the Community's steel production was under government control (Jones, 1985, p. 66). Major producers in Belgium, France, Italy and the UK had been nationalized, or were only nominally in private hands, while state subsidies to private firms were a common practice. And, where public ownership was extensive, policy-makers were reluctant to urge cuts in capacity. One result was that the problem of excess capacity eventually became acute and jeopardized the cartel's entire operation.

As the costs of subsidies mounted, the need to reduce existing capacity was addressed with greater urgency. British steel capacity was cut by 4 million tonnes during 1980–3. In France the corresponding reduction was 4.7 million tonnes and cash injections for the two large state-owned steel companies were slashed by one-third. Italy's steel industry, however, survived intact until late 1982 and a programme to reduce capacity was not put together in Belgium before 1983. But the Community's efforts to reduce capacity were most firmly resisted in West Germany. German suppliers argued that their firms were efficient, privately-owned companies, while many of their less efficient competitors survived only with the help of generous government subsidies. At German insistence, it was agreed to terminate most steel subsidies in the EC by the end of 1985. Altogether, steel producers in the EC succeeded in reducing capacity by only 16 per cent during the first half of the 1980s (IISI, 1985, Annex 4). European capacity in 1985 was approximately 142 million tonnes, although estimated demand (European consumption plus net exports) was roughly 109 million tonnes. Thus, the problem of excess capacity will persist.

While European attempts to rationalize were complicated by the industry's heterogeneity, American steel producers had their own set of special problems. Small, non-integrated mini-mills had rapidly captured certain segments of the American market. The major producers mine their own ore, turn out a wide range of products and want to remain vertically integrated. In contrast, mini-mills melt scrap to make steel, buy in supplies and are seldom unionized. These practices accord the latter firms a significant cost advantage over their larger competitors. Most began by focusing on narrow geographic market areas where they established close working relations with their buyers. Even those which have now enlarged the market they serve continue to specialize in products such as seamless pipe, steel roofing and wire rod. This enables them more easily to adapt the product to the user's needs and to devote a relatively large portion of their funds to R and D. In the 1960s, mini-mills accounted for only 3–5 per cent of the American market but by 1983, their share had soared to 18 per cent (*International Business Week*, 13 June 1983).

The inroads made by mini-mills, coupled with the industry's other problems, forced even the most unwilling firms to accept some forms of rationalization. Between 1974 and 1984, employment in the industry fell by almost 60 per cent. Reductions in production capacity were less brutal – a cut of 16 per cent in 1977–85 (IISI, 1985, Tables 6 and 9). Unlike their European competitors American firms have no experience with formal, cartel-like arrangements. Moreover, government programmes to assist the industry were not contingent on capacity reductions in any form – a fact which some observers regard as a serious flaw (e.g. Reich, 1982, p. 859).

The American steel industry's efforts to rationalize have involved cuts in wages and supplementary benefits as well as attempts to reduce production capacity and the number of workers. The desire to cut labour costs is not surprising. In the mid–1960s, the industry's wages exceeded the average for all manufacturing by 30 per cent, but the gap had widened to 70 per cent by 1980 (Kawahito, 1981, p. 248). Despite stagnating demand and profits steel firms offered only token resistance to the union's demands during this period. An explanation for this oddity was suggested by Lawrence and Lawrence (1985) and has been briefly noted in Chapter 6. In the case of the steel industry the ability of firms to negotiate favourable agreements with unions depends on several factors. First, when demand was buoyant and capacity was expanding, firms could introduce more capital-intensive processes and reduce the size of their work forces. Once investment programmes began to be cut back, however – either in deference to demand trends or because firms lacked the funds – this alternative was no longer available. Second, because the steel industry has long been relatively capital-intensive, the opportunities for replacing labour are probably more limited than in other industries. Finally, steel plants can have an extremely long life, which means that managers may have few opportunities to undertake modernization programmes to reduce the work force.

Taken together, these circumstances left the American steel industry in a comparatively weak position to bargain with the union. Nevertheless, steel firms continued to operate – even when wage increases raised costs to such an extent that losses were being incurred. Conventional micro economic theory shows that this behaviour is logical so long as firms can still recover some portion of their fixed costs since the alternative would have been to write off these assets completely. Some firms eventually reached a point where their financial position would not permit continued operation at existing costs. In the closing stages of what is called the 'end-game', unions were pushed into making concessions to keep plants open. The Lawrences suggest that such a phase occurred in the USA after 1982 when the union's wage demands were moderated in return for job security. This stage was still being played out in 1985, when the five largest US steel producers ended their twenty-six-year agreement which provided co-ordinated bargaining arrangements with the United Steelworkers Union.

In an effort to improve their negotiating position with labour unions, some firms have undertaken reorganizations. For labour the change often means a cut in wages in return for some form of profit-sharing. Other elements of the strategy are reminiscent of the tactics employed by mini mills, the major competitors of integrated firms. They include more flexible working methods, reliance on the unit's own scrap smelting facilities and establishment of a sales force to serve each specialized unit. While this version is regarded as a radical one by the American steel industry, several integrated producers have gone so far as to reorganize their operations into semi-independent units. The intention is that each unit will specialize and that labour negotiations with unions will be on a product-by-product basis.

Despite their acknowledged leadership Japanese steel firms have also been forced to rationalize. Although the industry had long been a profitable one, domestic suppliers began encountering foreign competition in their home and export markets during the late 1970s. Rates of import penetration were comparatively low, but competition from South Korea, Taiwan and other LDCs reduced the ability of Japanese firms to control their domestic and export prices. Japanese producers were (and still are) particularly concerned about Korean competition. The latter country's largest steel-maker, the state-owned Pohang Iron and Steel Company (Posco), plans to increase its capacity by more than 15 per cent by 1988. Heretofore, Japanese firms were the predominant suppliers throughout South-east Asia. Their export prices were sufficient to ensure comfortable profits but low enough to discourage competitors from further afield. Now, Japan's regional exports – currently more than 8 million tonnes per year – compete with South Korean exports which are about 1 million tonnes per year. Nippon Steel has estimated that competition from Posco has reduced export prices by about 15 per cent (*The Economist*, 10 March 1984).

Penetrating the Japanese market has posed greater problems for Korean suppliers. Steel buyers were initially unwilling to purchase imported steel because they feared that Posco was too small to replace Japanese producers. Moreover, local trading companies were accustomed to shipping steel to South Korea and were reluctant to consider a reversal of this practice. Posco eventually approached import-export firms run by Korean residents in Japan. These firms acted as stockholders and sold the steel (on 'spot' markets) to buyers with temporary shortages. Gradually more Japanese firms followed suit.

Japanese producers may have genuine reasons to be concerned about the competitive abilities of Korean suppliers which are probably based on real cost differences. In 1983, the share of steel-makers' wages in Japan was reported to be 18 per cent of total costs compared to 4–5 per cent in South Korea (*Far Eastern Economic Review*, 17 November 1983). Alternative estimates of average hourly compensation for steel-workers were $12 in Japan, compared with $3 in South Korea. (*International Business Week*, 5 March 1984). Posco's initial construction costs were also low, mainly owing to cheap government loans and government-built infrastructure. These cost differences are likely to persist because of the higher productivity of the Korean producer and the fact that its latest round of expansion is taking place when a bleak outlook for steel has created a buyer's market for steel-making equipment.

At the insistence of the government Japanese firms first began to reduce capacity in the late 1970s. Nevertheless, by the early 1980s profits first declined and losses were subsequently reported by all five major suppliers. Nippon, the world's largest steel-maker, embarked on its third round of capacity cuts in 1984 – this time on its own initiative. In addition to phasing out obsolete capacity, rationalization programmes have included salary and wage reductions, negotiations with foreign suppliers of iron ore (for example, Australia) to reduce prices and even the 'lending' of surplus workers to firms in the automobile industry. However, because these steps have been supplemented by the aggressive pursuit of other options, the strategy figures less prominently than in Europe or the USA.

Automobiles

The circumstances which have forced Western automobile firms to undertake rationalization programmes are several. One of the major reasons was the rapid emergence of Japanese firms as international suppliers. Prior to 1963, annual levels of production in Japan did not exceed 1 million units, which is less than the output of the UK or Italy. Twenty years later Toyota and Nissan were the world's third and fourth largest producers and together produced 4.5 million cars. Western competitors not only lost a significant part of their home markets to Japanese imports but were also displaced as major exporters to LDCs.

A second factor, and one which prompted some firms to consider rationalization of their product lines if not their production capacity, was the capricious nature of consumer demand. The volatility of petrol prices, interest rates and exchange rates all contributed to abrupt shifts in consumer preferences in the 1970s and early 1980s. Market instability, particularly in the USA, played havoc with the design of new cars. The cost of designing a new, small car in America was nearly $2 billion and the plans of US car-makers were repeatedly undercut by demand shifts. These and other trends eventually led many Western producers to adopt several strategies, one of which was rationalization.

By the early 1980s, American car-makers were faced with mounting competition at both ends of the product range. Japanese suppliers were increasing their US sales of small to intermediate models and studies revealed that they had attained a significant cost advantage over American producers. European rivals were simultaneously cutting into the American market for luxury cars. One of the first reactions of US firms was to search for ways to reduce costs. The United Auto Workers (UAW) and Ford agreed on cost-cutting measures in early 1982, while General Motors (GM) was able to negotiate a pay agreement for 1982–5 that was considerably tougher than its predecessor. Companies also put pressure on their suppliers to roll back earlier price increases. GM discarded its practice of buying steel on long-term contracts and began to buy on price tenders. By cutting variable costs in these ways, and by mounting similar assaults on fixed costs, firms significantly reduced the rates of capacity utilization at which they could break even.

GM subsequently took even more radical steps on a very large scale, entirely new to the industry. By 1984 the company had reorganized its entire North American operation. The five existing divisions, plus GM of Canada, were replaced by two new divisions, one for big cars and one for small cars. Each is seen as a self-contained company, responsible for its own engineering, manufacturing, assembly and marketing operations. The massive reorganization was partly a result of previous attempts to cut costs which had gone awry. In the mid–1970s each of the existing divisions was producing similar cars built on the same platform. The result was an indistinctive range of makes and models, often of inferior quality. The reorganization is intended to address this problem, to end duplication and to make management more accountable for its own performance. Another cost-saving feature of the reorganization which GM hopes to achieve is to reduce the degree of vertical integration. The firm currently produces as much as 70 per cent of its own parts. In contrast, its US competitors purchase a similar proportion from outside suppliers and this allows them to shop for the best price. GM now intends for its suppliers to compete with outside suppliers.

The problem of over-capacity is most apparent in Europe. In the early 1980s, Europe's market exceeded that of the USA by only 1 million cars. However, the European market was dominated by twelve major firms (six of them producing a complete range of models) while only six major firms operate in the USA. One consequence of excess capacity has been continuous pressure on firms to supply a wide range of models for each segment of the market. Some, notably Bavarian Motor Works (BMW), Jaguar and Volvo, are known for specializing in models for particular market segments but, in general, European firms have been reluctant to rationalize their model ranges. Efforts to retain a complete product line in the face of sluggish demand have weakened major producers. The effects are starkly apparent in the case of Austin Rover, the volume-car division of British Leyland. Although the firm produces a full range of cars, its annual output is less than specialized European producers such as Daimler Benz.

Drastic price discounts were another consequence of excess capacity as firms fought to maintain their share of the European market. The effects on profits were serious. Between them, European car-makers lost more than $2 million in 1980–2 alone (*The Economist*, 26 November 1983) and the losses of many firms continued to mount in later years. European governments have traditionally come to the aid of loss-making automobile firms. In fact, a great deal of the Community's industry was state-owned in 1985: Alfa Romeo, Austin Rover, Renault, Fiat and Volvo Holland were majority-owned, while 40 per cent of Volkswagen was in government hands. Government support was originally prompted by the belief that a healthy motor industry provides an important stimulus to other economic activities. However, that argument, although still valid, has been weakened by the steady decline in the industry's work force. The decline is not so much the result of explicit efforts to cut costs by rationalizing the work force. It is mainly due to automation which has significantly reduced the direct labour content used in the production of a car.

To date, the need to rationalize has been most emphatically stated in France where government studies have emphasized the need to reduce the work force. Excess capacity is clearly demonstrated by the fact that Renault and Peugeot produce roughly 3 million cars per year, while only 1.8 million (including imports) were sold in France in 1984. One result is that the cost of subsidies has mounted; between 1975 and 1983, French governments supplied Renault alone with FF3.5 billion of new capital. The firm hopes to reduce its work force significantly during the latter part of the 1980s, but previous attempts to enforce such measures have been deflected by opposition from trade unions. Moreover, it is unlikely that the government would contemplate a rationalization programme on a scale undertaken by some British or American firms. Other strategies, which promise to reduce costs while preserving the industry's standing as a major product of automobiles, are preferred.

In view of their significant cost advantages over international rivals Japanese car-makers have had little need to consider rationalization strategies. However, their success is largely based on export performance. Any deterioration of these markets would have serious consequences as the domestic market is inadequate to support the industry. Beginning in the mid–1960s, firms accepted low domestic prices and profit margins to stave off imports and the practice eventually became an established part of the Japanese market. In 1983, profits on each mass-produced car sold in Japan were only $85–$125 compared to more than $2,000 earned on the more luxurious cars sold in the USA (*The Economist*, 14 July 1984). By the beginning of the 1980s, the Japanese market was nearing maturity and competition for market share was intense. Profits earned through exporting have funded a vicious battle as nine domestic car-makers compete in a maturing market.

There are several reasons why Japanese firms have been able to avoid rationalization, despite poor conditions in their home market. The most obvious explanation is the phenomenal growth of exports throughout the 1970s which helped to stave off many incipient labour problems. During that decade Toyota doubled its output, while the firm's labour force rose by only 12 per cent. A second factor is that all firms rely heavily on sub-assemblies supplied by outside manufacturers. Some firms even sub-contract the assembly of entire vehicles. The practice allows car-markers a flexibility which their foreign competitors do not have. Japanese producers can easily absorb a larger share of these operations and thus adjust to a fall in demand without significant reductions in their own labour forces.

Moves to reduce the number of auto-workers have been undertaken gradually and consultation with trade unions is the usual practice when deciding on ways to automate assembly lines or locate new production facilities abroad. The Japanese industry has not had a major strike since the 1950s. Given the unions' docile attitudes, their main mission may be transformed into protecting existing jobs, so long as drastic cuts in the work force are not contemplated. The comfortable relationship of firms with trade unions is not likely to be disturbed, meaning that rationalization programmes will avoid cuts in the domestic work force such as occurred in the UK or USA.

Evidence from Other Industries

Various aspects of the chemical industry have already been described in Chapter 6. Following the boost to oil prices in 1979–80, demand for chemicals fell sharply and many firms began to rationalize their plant capacities. American companies withdrew from Europe and government-owned companies in France and Italy were forced to take over loss-making petrochemical plants. During 1980–84, up to 20 per cent of European capacity was shut for products such as ethylene, polyethylene, polyvinyl chloride or polystyrene. Because governments did not want to close plants when unemployment was rising, state-owned firms were the slowest to rationalize. Interestingly, state-owned firms accounted for roughly one-quarter of European production of petrochemicals in 1975, but ten years later the share was 40 per cent (*The Economist*, 16 November 1985). In Japan, rationalization efforts focused on the petrochemical branch of the industry and proceeded at a rapid pace. Mainly in order to accommodate cheap imports from Canada, Saudi Arabia and the USA, Japanese capacity was reduced by one-third during the first half of the 1980s.

Many companies found ingenious ways to cushion the effects of closures. The multiplicity of production routes and products afforded large firms a flexibility not possible in other industries. Several European firms negotiated rearrangements of their product lines with competitors to achieve a less expensive mix of products. Low cost-producers of certain chemicals tried to sell these to high-cost rivals. Producers were also careful in their selection of the sites to be closed in the case of bulk chemicals. For instance, ethylene closures were usually made in complexes where there was more than one plant. This meant that the company would still have 'captive' supplies for use as inputs in the production of downstream chemicals. However, owing to the cyclical nature of demand the industry's rationalization strategies have often been very short-term in nature. When some markets resumed their growth in the mid–1980s, many companies were again operating at full capacity and began to reconsider their rationalization programmes. They argued that the scale of commitments required was so great that the only option was to concentrate on specific chemicals and to become as large as possible in these particular fields.

Few industries have undergone a rationalization process so drastic as much of the world's shipbuilding and repair industry. During the early 1980s, several of the largest American shipyards were closed and almost 30,000 workers were laid off. The remaining US shipbuilders rely heavily on military customers rather than merchant orders. Japanese shipyards are reported to have cut capacity by 35 per cent in the decade up to 1985, while in Europe reductions during the same period reached 50 per cent (*Far Eastern Economic Review*, 10 October 1985). Japanese conglomerates have also redeployed labour from shipbuilding to other areas of heavy industry and, since 1982, have operated with a government-administered quota system which helps to spread the problems of excess capacity. Even comparatively modern operations in LDCs, such as government-owned shipyards in Singapore, have been compelled to rationalize.

Some of the reasons for over-capacity are not difficult to identify. As the exports of Japan and other Asian countries grew these countries wanted national fleets to ship their goods. The development of shipbuilding capacity has sometimes proceeded at a miraculous pace; for instance, South Korea is now the Western world's second largest shipbuilding country after Japan, but had almost no capacity at all in 1973 (*Financial Times*, 16 March 1984). At the same time, in traditional shipbuilding countries the desire of governments to maintain employment led them to subsidize selling prices. The result of these contradictory trends was that a growing number of ships were launched at a time when world seaborne trade was falling.

The drastic cuts in capacity which have occurred in the 1980s are not likely to bring immediate relief for surviving shipyards. The glut of available tonnage will continue owing to the long life of carriers and the fact that severely depressed prices of second-hand ships permits marginal operators – many new to shipping – to enter the business. Moreover, at the global level the benefits of rationalization have been partially eroded as China, South Korea, Taiwan and other LDCs have built up their capacity since the late 1970s. Altogether, more than 60 million deadweight tonnes of idle shipping capacity in the form of bulk carriers and tankers existed in 1984, while paradoxically world production was at its highest level since 1977 (*The Economist*, 17 August 1985).

Rationalization is a widely used strategy and there are few major industries which have not attempted some version of this in recent years. Critics frequently see the failure to rationalize as a central problem explaining the plight of many industries. Such comments are often justified, but other features of the strategy should also be noted. First, a rationalization strategy will seldom be sufficient for a lagging industry to reverse its decline and to overtake its competitors. An industry's first reaction to mounting foreign competitors is usually to search for ways to cut costs, but cost differences may be only one of the explanations. Shrinking industries are also likely to suffer from other problems; among them, inferior technologies, inadequate distribution systems, insufficient funding for investment or obsolete product designs. Such shortcomings will not be redressed through rationalization alone. Other strategies will be needed and the urgency to reduce costs will have to be weighed against these objectives.

Second, the options available to improve efficiency through rationalization may be limited by the very strength and scale of operations. Major industries will usually employ a large portion of the country's work force, or account for a significant amount of its capital stock. Plants are often widely dispersed throughout the country; they will have close links with other industries (both users and suppliers) and, in many cases, will be regarded as having strategic importance. All this power invites obligation. Such circumstances may deter the industry from implementing their cost-cutting strategies to the extent required – or even desired. Instead, industries and governments alike will be prone to search for alternative strategies which may seem to be less painful than rationalization.

Protectionism

Measures to restrict a country's import of particular goods can take many forms and serve a number of objectives. In large, mature industries the purpose of protection is usually 'defensive', a term used in Chapter 8 to describe policies intended to slow the pace of contraction resulting from structural change and international shifts in competitive abilities. Western countries have often justified the use of protective measures (tariffs, quotas, voluntary export restraints and similar policies) by contending that rapid growth of imports leads to adjustment costs of a magnitude that is politically unacceptable. LDCs, too, rely heavily on the use of tariffs and quotas, but justify their policies in different terms. For these countries the most common justification is based on the notion of an 'infant industry'. The argument stresses the need to protect new firms until they are sufficiently large and experienced to benefit from the economies of scale which their longer established foreign rivals enjoy. The following discussion of protectionist strategies is based mainly on evidence drawn from steel and consumer electronics, with brief examples taken from automobile and wood processing industries.

Steel

Many steel firms and their supporting pressure groups regard protectionism as an alternative to rationalization. Protection not only limits the amount of imports entering the country but also results in higher domestic prices. In the short-run, at least, such measures reduce the need to rationalize the industry.

Protectionist strategies have been widely used in the US steel industry. The USA first became a net importer in 1959 during the course of a prolonged strike. Since that time a major objective of the steel lobby has been to restrain the growth of imports. As imports rose protectionist sentiments grew stronger and, in 1969, voluntary export restraints were negotiated with the EC and Japan. These restraints were abolished with the passage of the Trade Act of 1974, but the steel lobby was later to resume its efforts.

Because the new campaign occurred in the midst of a serious recession, it benefited greatly from public support. The attack on imports also involved a change in tactics. It focused on a new test to determine whether foreigners were engaging in price discrimination between the USA and other national markets (a practice known as 'dumping') contained in the Trade Act of 1974. The shift in tactics was said to be on the advice of the Carter Administration which was anxious to deflect a new drive for import quotas (Mueller and van der Ven, 1982, p. 263). The American Iron and Steel Institute (AISI) played a leading role in this period. It filed a petition charging that Japanese producers had unfairly diverted shipments of steel to the USA as a result of an agreement to restrict imports to the EC. The AISI also attempted to document charges of unfair practices and forcefully advocated the need for stronger import restraints (AISI, 1978 and 1980).

In 1977, at the height of the protectionist drive, a steel caucus of about 150 Representatives and Senators demanded a more effective means of import restriction. Shortly afterwards the government introduced its new 'trigger price mechanism' (TPM). The mechanism set a minimum price for imports based on 'constructed costs' using Japanese data. Foreign steel could be sold in the USA at prices above the minimum, but imports priced below these levels would prompt a preliminary review to determine whether the government should launch a full-scale investigation of dumping practices.

American steel interests were dissatisfied with the levels of protection accorded by the TPM. They called for a two-tier system of construction costs – one based on Japanese data and another derived from European figures. The proposal, which was not accepted, would have led to much higher trigger prices for European exporters whose costs exceeded those of Japanese producers (although their landed American prices were sometimes lower). Firms subsequently resorted to litigation in an attempt to force the government to replace the TPM with a stronger form of import restraint. Anti-dumping suits were filed against several European producers, which led to the suspension of the TPM. The suits violated an agreement whereby the government had established the TPM in return for an industry pledge not to file anti-dumping charges. The government initially attempted to appease the industry, by establishing a higher TPM or minimum price of imports and by introducing new quantitative restrictions. However, when more firms resorted to legal actions the TPM was formally abandoned. The accusations implicated a host of suppliers and included some product categories – for example, semi-finished steel slabs – new to the dispute. Most of the EC's steel exports to the USA were affected by these suits. A compromise with European suppliers was reached in late 1982: governments and industries alike agreed to a quota system that would limit Europe's exports, on average, to 5.4 per cent of the American market.

The agreement led to a decline in steel imports from the EC. However, suppliers in other countries quickly stepped forward, boosting their exports to the USA by as much as 200 per cent during the following year (Wetter, 1985, p. 491). In 1985, the government put together a five-year relief plan. One element consisted of a series of VERs negotiated with the new steel suppliers in seven countries: Australia, Brazil, Japan, Mexico, South Africa, South Korea and Spain. In conjunction with a revised USA-EC steel pact, the new programme was intended to limit imports of finished steel to 18.5 per cent of the American market.

Trade restraints were then being applied to three-quarters of all steel imported by the USA (Wetter, 1985, p. 492). But the perceived losers in this arrangement are not necessarily foreign steel-makers. South Korea's restraint agreement, for example, calls for its share of the US market to fall by one-fifth. Under these circumstances Korean exporters will no longer have any incentive to undercut American prices; their market share cannot be increased. Instead, the tendency is for importers' prices to rise to US levels, which are perhaps 20 per cent higher. The total cost of the relief programme to the US economy was estimated to be $18 billion over the five-year period (*Wall Street Journal*, 7 January 1985).

Throughout this entire period the legal efforts of steel producers were actively supported by the United Steel-workers Union. Because of the high wages accorded steel-workers, the union had good reasons to endorse the protectionist drive. The only division between the various factions was that steel-workers and some of the smaller producers argued for a system of quotas, while most of the large, integrated firms initially preferred to seek relief through duties.

The campaign of the steel lobby did not proceed without opposition. At least some parts of the US bureaucracy were concerned about the effects on trade relations with the EC. Retaliation in the form of trade restrictions on American exports of chemicals, textiles or agricultural products was feared. The zeal with which steel firms supported the protectionist campaign also varied. Several firms had long-term commitments to import specific types of steel which were in short supply and they opposed at least some aspects of the campaign. Others had begun to diversify into oil refining, chemicals or activities outside the manufacturing sector and their enthusiasm for protective measures was also lukewarm.

In Europe, governments were initially hesitant to agree to any stringent protectionist measures. The steel industry called for the European Commission to establish production quotas, minimum prices and quantitative import controls. However, it was not clear that imports *per se* were the basic cause of the industry's problems. International agreements (specifically, Article XIX of the GATT) prohibited such moves if general market conditions, rather than imports, were the true source of the industry's problems. At the same time, European policy-makers feared that an overt protectionist stance might prompt the USA to take similar action. Rather than imposing unilateral quotas, policy-makers chose to negotiate some form of restraint agreement. Because they sought to provide some immediate relief from imports, Japanese suppliers were the most promising target. During 1975 that country accounted for more than one-quarter of the Community's steel imports, up from 13.8 per cent in the previous year (Jones, 1985, p. 22). Accordingly, the Commission concluded a voluntary restraint agreement with the Japanese in late 1975.

Pressure on the Community's steel producers continued as American opposition to imports from Europe mounted. Moreover, competition in European markets was intensifying owing to the efforts of producers in Spain and Eastern Europe. A more comprehensive set of import controls was required. Thus, shortly after the Americans introduced the TPM, the European Commission announced its own 'basic price system'. The system was very similar to the American version: minimum prices were determined on the basis of Japanese costs for traded carbon steel products; sales below the basic price would prompt a preliminary anti-dumping investigation and provisional anti-dumping duties would be assessed if results of the investigation supported the charges.

An important additional feature was that the basic price

233

system could be waived and the threat of anti-dumping investigations would be withdrawn if suppliers accepted a voluntary restraint agreement. In return, co-operating firms would be allowed to sell in the EC at less than reference prices while their European competitors would be prevented from matching these prices. Because the European market was highly protected, prices were high and the profits to be earned by participating foreign suppliers were substantial. With a strategy for 'inducing' voluntary restraint in place, the Commission moved quickly by filing a number of anti-dumping complaints in early 1978. Restraints were soon negotiated with all major steel suppliers.

These steps provided the Europeans with some measure of control over imports. Their cartel, Eurofer, worked reasonably well for a while. Price-cutting ceased, the market improved and minimum prices became irrelevant. However, in mid–1980, demand slumped again. Moreover, the Community's efforts to reduce excess capacity had made little progress. The existing set of policies were not adequate to restrain output and maintain prices at levels where the less efficient participants could operate. With demand slack, steel firms incurred heavy losses and the number of layoffs rose. These conditions forced the Commission to declare an official state of emergency, empowering it to set mandatory production quotas for individual firms.

At the same time, the American TPM was proving to be unsatisfactory to producers on both sides. The Community's acquiescence to the measure was obtained partly with the promise that genuine low-priced producers could gain an exemption from the TPM upon prior application and approval. American firms, however, were demanding even tighter import controls, while European suppliers found that the new trigger prices were too high and that they received too few exemptions under the pre-clearance procedures. In mid–1981, European suppliers reportedly forced the issue by boosting their monthly US exports to 800,000 tonnes, up from an average of 500,000 tonnes during 1980 (Jones, 1985, p. 74). The move led to the permanent abandonment of the TPM when American competitors responded with a series of anti-dumping charges.

The USA and the Community then undertook to negotiate another form of settlement. Their efforts eventually culminated in the US-EC Steel Pact. In exchange for dropping forty-five charges of unfair trade practices, filed by American producers, the Community agreed to a quota system limiting its exports to the USA. The first agreement ran until the end of 1985, a date coinciding with the Community's deadline for ending state subsidies. During that year a revised pact was negotiated. European steel-makers agreed to 'industry' limits on their exports to the USA for an additional four years. Europeans attempted to keep semi-finished steels out of the pact. They had long-term contracts to supply those items to buyers and to their own US-based subsidiaries, but the American proposal would have reduced imports of semi-finished steel to one-half the level in 1984. A compromise was reached after the USA temporarily stopped all imports of semi-finished steels from the Community.

The Japanese steel industry did not escape the effects of falling steel prices and new competition from LDCs. Like their American counterparts, some steel-makers proposed that their government file dumping charges against exporters in Brazil, South Korea and Taiwan. They also contended that heavy subsidies were being provided to their competitors. Estimates by the Japan Iron and Steel Federation put these subsidies at 40 per cent in South Korea and Taiwan (*Far Eastern Economic Review*, 17 November 1983). But the appeal for protection did not gain wide acceptance – even within the industry. Most Japanese steel-makers were reluctant to restrict imports because they shipped so much steel abroad themselves.

For LDCs, the danger of heightened protection is clearly illustrated by trends in the steel industry. The main targets of new protectionist measures were initially exporters in Western countries. However, the imposition of these restraints not only raised domestic prices (thereby making the market a more attractive one to all potential suppliers) but also 'froze' the ability of major foreign suppliers to exploit the market. Such policies soon proved to have implications for both the pattern of trade and the products concerned. First, new suppliers – many in LDCs – soon stepped forward to replace the newly restrained exporters and additional limitations were sought. Following agreements with European and Japanese steel suppliers, the USA had to negotiate export restraints with Argentina, South Korea and other LDCs. Similarly, Brazil, Indonesia, Mexico and South Korea were involved in negotiations with the EC. Second, the imposition of restraints on various products encouraged foreign suppliers to shift their exports to other steel items. Thus, there was a tendency for the network of export restraints to widen and to cover more and more of the industry. As it did so, suppliers specializing in other steel products became involved and here again the LDCs were implicated.

Consumer Electronics

The consumer electronics industry is defined here to include familiar items such as television and radio receivers, phonographs, stereo and sound equipment, video-tape recorders (VTRs) and major components such as picture tubes. Several characteristics applying to a major part of this industry, that is, television and radio receivers, have already been described in Chapter 6.

During the past three decades, the world's consumer electronics industry has experienced changes in patterns of production and trade of a magnitude much greater than that in most other industries. A very rough impression of these developments can be obtained from Table 9.1. The comparability of the data is, however, impaired by two facts. First, production figures are available only in numbers of units, while trade statistics are recorded in US dollars. Second, product characteristics changed significantly between 1970 and 1982 as consumer preferences shifted from monochrome televisions to colour, from bulky radios to transistor sets, and so on. Because of these distortions, no precise assessment of changes in world leadership in the industry or even in a particular product category, can be made. However, the general directions of change are still clear. The position of both the EC and the USA deteriorated as rapid gains were recorded by Asian LDCs and, to a lesser extent, Japan. These broad trends are confirmed by more detailed information. In the USA, for instance, twenty-seven firms were assembling television sets in 1960 but, by 1976, there were only twelve and several were foreign-owned (Grunwald and Flamm, 1985, p. 19). Europe's largest electronics firm, Philips, responded to Asian competition by reorganizing its entire operation and rationalizing in various ways. Altogether, more than twenty of the firm's plants have been closed since 1980, including three supplying television tubes and four producing television sets (*Financial Times*, 29 October 1982 and 7 May 1985). French, Italian and German firms have followed suit. In the UK, Thorn is the only domestic company which is still a volume producer of consumer electronics, although four firms were operating fifteen years ago.

Given the extensive penetration of American and European markets, it is somewhat surprising that protectionist campaigns have not been more vigorous. Rather than opting for a broad, industry-wide system of protection, most firms have pressed for trade restrictions on specific products (usually television sets). Nevertheless, the characteristics of trade restrictions in major importing markets differ in certain important details. Europe's unique transmission and reception technologies provided an effective means of deterring foreign producers of televisions during the 1960s and 1970s. However, as licences began to expire in the 1980s this barrier was swept aside. Various other forms of non-tariff barriers were also employed. Some were bilateral – for example, a privately negotiated voluntary export restraint between the UK and Japan dating back to 1973 – while others were imposed unilaterally by France and Italy. The EC also introduced restrictions on behalf of certain countries, mainly with the intention of reducing Japanese imports entering via member countries.

By the 1980s more ingenious forms of trade restraints had emerged. One of the most publicized was the short-lived French regulation which required imports of video recorders to be cleared through the small town of Poitiers.

As European opposition to imports mounted, a complex

Table 9.1 Global Trends in Production and Trade in Consumer Electronics (as a percentage of reported world total)

	EC 1970	EC 1982	USA 1970	USA 1982	Japan 1970	Japan 1982	Asian LDCs[a] 1970	Asian LDCs[a] 1982
Television receivers:								
Production	21	16	19	15	28	18	2	15
Exports	31	29	7	5	47	37	1	16
Imports	19	36	42	21	...	...	6	7
Radio receivers:								
Production	15	7	12	6	29	12	30	52
Exports	17	10	2	2	62	51	10	30
Imports	16	27	46	38	...	1	6	7
Sound recorders and reproducers[b]								
Production	34	17	19	8	35	57	1	4
Exports	28	9	7	4	50	80	...	5
Imports	23	39	43	29	1	...	4	7
Tubes, transistors and other components:								
Production	...	...	...	...	...	...	...	...
Exports	31	20	37	29	6	19	6	25
Imports	45	25	15	28	7	5	3	27

Sources: United Nations, *Yearbook of Industrial Statistics*, Vol. 2 (various issues); United Nations, *Yearbook of International Trade Statistics* (various issues); United Nations, *Commodity Trade Statistics*, series D (various issues) and related UN sources. [a] Hong Kong, Malaysia, Philippines, Singapore, South Korea and Thailand. [b] Sound reproducers only. *Note:* Figures are not directly comparable. For a discussion, see the text.

trade agreement was negotiated with Japanese suppliers of both finished and knocked down sets in 1984. European firms are first allocated a minimum production level. Based on a forecast for each year, Japanese suppliers were then allocated the difference between expected sales and European output. In return, Japanese suppliers pledged not to undercut the prices of European-produced video recorders. Contrary to agreements in other industries, the number of units to be sold by the Japanese was not predetermined. As the European market matured, forecasts proved to be overly optimistic and Japanese exports were cut. This trend, coupled with the fact that after 1985 Korean firms were no longer restrained from exporting recorders built with Japanese technology, may bring about the collapse of the entire arrangement.

Two of the three largest European firms, Philips and Thomson, have pressed the EC to raise its tariffs on popular audio and video products to 14 per cent, the same as the tariff currently applied to colour televisions. This would replace tariffs ranging from 4.9 per cent on hi-fi systems and video cameras to 8 per cent on video recorders. In addition, Philips has proposed an 'infant industry' tariff of 19 per cent on new products. These requests have yet to win the support of Thorn, the only other major European firm, which favours more bilateral restraints. The European Commission is also reluctant, fearing that with additional protection firms will merely relapse into complacency. The Philips-Thomson proposal was also opposed by some of the smaller firms. They contended that a better solution would be to cut the 17 per cent tariff on imports of semiconductors and thus reduce the costs of European producers of consumer electronics.

The protectionist campaigns by American firms have generally been in response to changing market fortunes. During periods of buoyant demand, imports soared, but rapid growth provided a sufficient substitute for a declining market share. By the late 1960s, however, Japanese successes in American markets had led to sporadic charges of dumping and a number of lawsuits. When demand again slumped in the 1970s, American firms began to press more vigorously for protection. The products involved in these trade disputes during the 1970s included resistors, transformers, capacitors, tuners, monochrome and colour television sets, tubes, microwave ovens and citizen band radios. However, conclusive findings of trade violations were mainly confined to television receivers. Eventually, an orderly marketing agreement with Japanese producers of television sets was introduced for the period 1977–80. This step was followed by the negotiation of a VER with Japanese subsidiaries in Taiwan and an OMA with South Korean suppliers of televisions. After the latter agreement expired in 1982, Korean exports to the USA soared from 630,000 units to 1.93 million in the following year. Dumping charges were again filed – by trade unions and US firms – and moderate duties were imposed on several Korean suppliers in 1984.

Unlike the situation in Europe, the protectionist stance of US firms is complicated by the fact that many operate a far-flung network of offshore production sites. These firms naturally favoured free trade in the finished and semi-processed items exported by their subsidiaries, associates and affiliates in LDCs. Zenith, the only major producer which had no offshore facilities, took a leading role in the American protectionist campaign. It supported the union-sponsored move to repeal the offshore assembly provision of the US Tariff Act of 1930 and endorsed the efforts of a lobbying group called the Committee to Preserve Colour Television. Interestingly, Zenith's first major move after the successful conclusion of the OMA in 1977 was to move much of its colour television production offshore.

Evidence from Other Industries

There are very few – if any – industries where protectionist strategies have not played some role. The US automobile industry provides an interesting example of the conditions which may divide major firms and interest groups in their approach to protection. After the entire American complex of automobile-makers and component suppliers lost 2.5 million workers during the late 1970s, Ford and the UAW joined forces and appealed for import quotas. When their request was rejected by the government they appealed to Congress to empower the Administration to negotiate restrictions on the imports of Japanese cars. It is significant that GM did not participate in this exercise. If imports were to fall, GM's dominance of the domestic market would have posed serious anti-trust problems.

Congress subsequently considered several alternatives to import controls, while the Reagan Administration provided mild forms of assistance by abolishing or postponing thirty-four government standards for pollution and safety. But pressure from the auto industry did not abate. In 1981, a voluntary restraint was negotiated limiting Japan's annual exports to the USA to 1.68 million cars. In return, congressional supporters of the car industry attempted to extract concessions. The UAW was expected to be more modest in its wage demands, while producers were encouraged to plough back their profits into the industry.

As car-makers pursued their cost-cutting efforts the situation of the country's auto workers steadily deteriorated. In 1982, the UAW embarked on an elaborate campaign for enactment of a domestic content law. The proposed law stipulated that the domestic content of autos should be as high as 90 per cent for firms selling over 900,000 vehicles. The union's argument that the employment benefits would be considerable found a sympathetic audience in Congress. At one time the proposal had as many as 200 sponsors but was never approved by Congress. Because of its extensive reliance on foreign suppliers of components and cars GM would have been hard pressed to meet such a standard and therefore opposed the bill.

Instead of regulating domestic content, the life of the existing export restraint was merely extended until 1985. Once it expired, the Japanese government announced that it would continue to impose a limit on exports to the USA, albeit at a higher level. American automobile firms subsequently resumed their pleas for protection against imports but with little success. Ironically, the same firms were busily developing new agreements with foreign producers to import cars, parts and production technologies (for example, through joint ventures) to reduce their costs. The latter strategy, which is described in Chapter 10, depends on the free flow of automobiles and components and could have been undermined had the pleas for protection been heeded.

Evidence from the wood products industry provides a different aspect of protectionism. The industry, which includes the manufacture of shaped and simply-worked wood items, plywoods and veneers, depends heavily on raw materials. The major sources of supply for tropical timbers (mahogany and teak) are Asian LDCs, while Canada and Scandinavian countries produce coniferous woods. During the 1970s considerable timber-processing capacity, which was dependent on imports of raw materials from these countries, was built up in Japan, South Korea and Taiwan. Asian producers of tropical timber hoped to emulate this step by restricting their own exports of logs. Producers in Indonesia, Malaysia, Papua New Guinea and the Philippines therefore formed the Southeast Asia Log Producers Association (Sealpa) in 1975.

The organization apparently hoped to force importers to provide technical and financial assistance needed to establish processing facilities at the source of supply. However, sizeable processing industries existed in several of the importing countries. These operations were relatively labour-intensive and often carried some political influence. Firms which relied on imported timber were also protected by a typical system of 'escalating' tariffs. For example, Japanese import duties on logs are nil but amount to 5 per cent for sawn lumber and are 20 per cent for plywood. Such a pattern favours the import of unprocessed timber and makes it difficult for foreign firms to export more processed forms of wood.

The operation of Sealpa was plagued by serious divisions between its members. One group comprised those producers who either wished to export unprocessed timber or were unable to do otherwise. Pitted against these were other firms which insisted on exporting processed timber or sawn wood. Countries determined to export only processed tropical timber (mainly plywood) have not only to undercut prices of Japanese processors but also absorb additional costs reflected by existing tariffs. Indonesia, in particular, has been successful in this regard and has boosted its share of the Japanese plywood market. In response, however, Japanese manufacturers have been able to extract price cuts of up to 30 per cent from other Southeast Asian suppliers of logs. At the same time, the aptly named Japan Plywood Political Federation has pressured the government to retain the existing tariff structure. The division between Sealpa members gradually widened. By 1985, Indonesia and the Philippines had subsequently banned the export of logs while Malaysian state of Sabah reduced its exports of unprocessed timber. By that time, however, improvements in the efficiency of the Japanese industry had greatly reduced its raw material needs and, despite the export ban on unprocessed timber, the prices of logs changed very little.

The end of Sealpa was signalled in 1985 when the International Tropical Timber Organization was established at the behest of Japan with purposes which largely usurped Sealpa's role. The new organization is a governmental one, comprising a large number of both consuming and producing countries. Its objectives include improved access to markets, increased processing of timber in the home country and provision of information to ensure 'greater transparency' in the international tropical timber market.

Supplementary Reading

In contrast to economists, analysts of business policy have long emphasized the importance of the firm rather than the industry. Economists have partly adopted this perspective by focusing on 'strategic' groups within an industry. The suggestion in Chapter 9 that a certain degree of commonality exists between major firms is carried much further by other analysts who attempt to identify strategic groups of firms according to key decision variables such as investment, R and D and advertising. Examples of this approach are provided by Porter (1979) and Oster (1982). A survey of the literature on business policy has been carried out by Caves (1980) who suggests that economists have much to learn from this field. Hirschman's views on the behaviour of firms in contracting industries (1981, especially pp. 209–65) draws together ideas from a range of disciplines.

With regard to the steel industry, it is important to distinguish between integrated producers – the major focus of this discussion – and the mini-mill producers. The significance of the latter set of firms is described in Barnett and Schorsch (1983). Acs's (1984) study of the American steel industry suggests several reasons why large, vertically integrated firms may actually be less efficient than their smaller competitors. Jones (1979, 1985) provides an account of the current European steel cartel and relates it to earlier attempts during the 1920s and 1930s. The same author (Jones, 1986) has analyzed the circumstances leading up to the US-EC steel pact of 1985.

Maxcy (1981) conducts a thorough survey of the automobile industry while Altshuler *et al.* (1984) have carried out an extensive analysis of the industry's prospects. Abernathy's study of the American automobile industry stresses the need to retain flexibility in products and processes in order to respond to external forces for change (Abernathy, 1978). Jones (1981) discusses the maturity process in the European automobile industry and the impact on public policy. In the Latin American automobile industry, Kronish and Mericle (1984) stress the relationships between the host-country governments, multinationals and trade unions. A discussion of the Asian automobile industry is provided by Odaka (1983).

The consumer electronics industry has been studied by Cable and Clark (1981, 1982) who look at the industry's development in LDCs with particular emphasis on the role of technological change and trade protection. One of the most widely studied parts of this industry is the field of radio and television. Turner (1982a, pp. 48–68) offers an interesting analysis of this branch of the industry. Peck and Wilson (1982) are concerned with the factors contributing to the successful Japanese penetration of the American market for television sets, while Walter and Jones (1980) focus on the protectionist tactics used in this part of the consumer electronics industry. Hazewindus (1982, Chapter 3) considers the application of microelectronics to the consumer electronics industry. Ballance and Sinclair (1983, pp. 130–43) provide an introduction to global trends in the development of consumer electronics. Kotler, Fahey and Jatusripitak (1985) chart the rise of Japanese exporters in various types of consumer electronics.

CHAPTER TEN

Competitive Strategies in International Industries

The discussion of industry strategies continues in Chapter 10 with a look at offshore processing and diversification. The use of either set of tactics may result from international shifts in competitive ability. In the case of offshore processing, firms located in certain countries may find they can no longer match the production costs of international rivals. A decline in competitiveness can result from a change in the relative price of factors of production in the country (for example, a rise in wage rates), a shift in the industry's factor requirements, or both. Some producers may have the option of reducing costs by moving parts of their operation – usually, labour intensive processes such as assembly of components – to low-wage sites in LDCs. Alternatively, the impetus for relocating or investing abroad can be attributed to growing protectionism and resistance to imports in major consuming markets. In this case, the motive is not likely to be a reduction in production costs. Foreign suppliers may simply find it 'expedient' to establish a presence in the markets which they previously served only through exports.

The reasons why an industry may embark on a strategy of diversification are equally varied. They include the desire to stave off the effects of market saturation, to find a more profitable market niche, or to secure the supply of vital inputs and components.

A strategy of offshore processing is illustrated by refer-

ence to the consumer electronics and semiconductor industries. The discussion of diversification strategies is based on
evidence from three industries: consumer electronics, steel
and computers.

Offshore Assembly and Processing

The internationalization of industries by stage of processing
is not new. Helleiner (1973, p. 31) foresaw this development
as the 'new frontier' for international business. For LDCs he
regarded as an alternative to import substitution, domestic
processing of raw materials, or exports of labour intensive
products in their final form. Some of the evidence cited in
Chapter 5 underlines the significance of Helleiner's earlier
impressions. The ability of several Asian countries to
establish themselves as processors of imported materials
appears to be a major reason for their successful integration
into world industry.

Firms may seek to establish offshore processing facilities
to retain some degree of competitiveness once their products
have entered the 'down side' of the product cycle. So long
as the associated transport costs are not high, these
producers can continue to compete by moving the labour
intensive parts of their operations to low-wage countries.
But they also require some additional cost advantage, such
as preferential access to capital, marketing prowess or
technology leadership. Otherwise, indigenous firms in the
LDC could match, or even lower, the costs of production by
the multinational (Grunwald and Flamm, 1985, p. 7).
Foreign assembly began with traditional products such as
textiles, clothing, radios and television receivers. As the
technologies permitting the separation of production stages
were developed, and the appropriate market conditions
emerged, the practice has spread to other industries,
including automobiles and semiconductors.

The popularity of an offshore processing strategy appears
to vary systematically among manufacturers in each of the
major Western markets. The strategy is most common
among American and Japanese manufacturers. US firms

adopting this practice are primarily geared to serve their home market. As a result, American imports are significant, exceeding \$20 billion per annum throughout the 1980s. American tariff regulations have encouraged the tactic. They allow the reimport of 'fabricated', but unfinished, products and the foreign assembly of finished goods which are to be re-exported to the USA. The original 'US value' contained in the materials prior to their export is not subject to duties when the processed or finished items are returned.

Similar tariff regulations can be found in the EC and Japan, but the approach to offshore processing has been different in each case. In contrast to the American version, Japanese firms have employed the strategy primarily as a means of penetrating foreign markets. They use their offshore sites as platforms from which to launch an export drive and a negligible amount of production is reimported to the home market. European manufacturers have shown a lesser propensity to engage in offshore processing. Grunwald and Flamm (1985, p. 5) suggest several reasons for the European reluctance: high tariff and other trade barriers which discourage foreign production, opposition from well-organized trade unions which fear the loss of jobs and the fact that state participation in many European multinationals discourages the practice. These and other characteristics become apparent in the following discussion of the consumer electronics industry.

Consumer Electronics

Beginning immediately after the Second World War, the industry established itself as one of the most dynamic growth fields in the manufacturing sector. Producers bene-fited from the rapid expansion of post-war demand and a rise in real incomes. The spread of national broadcasting networks, the development of colour television, FM broad-casting and international events such as the Olympic Games also helped to establish worldwide markets for consumer electronics. Additionally, the industry was a beneficiary of wartime advance in communications and electrical equip-ment which were readily adapted to consumer applications.

The post-war successes of many firms were founded on international differences in pay scales. Japanese firms enjoyed a significant labour cost advantage, since the relevant wage rates were roughly one-fifth the prevailing US pay scale (Majumdar, 1979, p. 563). They began at the bottom of the technological range by exporting small transistor radios. Their approach, which was largely imitative in nature, served them well throughout the 1950s and 1960s. The range of Japanese exports was steadily extended in later years to include all types of consumer electronics and their principal components.

Part of the initial response by American and European competitors was an attempt to move upmarket in an effort to gain buyers in the more profitable ends of their product lines. In doing so, many firms abandoned the lower range of their product lines and gave little attention to improvements in productivity or to development of new products. The subsequent costs of this decision were considerable. Much of the market for small, household electronics was eventually lost to Asian competitors in Japan and elsewhere. The difficulties of some American and European firms were compounded by their inability to produce components for these rapidly growing markets. For instance, very few picture tubes for colour televisions of less than twenty inches are now produced in Europe. Such tubes can account for at least one-third of the cost of a finished set, but most are imported – chiefly from Japan.

Beginning in the mid–1960s, various trends within the industry forced producers to undertake a search for low-wage locations for the later stages of production. Numerous producers (mainly Japanese) had established highly successful export programmes. Their success resulted in a prolonged period of fierce price competition in major markets such as the USA. As pay scales rose, however, Japanese firms feverishly sought to develop offshore processing facilities in lower-wage countries. They first moved their assembly operations to South Korea and later to Singapore and Taiwan. American producers countered in several ways. Usually they resorted to the same tactic by locating many of their assembly operations in Mexico and South-East Asia.

Offshore processing eventually became a common practice throughout the industry.

The existence of aggressive price competition was not sufficient, however, to explain the strategy's popularity for producers of consumer electronics. Other industries facing similar conditions have not necessarily turned to offshore processing. In fact, it was the growing ability of firms to separate physically the production stages that made the strategy viable. This ability, in turn, was the result of greater standardization of products and production methods. Producers of television sets, for instance, were able to reduce the number of components by up to two-thirds between 1970 and 1980 (*Financial Times*, 18 November 1980). Likewise, the components used in electronic calculators was eventually cut from 5,000 to less than 40 (Majumdar, 1979, pp. 562–3). Such trends are indicative of similar experiences in other parts of the industry. And, as production methods were simplified, the amount of skilled labour required for certain operations was reduced. Gradually, the input requirements at each stage of production became more and more distinct.

This turn of events had a profound impact on the selection of industry sitings. The production of most consumer electronics eventually came to fit easily into three stages. The first, which involved the conception and development of new products, made use of considerable engineering skills and required significant outlays for R and D. A second stage entailed the production of components and parts. In this phase firms were able to minimize their unit costs through mass production. As the number of components were reduced and the size of production facilities grew, many operations were automated and input requirements became relatively capital intensive. The third stage involved the testing of parts and components and their assembly into finished goods, all tasks which were labour intensive. By the late 1970s, roughly 70 per cent of all sitings in the electronics field (including industrial goods and components) were thought to be 'footloose operations', meaning that producers were free to locate where the costs of inputs were cheapest or where strategic marketing was dominant (Interfutures, 1979, p. 344).

Multinationals have been the real beneficiaries of these trends. They enjoy considerable leeway in the choice of location and almost all these firms operate offshore facilities for mass production as well as sites for assembly and testing. Numerous variations of the strategy can nevertheless be found. Some firms have used the strategy as part of a wider ranging and aggressive approach, sloughing off aging, uncompetitive products while securing a supply source for cheaper components or a new, low-cost export base. Others have chosen a more passive version of the strategy. They have relocated parts of their activities to reduce overall production costs but, at the same time, have retained much of their home-market operations.

European producers have been slowest to embrace the strategy. In addition to the policy aspects and other conditions noted at the beginning of this section, the fragmented nature of European markets has meant that most plants are comparatively small. Viable production of television sets, for instance, is thought to exceed 400,000 units. Yet, in the early 1980s, several dozen European plants were each producing only 10,000 units per year. For small firms, the cost savings to be derived by locating later stages of production in low-wage countries are limited. Even Philips, Europe's largest producer of consumer electronics, has few offshore processing facilities. The firm operates over 400 factories in 60 countries, although the bulk of its overseas investments are concentrated in Europe and North America. In 1985, only 6 per cent of Philips' foreign assets were in Asia – mostly in Singapore and Taiwan (*The Economist*, 27 April 1985). And, when European firms have established offshore facilities, there is indirect evidence that they have concentrated on the assembly of consumer items. In contrast, many of their competitors' overseas operations also include the standardized production of components and parts. This difference in orientation can again partly be attributed to the larger size of Japanese and American firms and the markets they serve.

Although the search for low-cost production sites continues, several factors have diminished the appeal of offshore processing. Rising wage levels in favoured coun-

251

tries such as Singapore, South Korea and Taiwan have forced firms to look elsewhere. Various producers, both European and Japanese, have turned to China. The motive for these moves is the low wage scale of Chinese labour; in 1984, the average wage paid by foreign investors was less than one-half that earned by Singaporean workers. Video recorder kits are now assembled in China under licence from Grundig, which also has a collaborative agreement to produce colour television sets in the country. Other electronics firms plan similar arrangements or have sought such tie-ups. Most agreements have stipulated that output from such investments must be exported.

Changes in the policies of host countries are another reason for the strategy's waning popularity. Asian LDCs currently have ambitious plans to develop their own electronics industry. Rather than serving as an offshore site for assembly and testing of components and products, they have begun to licence foreign technologies (mainly American) and to export their own parts, components and completed goods. At the same time, local firms in LDCs have aggressively moved into the production of more sophisticated components and products with applications in industrial as well as consumer electronics.

Trade restrictions imposed by Western countries have forced some suppliers to revise their tactics. In the mid-1970s, the US government exacted a series of orderly marketing agreements with Asian countries which limited the latter's exports of colour television sets to the American market. Japanese producers responded by moving 'behind' this trade restraint; they set up assembly operations in the USA. Because sub-assemblies and parts were not covered by the marketing agreements the new American-based subsidiaries continued to import these from Japan and low-wage LDCs. By 1979, all the principal Japanese producers of colour televisions – as well as some Taiwanese firms – had established assembly plants in the USA. In order to compete, American firms moved even more of their operations abroad (mainly to Mexico). Japanese subsidiaries may soon be in the peculiar position of performing a greater portion of their assembly work in the USA than many

American-owned competitors which assemble sets at off-shore sites. In the future, Japanese producers will probably continue to automate their US plants to reduce labour costs, while American firms compete for their home market on the basis of more labour intensive technologies which are most applicable in LDCs (Grunwald and Flamm, 1985, p. 20). By forcing firms to locate much of their operations in high-wage countries the ironic result of these policies may be to accelerate the pace of automation, although their intended purpose was to preserve employment opportunities.

Electronic Components

The production of active electronic components – semi-conductors and integrated circuits – began only after the Second World War. Transistors were invented in 1947 and soon replaced the vacuum tubes that had been commonly used in electronic equipment. The electric current which connects the electrodes in transistors flows through solid materials known as semiconductors. Full-scale production of such devices began in the late 1950s in California's Santa Clara County, now nicknamed Silicon Valley. This development was quickly followed by the first integrated circuit in 1959. Each circuit, or chip, contained many interconnected functions such as transistors. All functions are on a piece of silicon, making it possible to produce fully transistorized products.

Silicon Valley retained its position as the centre of innovation and development of the industry in later years, although production was also begun in Japan. The latter firms were usually newly created divisions of larger conglomerates which supplied a wide range of electrical products. This organizational arrangement helps to explain why Japanese firms were the first to use semiconductors in consumer electronics and calculators. American producers concentrated on selling a broad range of devices to cover a large segment of the market, while Japanese suppliers were specialized to meet in-house requirements.

Product improvements and steady price reductions were

instrumental in establishing a worldwide market for semi-conductors. Researchers succeeded in doubling the number of transistors or logic functions implanted on a chip in each year during the period 1960–80. Today, chips with more than 200,000 components are no longer state of the art, while in the early 1960s, each chip consisted of no more than ten transistors. The increasing ability of producers to miniaturize circuitry led to the rapid development of new products for use in both households and industries. World sales of semiconductors were $1 billion in 1970, but rose tenfold by the end of the decade. The volume of output simultaneously doubled in every year during the 1970s, enabling producers to achieve substantial reductions in cost. The price of a transistor was $10 in 1960 but was reduced to less than one cent twenty years later. Similarly, the price per integrated circuit function declined, on average, by 27 per cent per year during the 1970s.

Because of these events the producers of semiconductors and integrated circuits passed through a comparatively brief period of adolescence. Production methods quickly came to fit easily into a series of distinct stages. The first of these entailed the design of a new device and obviously required a highly skilled staff. Prior to the development of special computer-aided systems for design, teams of up to six engineers often required one to two years to create each new device. Once this task was completed, the production of integrated circuits involved three additional steps: fabrication, assembly and testing. Fabrication is a delicate process which begins with the production of a 'master' of the design. Using the master, the pattern is transferred on to many individual chips in the silicon wafer. Later steps in the fabrication process are the inclusion of insulators and metals and the etching away of bits of each layer that are not wanted in the finished chip. The assembly process consists of bonding the chips to leads and packaging them, after which the finished device is then tested for defects.

As the industry expanded, costs incurred at certain stages proved to be especially dependent on the volume being produced. Based on technologies in use during the late 1960s, unit costs for producing a finished semiconductor

254

device were thought to decline by 20–30 per cent each time output was doubled (Tilton, 1971, p. 85). The bulk of these savings were confined to the fabrication stage where mass production enabled firms to reduce costs significantly. The need to achieve greater economies of scale meant that initial capital outlays for a fabrication plant rose. Firms entering the business in the late 1960s needed only $1 to $3 million in capital equipment to begin fabrication (UNIDO, 1981c, p. 102). However, the capital outlay required of a new entrant for a basic chip-making facility had risen to at least $50 million by 1980 and was to become even more expensive in later years.

The arguments for extending mass production techniques to the assembly of semiconductor devices were less compelling. Machines to automate the assembly process became available in the 1970s, but several factors inhibited their use. Automated assembly required substantial expenditures for equipment and installation. And, because the design of chips was being continuously changed, the expected lifetime of the equipment was comparatively brief. The decision to automate also meant that firms needed to produce in large quantities, although this was risky when markets were uncertain or when demand behaved in a cyclical fashion. Manual assembly, on the other hand, required only modest capital outlays and offered producers more flexibility in choosing the size of their production runs. As a result, the assembly of integrated circuits continued to be a relatively labour intensive operation throughout the 1970s. The preference for manual assembly meant that few economies of scale could be realized. For mature products, the unit costs of assembly were high in comparison with those incurred during fabrication. This distinction between the two stages provided a strong economic motive for the transfer of assembly operations to low-wage sites.

Patterns of trade and national policy combined to make a strategy of offshore assembly especially attractive to US producers. Following agreements reached during the Kennedy Round of trade negotiations, US tariffs on semiconductors were cut to 6 per cent in 1972 – the lowest in all Western countries. By that time American producers were facing stiff competition in their home market from Japanese suppliers. The potential cost savings from foreign assembly were enhanced by other tariff measures. Products assembled from American-made materials at overseas locations could be re-exported to the USA without paying duty on the 'original American value'. Although similar regulations existed in the EC and Japan, the US arrangement proved to be the most liberal. Throughout the 1970s, between 80 and 90 per cent of American imports of integrated circuits and other semiconductor devices were brought into the country under these provisions (Grunwald and Flamm, 1985, p. 65 and p. 73).

For these reasons the chip-making industry was the first in the USA to adopt offshore processing on a large scale. The tactic was first utilized in the early 1960s. However, as information about costs was accumulated and production methods were standardized, the same procedure was repeated again and again during the next twenty years. Hong Kong, South Korea and Taiwan were the favoured sites for overseas plants. Later, when wage rates in these countries began to rise, offshore investment spread to Indonesia, Malaysia, Mexico, the Philippines, Thailand, Central American and Caribbean countries. Offshore assembly eventually became an important part of the manufacturing sector in several of these LDCs. Malaysia, for instance, has no indigenous chip-makers. However, in 1983 value added in this Malaysian industry was $1.1 billion, equivalent to roughly 4 per cent of the world semiconductor market (*The Economist*, 10 March 1984).

The strategy proved less popular among Japanese and European producers. As in the consumer electronics industry, comparatively little of Japan's offshore production of semiconductors was re-exported to the home market. Major buyers were often 'related partner' firms operating in the foreign country. The components were installed in various electronic products (mainly consumer items) and then exported to other markets. Because output was destined either for local markets or foreign markets other than Japan, the desire to cut costs was not the only motive for offshore assembly. Issues relating to market access in the host country and nearness to equipment industries also influenced the choice of overseas sites. The Japanese industry's dependence on overseas assembly of integrated circuits was never great. Throughout the 1970s, imports from these sources were equivalent to no more than 15 per cent of Japan's total shipments of integrated circuits and by the end of that decade the share had fallen to 5 per cent (Grunwald and Flamm, 1985, p. 86).

European policy-makers were comparatively slow to appreciate the significance of the semiconductor industry (Dosi, 1981, p. 28). Government policies employed during the 1960s were primarily intended to speed the development of the computer industry, though they probably reduced the appeal of an offshore strategy for Europe's chip-makers. Policy-makers later rushed to provide support to their lagging semiconductor industry. By the early 1970s the Community's external tariff on imports of integrated circuits and related semiconductor devices was considerably higher than the corresponding Japanese or US rates. Buyers of chips were urged to favour domestic firms for reasons of national security and a few state-owned producers of semiconductors began operations. All the largest European producers assembled offshore, but the strong protectionist measures imposed by the EC and its member states probably eliminated a significant portion of the cost savings to be derived from this option. The Community's imports of integrated circuits assembled abroad rarely exceeded one-fifth of total shipments during the 1970s. Furthermore, the foreign subsidiaries of European firms – unlike the Japanese – had few local buyers for their production.

The world's semiconductor industry entered a new phase during the 1970s which eventually had implications for an offshore strategy. As markets for semiconductor devices matured, demand became more sensitive to the business cycle. Integrated circuits could then be found in various types of capital goods and producers' fortunes were more closely linked to the investment decisions in user industries. Annual variations in demand, often amounting to 10–20 per cent, were common. And, with the growth in worldwide capacity, each subsequent downswing in demand brought a vigorous round of price-cutting. This erratic pattern was aggravated by the fact that many large users of chips had set up their own captive operations. Production problems were recurrent – largely because of the users' inexperience – and the firms were periodically forced to buy chips on the open market. During the early 1970s, the industry passed through several minor crises as the demand for chips and integrated circuits plummeted.

The operation of existing American-owned subsidiaries was not significantly affected by this volatility. With each recession, the foreign share in the industry's total value added rose relative to domestic production. More important, however, was the impact on new American investment in additional capacity. Late entrants continued to establish operations in LDCs but the pace of offshore investment by more mature firms slowed. Japanese firms were more fortunate than their American competitors, since they were able to finance new investment from the profits of other (much larger) production divisions. Most US producers were solely dependent on revenues earned from the sale of chips and integrated circuits.

By the beginning of the 1980s, the cyclical behaviour of demand had made all investment programmes (whether overseas or at home) a precarious venture. By that time the cumulative effects of technological improvements had drastically changed the industry's profile, with significant implications for an offshore strategy. These effects were most evident in the industry's greater product sophistication and increased market segmentation. Memory chips capable of storing more than one million pieces of data became available, while the number of customized, semi-customized or other specialized products increased many fold.

There are several reasons why such technology-induced trends have forced chip-makers to reconsider their locational practices. First, buyers began to exert greater pressure on their suppliers to provide additional services. Producers were required to supplement the engineering skills on which their growth had been based by new service-oriented functions to help buyers adapt products to their needs. Examples include the design of the microprocessors which use the basic chips and the development of subsidiary chips to suit the needs of different customers. Such activities depend on close liaison with buyers and required producers to locate some of their operations in the major markets.

Second, as the industry's products have become more complex, the relative composition of production costs at each stage have changed. In the design phase, the creation of more intricate chips has become a time-consuming task which requires skilled personnel that is both expensive and in short supply. Without radically new technologies, the investment needed to design a chip for today's markets could reach $75 million. At the fabrication stage the reduction in the size of chips has forced producers to automate; the mere presence of a human being can contaminate the process when single chips contain more than 1 million components. The cost of erecting a high-volume plant to produce today's chips is now ten times greater that it was a decade earlier (*International Business Week*, 10 June 1985). Greater product complexity has also meant that testing must often be done by computer and requires relatively expensive investment in testing facilities. To justify these investments firms must take advantage of any economies of scale, meaning that they are more likely to centralize these facilities, either in their home market or closer to their foreign distribution centres. Such trends as these have created an industry where strategic options give priority to issues relating to investment, R and D and marketing. In these circumstances, locational patterns primarily intended to reduce the costs of unskilled labour (for example, through offshore assembly) are more the result of historical practices rather than of immediate concern.

Major parts of the world's semiconductor industry were originally founded on the production of 'standard' memory chips which could be mass-produced. With this approach, the firm's typical goals of enlarging market share or retaining cost leadership were compatible with various locational strategies. Domestic plants could be geared to serve foreign markets or, alternatively, firms could rely on offshore processing. Even today, American producers continue to assemble most of their chips overseas, while

Japanese firms are predominantly exporters rather than multinationals. As firms have widened their product portfolios and sought to achieve greater economies of scale, however, the attraction of investing in LDCs has been partially supplanted by the need to establish a presence in other Western markets.

The shift in investment preferences is not necessarily motivated by a desire to cut costs but is more often a response to protectionist threats linking Japanese and American producers. In contrast, European firms supply comparatively few of the industry's key products and are already well insulated from the effects of overseas competition. The EC imposes a 14 per cent tariff on semiconductor imports, which are further limited by a series of voluntary restraints negotiated with suppliers. Major parts of the American industry, however, are much more vulnerable to cheaply priced imports from Japan. And, as the benefits of an offshore strategy have been eroded, these firms have turned to Washington for relief.

The protectionist drive in the USA ultimately forced a change in the investment practices of Japanese producers. The campaign was led by the Semiconductor Industry Association (SIA), a group of nearly fifty producers and users of chips. The group's efforts were initially handicapped by the far-flung character of the American industry. Several members of the Association were regular buyers of Japanese chips. They benefited from the low prices and were reluctant to support the protectionist drive. The organization's position was further complicated by the fact that the two leading US producers of semiconductors, IBM and Texas Instruments, have operations in Japan – and neither are members of SIA.

The pricing tactics of Japanese exporters were the initial focus of the protectionist drive. Producers repeatedly charged that their Japanese competitors were dumping products on the US market and declines were often drastic. During a thirty-month period beginning in 1980, the price of one widely used chip, the 64K-RAM, fell from $20 to $5. The same pattern was repeated in later generations of memory chips, such as the 256K DRAM when the price was cut from

$17 to $4 between 1985 and 1986. As Japanese suppliers enlarged their share of the American market the protectionist drive gathered support from outside the semi-conductor industry. The price of the chips was seen to be of minor importance, since the components usually account for only a negligible portion of the total cost of most products. The focus of the debate has shifted to broader issues, involving the security of supplies and access to the latest models.

American protagonists hope to avoid the type of voluntary restraints employed in other industries such as autos or steel, since they believe these would only ensure higher profits for their Japanese rivals. They are equally reluctant to accept the imposition of duties on Japanese exporters who are thought to have dumped products on the US market. The machinery to implement these measures is cumbersome and is not effective against 'downstream dumpers' – for example, South Korean manufacturers producing computer subunits with cheaply priced chips from Japan. Whatever the outcome of this conflict, protectionist pressures have forced firms to move some of their facilities to the markets which they supply. Japanese expansion into other Western markets began in the 1970s. By the mid–1980s, firms such as Fujitsu, Hitachi and Nippon Electronics Corporation (NEC) were operating nearly twenty chip making centres in the USA and Western Europe (*Financial Times*, 24 October 1985). In a like manner, US firms have established a significant European presence, although their operations in Japan are still modest.

Diversification

Efforts to diversify may take many forms, depending on the industry concerned. Often the strategy will merely reflect a desire to reduce dependency on products which constitute the slower growing parts of the market. A variation on this same approach would be a strategy of gradually moving up market into higher valued or more profitable items. Either version may be very similar in spirit and impact to a strategy of rationalization through product specialization but it may also be pursued for reasons other than cost reductions – for example, to stave off the effects of market saturation or to obtain a more secure or profitable market niche. Another form of diversification is to move into related fields, either upstream or downstream, which are closely linked with the industry's original operations. Also, diversification into activities not directly related to the firm's original markets can be tantamount to partial exit.

Consumer Electronics

Intense price competition and the threat of market saturation are two of the characteristics that forced producers of consumer electronics to search for ways to extend both the range of products and their functions. A strategy of moving up market into higher valued items is attractive and several variations can be observed. In the simplest form, the approach is a purely imitative one, frequently attributed to Japanese producers during the 1950s and 1960s. Exporters began with the simplest products, but gradually extended their product mix to match that of their Western rivals. The export of monochrome television sets was followed by small-size colour models and, later, larger ones. Eventually, tape recorders, stereo equipment, VTRs and all the principal components for these items were added to the product line.

The Japanese experience suggests that a successful strategy of imitation is dependent on several factors. First, the tactic itself offers no prospect for firms to achieve a premier position in the field; some degree of technological independence is eventually necessary. Significantly, the Japanese combined their imitative approach with other strategies to emerge as the world's leaders in the field of consumer electronics. Second, a successful strategy of imitation requires a large and rapidly growing domestic market. In comparison to Japan, today's imitators – Hong Kong, South Korea or Taiwan, for example – are excessively dependent on export markets. Moreover, to protect their domestic industries, several LDCs severely restrict imports of consumer electronics. This practice results in local prices which are sometimes double the world price and further limits the home market. Thus, the current group of imitators have to confront a more difficult range of public policy choices than did their predecessors.

Basic changes in the industry have raised another set of problems for latecomers who wish to follow the technological leaders. As long as there was a number of possible suppliers of technology, latecomers could easily change their foreign partners. Because the European and American producers have yielded so much ground to the Japanese, however, this alternative is not always possible today. Established producers have also become much more cautious about providing their technologies to new entrants. For instance, the leading Japanese producers of VTRs licensed their technology to South Korea on condition that the junior partner would not export before March, 1985. By that time the world market was expected to be relatively mature. Also, current imitators are more dependent on foreign suppliers of complex parts and components than was the case in the 1960s. They complain that their suppliers (mainly established Japanese competitors in the same field) frequently withhold or delay crucial orders. For such reasons a purely imitative approach offers less promise today than it did twenty years ago.

For producers in countries with a relatively sophisticated technological base, a strategy of moving up market offers a different range of options. Here, the most common version calls for firms to introduce minor improvements as a way to boost sales or to extend the lifetime of the basic product design. Parochial examples from the field of television currently include sets which are cable-ready, equipped with stereo sound or digital systems to enhance reception. More significant product improvements are leading to the merger of audio and visual equipment as colour television sets are linked to stereo video casette recorders, video disc players, AM/FM stereo tuners and home computers. Another example of 'equipment clustering' is a home control centre responsible for the regulation of energy consumption and supervision of domestic appliances. Such trends may have at least two consequences. First, the merger of different

263

products would tie the consumer's purchase of the entire system to a single supplier. Second, firms which have previously specialized in either audio or visual equipment may find it difficult to produce an integrated system (Hazewindus, 1982, p. 23–6).

The desire to prolong the life of a basic product design is not the only reason to move up market. In the 1960s, major firms made several fundamental decisions based on this rationale, which later changed the industry in unexpected ways. American and European producers implemented the strategy largely in terms of its marketing implications and attempted to push consumers toward the upper and more profitable ends of their product lines. This tactic, which effectively ceded the lower range of product lines to foreign suppliers, had dramatic consequences for the producers of television sets and components. Japan soon emerged as the major exporter of small sets (less than twenty inches) – a market which later proved to be very important and now accounts for the bulk of sales in Western markets. A related consequence was that Western firms lost much ground in the vital area of components for small household goods.

Steel

For major steel firms, the attraction of a diversification strategy is a consequence of the industry's changing fortunes, which were described in Chapter 9. Producers of bulk steel suffer disproportionately during any slump. Diversification into higher quality or speciality steels offers improved demand prospects and a lesser threat from competitive substitutes such as aluminium or plastics. Diversification into related fields is commonly practised by large, integrated firms which choose to move downstream into engineering activities. This arrangement can work to the benefit of the firm, because both the engineering and metalworking parts of its operation are assured that the types of steel required will be available. Also, diversification into other fields not directly related to steel became common in the USA during the 1980s. Steel producers sought to increase their earnings by buying into other businesses, which were either more profitable or provided the purchaser with greater borrowing ability and tax advantages.

With the slump in world demand, some Japanese steel-makers quickly moved up market. They began to produce greater amounts of special steels for the oil industry, 'high-strength' steels that would compete with aluminium in the manufacture of automobiles, containers and other mass-produced items, and other, more sophisticated, products. Japan's consumption of ordinary steels declined during the 1970s, while usage of these speciality steels was steadily rising (UNIDO, 1980, p. 18). Because Japanese exports to many markets are now heavily restricted and are under pressure from producers in LDCs, firms have also begun to reduce their dependence on steel. An emerging trend is to produce other materials – for example, a range of fine carbons for use in nuclear reactors, electrodes and semi-conductor machine tools. Some firms have created additional divisions to handle these new materials and almost all – that is, Nippon, Kobe, Kawasaki and Nippon Kokan – hope that these markets will account for 30–40 per cent of total sales in the next decade.

In the USA, diversification has been led by small firms rather than by integrated producers of steel. Some of these firms concentrate on production of stainless steels which are stronger and more resistant to corrosion than ordinary carbon steel. Others have sought a market niche in the production of steel alloys used to make valves and engine parts for automobiles and aircraft. Numerous examples of this type of firm can be found and most of the diversification programmes share one common characteristic – the firms have supported these moves by establishing very close contacts with their buyers and with aggressive marketing efforts.

Among the integrated American steel-makers, diversification out of the steel industry was the predominant version of the strategy in the 1980s. The approach has been epitomized by the purchase of Marathon Oil by United States Steel. The transaction – at a price of $5.8 billion – was the largest acquisition in US history. In 1984, steel accounted for only one-third of the company's total sales. And among other major steel producers, such as Armco, LTV and National Intergroup, the share was between 50 and 70 per cent. Such moves have been expensive, however. The debts assumed in order to diversify have sometimes carried interest charges which occasionally exceeded the tax write-offs and earnings of the newly acquired firms. In other instances acquisitions went awry. Soon after steel firms bought into fields such as insurance, oil and oil-field services, the markets for these activities collapsed.

Evidence of diversification programmes in Europe can be found, but the approach differs from that observed in other markets. The possibilities for diversification have been largely overshadowed by the problem of excess capacity, leading firms to focus most attention on opportunities to move downstream. In theory, this form of diversification promises to provide more secure markets for the steel-producing parts of the firm and, it is to be hoped, a source of profits which will offset the losses incurred. The leading German producers of steel moved downstream into metal-working during the 1970s. Their steel-using operations were of sufficient size to absorb demand fluctuations and to subsidize some of the losses in the steel-producing activities, but subsequent trends proved these factors to be inadequate. In 1981, the French government began to push its state-owned firms up market to compete with their more diversified German and Japanese rivals. The country's widely dispersed producers of speciality steels were consolidated into two more homogeneous groups. European attempts to move downstream into engineering and metal-working have often been taken through mergers. However, because these proposals would have entailed layoffs, plant closures and reductions in capacity, they have been opposed by pressure groups in the older steel-making regions of Belgium, France and Italy.

For American and European firms, a move into sophisticated steel products may offer advantages in addition to improved market prospects. Buyers of sophisticated steel products have more varied and exacting requirements than those using simpler forms of steel. Automobile makers, for instance, increasingly demand steels which are more resistant to corrosion and heat or are more easily formed and welded in order to obtain a better fit and finish. These trends mean that marketing becomes a more critical part of the steel firm's operation. In their home countries, integrated steel producers should have an advantage over foreign competitors – particularly those in LDCs – in the marketing phase.

Nevertheless, diversification strategies, even modest ones entailing a change in product mix, can also pose problems. A potential drawback is that if too many firms choose to diversify, competition will be increased in the new product fields. For instance, Swedish producers of speciality steels may account for as much as one-third of that country's national output (compared with only 1 per cent in the UK) and increased competition in these higher value added items has driven a number of firms out of business (*Financial Times*, 2 June 1982). The huge investment costs required for diversification are a major constraint. The financial position of several firms in the USA (and some in Europe) has been weakened by heavy losses in steel and ill-advised purchases in other fields. The position of these firms may now be so precarious as to impinge on their ability to diversify.

Computers

Firms producing computers have diversified into related industry for reasons other than a sagging market. The manufacturers require a large number of semiconductors or chips. Their ability to bring out new models and to keep pace with demand often depends on adequate sources of these components.

In the USA and Japan, computer manufacturers are believed to take up to 40 per cent of all the chip-makers' output. Because their operations are heavily dependent on adequate supplies of semiconductors, computer firms were forced to move into this industry and began to produce chips for internal use. International Business Machines (IBM), for instance, has not only spent huge sums for research on semiconductors but is probably the world's largest producer of these devices. Similarly, Japan's four largest producers of chips – NEC, Hitachi, Fujitsu and Toshiba – are its largest computer companies. To a lesser extent, other larger users of chips and integrated circuits in the automobile, consumer electronics and office equipment industries are also producers of these items. Captive operations such as these run the risk of failing to keep abreast of the rapidly changing state of technology.

There are other reasons why users began to design and produce their own chips. First, very large-scale integration has meant that virtually entire systems are implanted on a chip, leading many equipment-makers to prefer in-house development to protect proprietary designs. Second, the newer, system-wide chips must be customized for specific applications, but the volumes produced for each design will be low.

Computer firms have also diversified by buying into related industries. Traditionally, the producers of mainframe machines preferred to follow a policy of designing and producing almost everything in-house. However, as the range of computers, office automation equipment, tele-communications equipment and auxiliary devices have multiplied, even the largest firms have found themselves unable to keep abreast of all the changes. By purchasing smaller firms having a technological lead in specific fields, the new owner may hope to acquire technologies and products which it could not develop internally.

Another reason for buying into other industries can be the desire to determine industry standards. These standards, which are simply agreements about the way things should be done, may be fixed between some of the manufacturers themselves, by government order or through pressure from buyers. Occasionally, because one company is so important, others have to design and build their own products the way the leader does. The ability to set industry standards in fields characterized by both rapid change and converging markets can confer significant advantages on the successful firm. An important test of a computer's usefulness is how easily it communicates with other parts of an integrated system being used for research, production or information. For example, the integration of computers with office equipment, voice and data communications and other fields requires networks designed and built to certain standards. By purchasing firms with a technological lead in key components or designs, the firm manufacturing computers can help to ensure that its own products and systems are not only compatible with those produced by the newly acquired company but also have a better chance of being accepted as the industry standard.

Some of the larger American computer firms have also bought into related industries for 'defensive' reasons. The competitive position of several domestic suppliers of semiconductors deteriorated as Japanese firms cut prices and moved aggressively into the American market. One response was the purchase by IBM of a stake in Intel, a producer of chips particularly hard hit by Japanese competitors. The move reflected IBM's concern that the commercial failure of domestic suppliers would make it too dependent on foreign suppliers of chips. Other independent American chip-makers have been purchased, either partly or totally, by large users of chips and a fear of greater dependence on foreign suppliers has been at least one of the motives for this move.

In conclusion, the computer industry is extremely complex and efforts to diversify represent only one dimension in the range of strategic and technical choices available to leading firms. Discussion of the computer industry is continued in the following chapter, with a survey of alternative strategies.

Supplementary Reading

With regard to the semiconductor industry, Tilton (1971) offers a good account of the international diffusion of technology during the early phase of the industry's development. Wilson, Ashton and Egan (1980) conduct a microeconomic study of innovative behaviour among semiconductor firms. A complete history of the industry is provided by Braun and Macdonald (1982). Flaherty (1984) emphasizes the importance of the international transfer of know-how in the industry, compared with more common measures which focus on the race to patent and the expenditure level for R and D. Grunwald and Flamm (1985, pp. 38–136) have compiled a detailed study of offshore processing activities in the industry. For additional literature on the computer industry see the readings suggested at the end of Chapter 11.

CHAPTER ELEVEN

Collaborative Strategies in International Markets

The survey of industry strategies is concluded in Chapter 11 with a discussion of two additional versions. The strategies described here are commonly observed in industries which have yet to reach maturity. The first of these, the selection of a national champion, is heavily dependent on the role of government. The second strategy is characterized by the extensive network of interfirm alliances and collaborative agreements built up by firms within the industry. Both tactics may be pursued simultaneously, although for reasons discussed in this chapter a government's selection of one or more firms to serve as a national champion, or champions, is a decision usually postponed until the industry concerned has passed through the earliest stages of development. To illustrate the two strategies, the following discussion draws upon the experience of the computer industry and the closely related field of industrial automation.

Promoting a National Champion

The practice of selecting industries to serve as national champions is linked to the idea that governments may be able to 'pick the winners'. In comparison with other strategies already described, the approach can be distinguished by its emphasis on fields of high technology, by the degree of commitment on the part of policy-makers and by the close relationship prevailing between the government and the industry (Ohlin, 1978, p. 320).

The preferential treatment that policy-makers accord a national champion includes efforts to channel resources into the favoured industry, measures to boost demand for the industry's products, or both. In the first instance, governments may provide funding for R and D, generous tax write-offs, cheap loans and other forms of material and technical assistance. In the latter case, they try to allocate a part of domestic markets to indigenous firms and exclude foreign competitors. Governments may do this through a set of policies which ensure that methods of public procurement will favour domestic producers. At the same time, other policies will be used to discourage foreign investment, restrict imports and otherwise limit foreign competition.

Reasons for active government support for a particuar industry are generally similar throughout the world. Many policy-makers, for example, see the development of new systems of electronic capital goods as a way to reverse the long-term decline in growth of productivity. They hope the systems will provide a basis around which their lagging industries might reorganize. The following discussion focuses on government policies intended to hasten the growth of the computer industry, an industry which lies at the heart of the electronics complex. Because it was well established in several Western countries before the 1960s, there is now sufficient evidence available to gain some impression of the evolution of this particular strategy during the post-war period. The discussion of policies in Western countries is followed by a description of the policies and tactics employed in LDCs.

The Computer Industry in Western Countries

The production of computers was an early choice as a national champion in many Western countries. The provision of state funds for R and D, preferences in public procurement for domestic firms, government-assisted mergers and favourable loan terms are only some of the policies which have been employed by governments in

France, Japan, the UK, USA and West Germany to foster growth of computer firms.

At the time when the industry was being established, the most vital form of assistance provided by governments was to serve as a buyer of its products. In 1954, the government was the only major buyer of computers in the American market and eight years later it still accounted for nearly one-half of all computer sales (Reich, 1982, p. 865). The Ministry of International Trade and Industry (MITI) aggressively encouraged government purchases of computer systems manufactured by domestically owned firms. Almost 90 per cent of the total value of computer systems operating in the public sector were supplied by indigenous firms in 1970 and the share had risen by the end of the decade (Pugel, Kimura and Hawkins, 1982, p. 58).

Because Japanese manufacturers were some years behind their American rivals, the issues of foreign investment and technology transfer were among the first to be addressed by the Japanese government. Foreign investment in the computer industry was closely controlled from the time that Japanese firms began to develop their own computer technologies. Applications to invest required screening by MITI, related government agencies and the Foreign Investment Council. Controls were so stringent that only one US manufacturer, Sperry-Rand, attained entry during the period 1958-75. This feat was achieved through a joint venture which, in turn, was contingent on the American firm's provision of technological know-how.

IBM was somewhat unique in avoiding Japanese controls. The firm had entered Japan prior to the Second World War and had resumed operations during the occupation – before the regulations for foreign investment were put into effect. By the time Japanese manufacturers were ready for commercial production, it was clear that any of the basic technologies they had developed would infringe IBM patents. Japanese firms were required to obtain licences from IBM. Shortly afterwards, IBM Japan requested permission to remit dividends and royalties to its parent company and to begin local production of several systems. By linking the request for patent licence with the applications from IBM, the

Japanese government took the lead in these negotiations which were concluded in 1960.

The Japanese were also early practitioners of publicly directed programmes to accelerate R and D. One of the first of these, a project to develop a pilot model for a large-scale computer system, was begun in 1961. The government subsidized the research but required recipients to form R and D cartels. Patents resulting from the projects were then granted to all the cartel participants. The amount of government funding involved was modest, both in comparison to private expenditures on R and D and relative to the funds provided by other governments. Instead, the distinctive feature of the approach was the clear demarcation between the cartelization of R and D activities and the subsequent commercialization of the research which was highly competitive.

Once indigenous production of computers was established, Japanese policy-makers cast about for ways to bolster the use of Japanese computers in private firms. The practice of leasing, rather than selling, hardware had become a common method of product differentiation among computer manufacturers. However, the costs of leasing proved to be a greater burden for the newly established Japanese firms than for their larger American competitors. The government's response was to 'guide' manufacturers into the formation of a joint venture, the Japan Electronic Computer Company (JECC). By financing all leasing costs, JECC spared the firms from the associated capital requirements. JECC also played an important role in the 1960s and 1970s in expanding the market shares of indigenous firms (Pugel, Kimura and Hawkins, 1982, p. 60).

In comparison to the Japanese, the US government was reluctant to sponsor formal programmes for collaboration – even those which were confined to R and D. One reason for the government's hesitancy was that such an approach could violate American anti-trust laws. These laws were later applied less stringently, but even today joint programmes are frequently undertaken at the initiative of private firms. Another reason for the lack of government-sponsored collaboration in the USA was that most of the relevant firms have close links with the defence establishment. The Department of Defense often discourages close collaboration between firms on basic research and is not concerned with efforts to develop new commercial products.

Once the Japanese and American markets were successfully established, the industry began to exhibit certain characteristics of maturity which led policy-makers to alter their tactics. There was no longer a serious need for public programmes to develop and nourish a budding domestic market. The leading firms were bent on attaining an international (rather than domestic) presence and policy-makers adjusted their approach in order to support this drive. Collaboration between firms and governments began to assume a more specific focus. Public support for R and D became more pragmatic, entailing a search for strategic technologies which could confer international leadership on the innovator. The Japanese practice of creating state-organized cartels for R and D was applied more selectively but drew upon a larger pool of scientific talent, bringing together researchers from industry, government and academia. Two such projects, funded jointly by Nippon Telegraph and Telephone (NTT) and MITI, were intended to develop new generations of advanced integrated circuits, microwave systems and computers. Engineers from NTT collaborated with researchers from three large private companies which received no public funds to cover their participation costs. Instead, the firms expected to receive orders from NTT once the programme yielded results. The MITI project was organized around a co-operative research laboratory where more than 100 researchers from five companies worked to develop 'very large-scale integrated circuits'. The project resulted in more than 1,000 new patents. Private firms were obliged to repay MITI's outlay if they earned money from the patents. To do so, of course, they had to convert their newly found knowledge into marketable products. In this highly competitive phase, each firm worked by itself.

Dramatic improvements in computer technologies during the 1970s conferred many benefits on both originators and 'fast' imitators, but they also created new problems. For example, steadily declining prices for hardware (especially computer memory) led engineers to design systems so powerful and complicated that the writers of computer software could not cope efficiently. The growing complexity of the software created serious difficulties for major users, including the government and the military. In response, the US Department of Defense urged its largest contractors to form a joint venture for software research. Although such a step might have violated anti-trust regulations, the proposal provides evidence of support for a less stringent application of these laws.

As competition between Japanese and American computer firms became more intense, the desire to protect proprietary rights and to prevent rivals from acquiring vital technologies assumed greater importance. Government and industry have collaborated, sometimes in extraordinary ways, to preserve proprietary rights where foreign competitors are involved. In the USA, the joint efforts of the Federal Bureau of Investigation (FBI) and IBM to prevent procurement of commercial technology in 1982 is an extreme example. Foreign computer firms, mainly Japanese ones, were the primary target for both civil and criminal suits, in what become known as the 'Japscam' trials. In the criminal suit of the Department of Justice against Hitachi, the government refused to comply with a court order to reveal the details of its relationship with IBM. Soon after the affair began, the FBI awarded IBM a $17 million order, even though the firm was not the lowest bidder. The Bureau argued that the bids submitted by competitors included technology which had been 'improperly obtained' from IBM (*Financial Times*, 4 August 1982).

Japanese and European competitors see other features of the American policy for technology transfer which, in their opinion, provide an unfair advantage to the US computer industry. Most countries limit exports of high technology goods for reasons of national security, but the USA has also banned the export of computers and related equipment for reasons of foreign policy. In order to limit the flow of technology into socialist countries, American policy-makers attempt to regulate the re-export of goods by other Western countries. Producers in Europe and Japan, whose products incorporate American technologies, argue that the restrictions favour US firms whose applications for licences to export often receive more lenient treatment.

Like their Japanese and American counterparts, European policy-makers were quick to accord the computer industry the status of a national champion. However, the problems faced by the Europeans were somewhat different from those of their competitors. One difficulty was the extent to which the market for computers in the EC was divided according to national boundaries. A second was that vital parts of the computer industry – especially the production of large mainframes – had already been pre-empted by international rivals. A third characteristic of the European dilemma was that most of their markets were already occupied by subsidiaries of Japanese and American firms. The extent to which these 'intruders' have penetrated European markets still complicates the efforts of governments to promote their own national champion.

During the 1970s, European policy-makers struggled to assemble an overall plan for the development of computers, microelectronics and telecommunications equipment, as well as a common policy on public procurement. The inability of governments to agree on the treatment of American subsidiaries was a major handicap in putting together a common set of policies. Countries with no domestic computer industry of their own argued that American subsidiaries should qualify as 'home' producers. Other countries – in particular, France – opposed the involvement of foreign subsidiaries in any EC-wide programme. The initial programme emerging from these negotiations was a modest one. It called for direct financial assistance to hasten the development of European firms engaged in the production of computers and microchips. Indirect support was provided through the creation of a European network for advanced communications. In addition, public procurement policies would allow all 'qualified' EC firms the opportunity to tender bids, while EC governments were requested to allocate a small percentage of their annual equipment purchases to suppliers in other member countries.

Efforts to reduce IBM's domination of European computer markets constituted another element in the strategy. In 1980, following an eight-year investigation, the European Commission filed anti-monopoly charges against the US firm. IBM was accused of abusing its position of leadership and restricting competition. By refraining from prompt publication of the specifications for its new products, the firm allegedly prevented other producers from developing competitive models. Eventually, both the EC and IBM found good reasons for reaching a compromise in the dispute. There was no threat that the firm would withdraw from the European market, which was an important one. Moreover, IBM was a major provider of jobs. Its European facilities consisted of fifteen factories and nine R and D facilities which, together, employed 100,000 people. The firm was also an important source of exports and technological know-how. Policy-makers feared that an unfavourable decision would mean that the firm would not be likely to expand its European operations. IBM itself had good reasons to seek a compromise. Such a ruling by the European Commission would have forced the firm to reveal extensive technical information as soon as it introduced products anywhere in the world. IBM was concerned that the disclosures would quickly find their way to Japanese competitors. Taken together, all these considerations eventually led to a solution to the conflict.

European resentment of IBM is only part of a wider concern with American and Japanese dominance which has influenced many of the Community's policies in the field of advanced electronics. Funding for R and D and production contracts have seldom been awarded to the new and smaller European entrants. It was feared that such a practice would divert support from the few firms large enough successfully to challenge non-European competitors. In adopting this approach European policy-makers have followed the practice of their Japanese counterparts who also favour support for large, established firms. Geroski and Jacquemin (1985, p. 195) argue that in some instances the tactic has been carried too far, contributing to a proliferation of different national champions in each member country. And, by making it more difficult for new entrants to obtain government funding, the approach runs the risk of stifling the advances of pioneering firms which may have developed viable new technologies.

An attitude of competitive coexistence has marked the industry's development during the 1980s. Various industry-government coalitions sought to develop key technologies for components, computer manufacture or applications to preserve or to surpass their international competitors. One of the most publicized of the new technologies is the development of fifth-generation computers. The distinguishing characteristic of these machines is that they would have some reasoning capabilities or artificial intelligence. While the goal of artificial intelligence has proved to be elusive, the development of machines with the ability to translate languages, diagnose medical problems or guide intelligent robots is still commercially promising.

In the prevailing atmosphere of international rivalry, when Japan announced that it planned a concerted, government-financed effort to develop a fifth-generation of computers it provoked a stream of government-sponsored projects in Europe and the USA. The Japanese programme is handled by the Institute for New Generation Computer Technology (Icot). The institute has a permanent staff for R and D and the results are transferred to private companies which build the prototype machines. Because of MITI's awesome reputation for central planning and its previous successes, the move was treated with great concern by competitors in Europe and the USA. However, the significance which Japan's competitors attached to this project may have been misplaced. As the industry has matured Japanese companies have acquired a greater penchant for secrecy and much of the more interesting work is carried out by private companies outside Icot.

The EC responded to the Japanese initiative in 1984 with the European Strategic Programme for Research and Development in Information Technology (ESPRIT), an ambitious programme to create an autonomous technology base for computers, semiconductors and related fields. The programme calls for a matching of public and private funds, but even so more than $1 billion in Community assistance will be offered between 1984–9. The money is allocated to 'clubs' of partners from different member states and is used for research at the pre-competitive stage. Five basic areas – microelectronics, software, information processing, office systems and computer manufacturing technologies – are included. In contrast to previous approaches, at least one-half the approved projects involve firms with less than 500 employees.

In addition to the desire to overtake the Japanese, ESPRIT is intended to serve a second purpose. Europeans hope to use the programme to build up their own companies' ability to compete against other international giants, in particular IBM. Although the firm holds over one-half the computer market in the EC and submitted proposals to participate in ESPRIT, it was nevertheless excluded from the initial funding allocations. Underlying the European distaste for IBM is a growing concern about the stringent export controls imposed on American technologies which can hamper foreign companies that use these technologies and components.

At the same time, European governments have come forward with their own plans to spur on the development of fifth-generation computers. West Germany intends to spend at least $1 billion on this goal before 1990, while the UK has an ambitious project of its own known as the Alvey programme. The British project is intended to redress specific problems relating to the country's base for information technology. Because Britain's research effort was thought to be too fragmented, a major objective is to draw together researchers from universities and the staff of large electronic firms. Most of the preferred areas of research concern specific problems encountered in the development of fifth-generation computers. In return for supporting a portion of the research costs, participant firms have access to all results and share in any copyrights, patents or licences.

The American response to Japan's fifth-generation programme was begun in 1983 under the Pentagon's Defense Advanced Research Projects Agency (Darpa). The programme is expected to have a life of ten years and funding for the first half is put at $650 million. While Japan's programme is aimed at developing commercial projects, Darpa's activities – although they include basic research on artificial intelligence – are primarily intended to develop technologies with military applications. Aside from Darpa, the American effort relies on the research of a consortium of major electronics and computer firms known as Micro-electronics and Computer Technology Corporation (MCT). The consortium, which currently consists of twenty-two firms, was made possible by a relaxation of the country's stringent anti-trust laws in 1984. Membership is restricted to firms which are at least 50 per cent US-owned. They can buy stock in any of four major research projects being carried out by MCT and the technologies developed by the consortium are available to all members.

The development of fifth-generation computers with artificial intelligence is only one of several areas where government and industry have banned together to hasten progress. The same process has been repeated in the case of supercomputers, a field which entails entirely different problems. Such computers are especially designed for rapid processing of information. Exceptional speeds are attained by using entirely new semiconductor devices and a different architecture from other computers.

By the mid–1980s, supercomputers still occupied a market niche similar to that of first-generation computers in the early 1950s. They have found only limited applications in scientific research, in large industrial corporations and in government agencies. While no more than a few hundred of these machines have been installed, their significance far outweighs the modest number in use. The technologies developed for the supercomputer have filtered down to higher-volume machines, enabling producers to turn out faster computers for commercial applications. The super-computer is also the vehicle enabling development of artificial intelligence. These machines promise to become a major competitive tool in fields as diverse as aerospace, semiconductors, oil and defence.

Because many Western strategists believe that improved information processing is crucial for economic growth and greater efficiency, governments aggressively support research on supercomputers. The Japanese regard the development of supercomputers as essential, not only to ensure efficiency but also for management of the ecosystem and for dealing with the myriad problems of an aging society. The Japanese programme, known as the National Superspeed Computer Project and operated under the auspices of MITI, is intended to challenge the two leading American firms, Cray Research and Control Data. A drawback of the American machines is that they have to be programmed differently from standard mainframe computers. Japanese rivals hope to take advantage of this characteristic by building their own supercomputers to operate on the same software as the standard mainframe produced by IBM. This improvement would extend the market for supercomputers, as users of existing mainframes could move up to the Japanese version without rewriting entire systems. Such an enlargement of the market would substantially reduce manufacturing costs and pose a threat to IBM's mainframe market.

While the supercomputer is seen in a techno-economic context in Japan, that country's efforts to push ahead are viewed in the USA as a threat to national supremacy in a crucial military technology. Research in the USA is largely undertaken by private firms and their efforts are supplemented by the private research consortium, MCT. Although the work of that group is not exclusively concerned with supercomputers, it is developing computer architectures which would be a significant contribution to the design of the new machines. The US government plays an important but indirect role in the development of the supercomputer because it is the largest procurer in that market and determines the performance standards for the machines.

Artificial intelligence and supercomputers are only two examples of computer-related fields where international rivalries and efforts to establish a national champion are prominent. Others include radically new types of semiconductor devices, variations in computer architecture, fibre optics and computer software. But while governments and firms have pressed ahead in their efforts to determine industry standards or to attain technological leadership in the more sophisticated parts of the industry, other parts of the market have begun to assume characteristics of maturity. Some of the latter aspects are considered in the following section which looks at the efforts of LDCs to establish the computer industry as a national champion.

The Computer Industry in LDCs

Despite the complex and sophisticated technologies involved, policy-makers in many LDCs regard the indigenous manufacture of computers as a desirable goal. Perhaps the most compelling economic argument for development of an indigenous computer industry is the desire to acquire and master these technologies. Ideally, investments by multinationals would not only boost overall economic activity but would also serve as an effective means for the host country to achieve greater technological competence. The LDCs obviously lack the resources and technical capabilities of Western governments and do not aspire to a position of international leadership. Their attempts to promote the industry as a national champion are piecemeal and are sometimes drawn together from other strategies outlined elsewhere in this book. However, at least one central feature of the original strategy – a strong commitment on the part of policy-makers and close collaboration between government and indigenous producers – is retained.

For governments of LDCs, one of the most difficult issues is to assemble a set of policies to govern the operations of mutinationals in their country. The political and economic conflicts which can arise are not unique to the computer industry, but they are accentuated when the industry in question is one based on high technology. Such investments may be questionable in countries with limited capital and few labour skills; they can prove controversial and, even if economically justifiable, may encounter opposition from vested interest groups in the economy.

The efforts of LDCs have been greatly influenced by the changing economics of the computer industry. In the industry's early stages of development, large mainframes accounted for an overwhelming portion of the computer market. The volume of each firm's production was very small, but the amount of value added attributed to each sale was considerable. Under these circumstances, the cost of components did not matter greatly and there was comparatively little pressure for competitors to bring out new products. With the advent of small computers and a steadily growing range of applications for business and industry, however, these hallmarks of the computer industry were swept aside. Major firms found they needed to produce in large volumes and to sell at a low price to keep abreast of a fast-changing market. Price became a more significant form of competition. The new circumstances meant that the LDCs became more attractive as production sites for cheap electronic components and assembly operations. Such opportunities may eventually be extended as major firms attempt to cut costs further by moving more of their operations to the source of component supply.

A second favourable trend results from the growing number of international competitors in the world's computer industry. By the mid–1970s, a significant number of producers had established operations in LDCs. No fewer than 16 American firms had subsidiaries in these countries, with a total of 134 sales units and 30 manufacturing units (Grieco, 1982, p. 622). Computer-makers based in Europe and Japan had also begun to establish overseas operations. For LDCs that chose to retain links with the international computing industry – even while simultaneously developing their own national champion – the number of potential foreign participants was steadily increasing. Moreover, because the cost of competing was declining, it became possible for LDCs to purchase the most vital components from any of several suppliers and then use these as inputs in their own, uniquely designed, small systems. Although the opportunities for developing an indigenous computer industry were improving, governments of LDCs nevertheless proceeded cautiously. Most continued to limit imports and to restrict foreign investment or require foreign entrants to accept joint ventures with local firms.

Among Latin American countries the Mexican market for computers was noted for its openness during the 1970s. Import permits were easy to obtain, tariffs were moderate and there were no quotas. At the beginning of the 1980s, however, the Mexican government set an ambitious new goal: local firms were to supply 70 per cent of the domestic market for computers by 1987. The simultaneous imposition of strict limitations on imports forced domestic prices up to levels which were roughly double those in the USA. The government supplemented its import policy by exerting pressure on international firms to manufacture in the country or to leave. Roughly forty companies were said to have responded with proposals to produce micro and mini computers locally (*Financial Times*, 5 May 1982).

IBM was among those that applied to establish a local subsidiary. The firm proposed to build top-of-the-line machines in a plant which would have been the largest of its kind in Latin America. Over 90 per cent of the output was intended for export. The remainder, equivalent to two-fifths of the local market, would be sold in Mexico at prices no more than 15 per cent above the US level. The project would obviously have boosted Mexican export earnings. But its attractiveness was diminished because the initial capital investment would have been only a moderate one and less than 100 assembly workers were to have been employed.

Two fundamental issues emerged in the ensuing dispute. One was the extent to which the Mexicans hoped to benefit from any transfer of technology associated with the project. Multinational production of mainframes and minicomputers in Mexico had begun before the government imposed restrictions on foreign-owned computer firms and wholly-owned subsidiaries. Policy-makers hoped to avoid the same situation in the personal computer market and to ensure that local producers would develop their own capabilities. However, most foreign firms saw Mexico not as a recipient of new technology but as an export platform; investors offered increased foreign exchange earnings and employment in exchange for cheap labour and the country's strategic location. In line with its general policy, IBM wished to retain complete ownership of its subsidiary. The country's code for foreign investment limited the computer industry to Mexican-controlled firms, a requirement that could be waived only in 'exceptional circumstances'. Furthermore, a precedent had already been set by other firms: the operations of Apple and Hewlett-Packard, although significantly smaller than that proposed by IBM, were minority partnerships in joint ventures with Mexican firms.

The second issue concerned the potential gains to be derived by the Mexicans from capital investment, employment and additional demand for local suppliers. IBM requested that the country's strict rules governing domestic content be relaxed. The firm contended that Mexico did not have sufficient suppliers of components to support an operation of the proposed size. But critics argued that expected benefits were not large enough to justify exemptions. They suggested that the modest size of IBM's proposed investment made it a classic 'suitcase factory' which would facilitate easy withdrawal. In 1984, the Mexican Foreign Investment Commission rejected the IBM proposal, although negotiations with the firm have continued on other proposals.

Both these issues were certainly crucial for any assessment of the proposal. However, the debate was complicated by the involvement of various special interest groups. The local electronics industry feared (with justification) that IBM could soon come to dominate the Mexican market. Other industries were wary that any agreement to set aside parts of Mexico's investment code and domestic content regulations would set a precedent. Such a ruling would have been seen as a threat to powerful, state-protected industries such as petrochemicals and mining.

Like Mexico, Brazil has steadily increased the degree of protection as part of its efforts to develop an indigenous computer industry. During the 1970s, import restrictions were only moderate and the number of domestic producers were few. In 1977, imports of all computers other than mainframes were banned. Nearly 150 small domestic producers emerged during the next seven years, with annual sales of roughly $1 billion (*The Economist*, 4 February 1985). Rapid development created tensions between the Brazilians and major international firms. The latter charged that many of the new Brazilian entrants were using technologies pirated from abroad (*International Business Week*, 19 November 1984). Nevertheless, an even more stringent law was approved by the Brazilian Congress in 1985. The existing ban on computer imports was extended, while only Brazilian companies would be allowed to sell most types of computers in the country until the early 1990s. Foreign firms already having Brazilian operations could continue their existing operations, but any new investment would be to produce for export only.

Among the more advanced LDCs, India's experience in the computer industry is one of the most extensive. The country's approach is dominated by three long-term goals. They include Indian control of foreign subsidiaries, indigenous production of all but the most complex sytems and participation in the manufacture of the most advanced systems available internationally (Grieco, 1982, p. 612). These objectives inevitably pitted the Indian government against several international firms, with the most publicized dispute again involving IBM. When the firm was first advised that the local subsidiary should share ownership with Indians, it contended that its international and interdependent operations required centralized co-ordination and control. These arguments served to forestall the government's initiative, but other firms – International Computers Limited (ICL) and Burroughs – eventually acquiesced. When discussions were resumed in the mid–1970s, IBM offered concessions which would have raised export earnings and accelerated the transfer of technology. However, no agreement on partial Indian ownership was reached and IBM withdrew completely from India in 1978.

Throughout most of the 1970s the only wholly-owned Indian computer firm was the central government's Electronics Corporation of India Limited (ECIL). Minority-owned subsidiaries of other foreign firms produced a few very large and expensive mainframe systems, or supplied minisystems which were beyond the capabilities of ECIL. Because of the stringent import restrictions applied, most users were forced to buy from ECIL, but the systems it was developing were not very efficient (Grieco, 1982, p. 628). The government subsequently permitted new, wholly indigenous, firms to begin production. These suppliers soon began to sell minicomputers at prices far below ECIL. By the late 1970s, ECIL's hegemony was being successfully challenged by a coalition of computer users and indigenous enterprises wishing to enter the field of systems engineering. Only a few years later, the market shares of both the new privately-owned Indian firms and foreign suppliers came to exceed that of ECIL. While the government's original intention to promote ECIL as the country's national champion has met with only limited success, the changing configuration of world computer markets has provided policy-makers with other means to shape the development of their domestic computer industry. By the mid–1980s, foreign firms – Norsk Data and Control Data – had joined up with ECIL to produce mainframes and super-minicomputers. Other foreign firms, including Hewlett-Packard, ICL, Prime and Texas Instruments, have simultaneously undertaken joint ventures with Indian firms to produce a variety of computer-related products.

Today, the LDCs which choose to single out parts of the computer industry to be a national champion have a widening range of choices in determining the extent to which they depend on international producers. Most conventional interpretations have suggested that rapid technological change can undermine a government's ability to negotiate and bargain with these firms. However, at least some of the foregoing experiences would seem to imply that the nature of innovation and changes in the industry's international structure have enabled some LDCs to bolster their negotiating positions. While the costs and inefficiencies resulting from a singularly autarchic approach to the development of indigenous technologies have been extensively documented, the more advanced LDCs may no longer face the stark choice between autonomy and dependency which is sometimes supposed. Governments can also learn to manage and to exert greater control over those elements of dependency which arise in their relations with international computer firms.

In contrast to the assertive tactics described above, other Asian LDCs – notably Hong Kong, Singapore, South Korea and Taiwan – have taken a much more accommodating attitude towards international computer firms. They rely heavily on foreign expertise and capital to develop their industry. These countries have all proved to be particularly adept in attracting foreign investors and have quickly emerged as important suppliers of computer parts and components. Evidence of their success is suggested by the fact that the cost of producing many of these items in the Asian Basin was at least 30 per cent less than in the USA (*Far Eastern Economic Review*, 21 July 1983).

Taiwan was the first of these countries to produce a government plan for development of the computer industry. Investors, both local and foreign, were granted a five-year waiver of taxes. Reduced tax rates were applicable once the waiver expired, while subsidised loans for capital investments were provided by Taiwan's Bank of Communications. The government was also quick to recognize the need for Taiwan to become more self-sufficient in computer technology. In 1972, it established the Electronics Research Service Organization (ERSO), a quasi-government body which collaborates with private firms as well as conducts its own product design and product development.

In terms of its technological capabilities, the Taiwanese industry may be the most advanced of the four Asian countries, but a lack of funds for R and D and research staff poses serious problems. Most engineers are trained abroad (virtually all in the USA) and only a small proportion return. As wage rates in Taiwan rose, its firms lost competitiveness to other Asian producers and the need for a more productive R and D programme became apparent. In 1979, the Institute for Information Industry was founded and given the tasks of developing software and training packages to encourage computer use. And in the same year, a publicly funded firm – United Microelectronics – began operation and now produces computer memory chips.

Taiwan's weaknesses in R and D activities can be partly attributed to the fact that indigenous computer firms mainly consist of small, family-owned enterprises. Their small size limits the ability of firms to innovate or to introduce any new product designs. This fact, coupled with their inferior technical capabilities, led many producers to opt for a strictly imitative approach. The tactic eventually gave rise to a different type of problem – a reputation for infringement of copyrights and trademarks of established producers. As Taiwan's international ambitions in the field of computers have grown, the need to shed this reputation has become imperative. Policy-makers responded by urging both foreign and domestic companies to set up local product-development teams and to allocate a minimum percentage of annual sales to R and D. These efforts were supplemented by the government's establishment of Taiwan's first venture capital company and by government-inspired joint ventures with international computer firms.

Of the four Asian LDCs considered here, the level of the South Korean government's commitment to development of a domestic computer industry far exceeds that of its regional competitors. The Korean approach is a three-pronged one, reminiscent of the earlier Japanese strategy. It includes protection for local firms, aggressive purchases of foreign technology and pressure on foreign firms to enter joint ventures. The government's strategy for its national champion is also made easier because the Korean market for computers – although comparatively underdeveloped – is larger than any of its other Asian rivals. Thus trade restraints can yield large profits for domestic producers, while exports account for a comparatively smaller share of total production. One drawback of the generous protection accorded the industry is that domestic prices have remained relatively high, inhibiting the growth of domestic demand. In order to boost their market, policy-makers attempted to liberalize restrictions on computer imports and foreign investment began in the early 1980s. Such efforts were resisted not only by indigenous firms but also by those foreign companies which had previously managed to establish operations in the country. Existing computer firms argued that any change in regulations would be unfair as these would violate the original terms and conditions for investment. In 1983, Korean import duties on computers were still 20 per cent, while components bore a 30 per cent tariff. In comparison, Taiwan's corresponding rates were 5 and 7.5 per cent respectively, while these items were subject to no tariffs at all in Hong Kong or Singapore.

South Korea relies on American computer giants such as IBM and American Telephone and Telegraph (ATT) for most of its technology. But with the government's help, several firms have negotiated joint ventures to produce computer components, terminals and related items. Most of these agreements leave the marketing and technology development to the American parties, while the Koreans offer cheap production costs and high quality. However, policy-makers recognize that without a substantial boost in the scope of the country's R and D such an approach relegates firms to follow in the shadows of the world's leaders. The government has attempted to reduce its dependence on foreign technology by establishing the Korean Institute of Electronics Technology (KIET). The institute conducts research in areas beyond the technical capability of private industry and collaborates with firms on other projects. If the results prove to be commercially successful the companies pay royalties to KIET. The Korean computer industry itself is better able to undertake R and D than their competitors in other LDCs. Because Korean producers are comparatively large, well diversified and vertically integrated, their approach is distinct from that of the smaller, family-run enterprises in Taiwan and Hong Kong. Korean firms can better afford to carry out R and D programmes of their own, using revenues for older lines to finance their development of the computer industry.

Each of these countries has attempted to expand its domestic market through government purchases and other policies to encourage computerization and the automation of offices and industries. None, however, has pursued this objective more zealously than Singapore. The city-state allows businesses to write off the full cost of a computer in the first year after purchase. Singapore also offers a range of incentives to attract foreign computer firms which goes beyond those of other Asian LDCs. These include a tax-free status for five to ten years, subsidies for the costs of worker training and financial assistance for capital investment. The policies are all implemented through the Economic Development Board which endeavours to attract producers of computers equipment and components.

The government's aggressive efforts to lure foreign investment to Singapore are one way to counterbalance its weaknesses in other fields. In comparison with the Asian LDCs, the city-state still lacks the manpower necessary to conduct a broadly based programme of R and D. The government is concentrating its limited human resources on the development of computer software in the hope of moving beyond operations such as assembly or production of the simpler components. The project, administered by the National Computer Board, is intended to establish the city's firms as the leading service centre for all data-using sectors throughout Asia.

A significantly different situation prevails in Hong Kong, where the extent of public policy intervention is comparatively small. Even without offering special incentives to foreign investors, Hong Kong still provides an attractive investment environment because of its free port, good communications, low taxes, efficient customs and banking systems and no restrictions on profit remittances. However, foreign investors are reluctant to allocate significant funds in view of the ex-colony's uncertain future. As a result, most of the investment has taken the form of assembly operations which require relatively little expenditure or capital equipment and promise a quick return. Despite Hong Kong's ambivalent future, the government has quietly but steadily increased its assistance to computer firms. The salaries of newly graduated electrical engineers are subsidized for the first eighteen months and research on computer components and microprocessors is publicly funded.

Certainly, the constraints and alternatives faced by these countries are somewhat different from those of their rivals in larger LDCs. Some Western analysts doubt that most computer firms in LDCs will be able to develop the R and D programmes and distribution systems necessary for them to become fully-fledged competitors. As Western firms (with the help of their own governments) accelerate their own search for new computer technologies and markets, the drawbacks of an autarchic approach to the industry's development may grow. For instance, strict controls on imports and foreign investment can perpetuate the use of technologies which are rapidly becoming obsolete or inferior. And when very few foreign firms are allowed to establish local operations, they have no need to compete against their other international rivals and are typically reluctant to share their best technologies. Lacking access to a steady flow of technological advances, indigenous producers may not only find it difficult to follow an imitative approach but could also fall behind rivals in other LDCs which operate in less restrained environments. A related danger may arise if a government goes too far by erecting an extensive network of trade restraints, investment restrictions and other measures to protect domestic firms. In doing so, it may create a whole new constituency of vested interests which then oppose any reversal in policy.

The efforts of governments and indigenous firms in LDCs in this field have been vigorous and sometimes imaginative. In global terms, however, their impact has been of very little significance; Western producers and markets continue to dominate in every phase of the world computer industry. In the latter countries, advances in computer hardware, software and electronic components are gradually extending the range of computer applications into fields such as industrial automation and telecommunications. For firms specializing in these new developing areas, the choice of an industry strategy is somewhat unique. One set of tactics is surveyed in the concluding section of this chapter.

Interfirm Tie-Ups and Collaboration

A strategy which relies heavily on an international network of firm alliances and/or close collaboration between domestic producers will often be intended to serve objectives similar to that of a national champion. For industries with many applications still at the conceptual stage, access to the results of R and D is crucial. Likewise, the rising costs of research can prove to be prohibitive to all but the richest firms and most generous of governments. These problems can be partially resolved by forming consortiums or undertaking other collaborative projects. Such steps may be government-inspired or taken at the initiative of private firms. Private firms in technology intensive industries may also have other reasons to seek collaborative arrangements, either at home or abroad. For example, the ability to set industry standards for major products, components or operating systems can be a powerful reason why firms seek alliances with users or suppliers which dominate their respective fields.

There are other, more fundamental, reasons why the collaborative initiatives of private firms will differ from the co-operative elements found in a government-inspired strategy for its national champion. Ultimately, it is firms, rather than government officials, which make investment decisions and take the other steps necessary to attain competitive leadership in both foreign and domestic markets. The information on which these decisions have to be based is seldom available to policy-makers themselves. Individual firms not only have better knowledge about the technologies, markets, consumer preferences and behaviour of computers, but also have a greater incentive to use this knowledge. The informational gap between policy-makers and businesses is usually greatest in industries based on high technology and it is here that a strategy of international tie-ups and interfirm collaboration, rather than one of a national champion, will be most likely to reflect the specific needs of individual firms.

Firms in mature industries will have different reasons for collaborating and seeking alliances. Some may specialize in particular products and even have a technological lead over competitors, although they may lack the facilities and staff to provide effective distribution and service in foreign markets. Others may wish to move some parts of their operation offshore to reduce costs, but would prefer to develop sub-contractual relationships with local firms rather than establishing a foreign subsidiary. Also, as industries mature and their markets become global rather than national, the costs of product design and re-tooling can soar, forcing even the largest firms into collaborative arrangements with one or more competitors.

Among maturing industries, several of these considerations have emerged in descriptions of various industry strategies. However, the following discussion of international tie-ups and interfirm collaboration focuses on an emerging industry: the design, production and installation of automated or computer-controlled equipment such as machine tools and robots. Both these devices are usually pictured as parts of a larger manufacturing configuration, sometimes known as a flexible manufacturing system. The term is commonly associated only with metalcutting operations, although this also includes references to systems for metalforming, assembly and other purposes.

Because the development of automated systems is still at such an early stage, there are no alternative definitions which are both widely accepted and general in scope. Many of the automated factory systems of the future will nevertheless share certain common features and these provide at least some notion of the industry's 'boundaries'. First, the machines will carry out a number of functions ranging from assembly, cutting, welding or painting to much more delicate tasks which require visual and tactile sensors. Second, all the operations must be closely integrated with the work of other automated devices designed to handle materials and tools and to carry out measuring and testing operations. Third, the systems would be computer-controlled, would operate with a minimum of manual intervention and should be able to process any item belonging to a specified family of products according to a predetermined schedule.

These general characteristics imply that the new system will have to satisfy several basic requirements. For instance, it must be capable of producing a variety of parts. Capital investments can seldom be justified when a system is designed to produce only a single part. And to produce a sufficient range of products, machines must have the ability to switch, under computer control, from one production step to another. Robots or, alternatively, a conveyor mechanism will also be required to speed the passage of materials from one machine to the next. The importance of this latter requirement is underlined by the fact that materials are worked on as little as 5 per cent of the time they are in a factory; during the remainder of the time they are pushed from place to place or lie idle (UNIDO, 1981a, p. 154).

Rapid technical advances in both computers and micro-electronics have provided impetus for development of automated systems. To integrate all the operations which these systems would encompass, a wide range of new skills and knowledge will be required. These include not only the development of new computer hardware but also advances in computer software, systems engineering, production scheduling and a detailed understanding of the manufacturing process within which the new system is to operate. The diverse range of abilities, technologies and products needed is one of the major reasons for the growing network of interfirm linkages and contacts described below.

Until the 1950s, the machines that turned, milled and ground metal were controlled by hand or by cumbrous gears and cams. The first step in the eventual development of factory automation began with the introduction of numerically controlled machine tools – programmable devices which received instructions from tapes. The new type of machine tools were operated as independent or stand-alone devices and were able to perform a limited range of very specific tasks. Because the tools were not flexible, the cost of their installation could be justified only for industries with long production runs. Most engineering industries, however, produce in very small batches – up to 75 per cent of the items manufactured are made in runs of 50 or less (ECE, 1985, p. 2). This characteristic severely restricted the market for numerically controlled machine tools.

Once the size of electronic components was reduced and computers became more powerful, engineers were able to do away with a tape form of machine instruction. The microprocessor – essentially a complex programmable integrated circuit – was introduced to the factory floor. This adaptation permitted the sequence of instructions to be changed, making it possible for the same piece of equipment to manufacture different parts rather than just a single component. Greater versatility meant that automation could be cost-effective for industries with production runs which were not especially long.

American firms invented the microprocessor, but Japanese competitors were quicker to realize that its use in numerically controlled devices could change the market for machine tools. One reason why American innovators failed to match their rivals was the lack of contact and co-operation between machine tool-makers and firms which supplied the microprocessor (Sciberras and Payne, 1985). The manufacturers of machine tools were slow to switch to solid-state electronics and resisted calls for cheaper, more flexible numerical controls. And, by the time they did, buyers had turned to Japanese producers, or had begun to make their own numerical control devices. A few Japanese firms had the additional advantage of having acquired experience in production of both machine tools and microprocessors. Fanuc, the dominant firm in today's market for numerical controls, was one of these. Begun as a division of Japan's largest computer-maker, Fujitsu, the firm was spun off in 1972. Although its speciality was the production of computer control equipment, Fanuc also produced machine tools. The firm's unique orientation served it well in the race to develop more flexible machine tools – a market which it eventually came to dominate.

With improvements in numerically controlled machine tools, attention turned to a related problem – how best to shuttle parts and materials from one part of a factory to another. Robots, along with pallet systems and gantries, were developed to deliver the workpiece to the machine, to take it from one machine to another and, after machining, to store the finished components. Robots are simply mechanical arms which can repeat a simple series of motions guided by a computer. They normally replace a human skill and are typically designed for a specific industry.

The first robots were developed by a US firm in the early 1960s to perform welding tasks. Like other automated tools, their high cost initially prevented widespread use. Based on costs and wage rates in 1971, a Japanese company would

have required over twenty-two years to recover its investment in a robot operated on a single shift basis (*Far Eastern
Economic Review*, 4 December 1981). In 1980, a basic robot
was still thought to cost $50–60,000, while depreciation,
interest and maintenance added an additional $20–30,000
(*The Economist*, 1 March 1980). Limited flexibility was
another shortcoming. Although programmable, robots were
not very intelligent and were dedicated to simple, straightforward tasks such as spray-painting or lifting heavy
castings.

In seeking to establish themselves in this newly emerging
field, Japanese and American firms followed different
tactics. Japanese firms moved quickly by relying on existing
technologies. They also made extensive use of conveyors
and pallets to transfer parts and materials from one machine
to another. Since conveyors required less sophisticated
controls than robots, the overall systems designed by the
Japanese were not complicated. In line with the same
approach, Japanese suppliers specialized in the simplest
types of robot. Even today, more than one-third of the
robots produced in Japan are merely pick-and-place
machines which have to be reset and adjusted by workers
(*The Economist*, 5 April 1986).

Most American users preferred to automate gradually by
employing their existing machine tools in combination with
robots. A typical plan called for the system to be built up
piece by piece, relying heavily on robots to be used in
conjunction with standard, single-function machine tools.
As firms extended their systems, the robots would be re-
programmed rather than a conveyor rebuilt. An advantage
of the gradual approach was that it avoided large capital
investments and production bottlenecks which might result
from poor planning. However, in comparison with the
Japanese version, a more advanced technology was required
because the system used a greater variety of machine tools
and a larger number of machines.

The contrasting approaches adopted in the two markets
help to explain some of the fundamental differences
between Japanese and American suppliers. In Japan robots
were not the preferred choice for an in-factory transport

system. And, by American standards, many were regarded as being very rudimentary. The suppliers, however, were willing to provide custom-built versions to suit the buyer's needs and to assist in their installation. With such encouragement, the Japanese market flourished and buyers soon came to use robots much more adventurously than in other Western countries. The result was an industry composed of numerous firms supplying a broad range of automated machines. American producers, on the other hand, emphasized links with software companies, computer-makers and other firms that were able to contribute to the development and integration of the necessary technologies. Many of the innovators in this field were soon bought up by more affluent companies such as Westinghouse, General Electric and Bendix. The structure of the US industry eventually came to comprise a small number of highly specialized firms. With hindsight, the American approach appears to have been the more technically innovative, while Japanese firms soon excelled in the fields of manufacturing engineering and marketing.

By the early 1980s, computer-controlled machine tools and robots had become common on many factory floors. In the automobile industry, robots performed not only simple jobs such as spray-painting, welding or lifting heavy castings but also more high-precision tasks like engine boring and assembly of car bodies. Producers of electronic products used them to assemble parts, insert components and provide quality control, while industries ranging from shipbuilding to textiles found similar applications. The later generations of numerically controlled machine tools were also much more adept. They were able not only to perform multiple but also much more intricate tasks, ranging from precision drilling and grinding to milling.

Once the industry passed from infancy to adolescence, the nature of interfirm collaboration began to change. At least three consequences should be noted. First, the markets for automated machinery were no longer composed of only a few buyers with limited experience. Many users of automated machines began to produce their own equipment. Others pressed their suppliers to make product improvements or to extend the function and capabilities of various machines. These developments gradually created a much wider basis for interfirm collaboration in which the user industries themselves were active participants.

Second, when the size of domestic markets had reached a minimum threshold, producers abandoned a purely domestic focus and sought to establish an international presence. Japanese firms created an extensive international network of subsidiaries and joint ventures and actively exported licences to the USA. American firms established numerous subsidiaries and tie-ups in Western Europe but were the initiators of comparatively few links with Japan. Significantly, the number of intra-European agreements, however, was virtually nil (ECE, 1986, p. 271–2). No substantial increase in the volume of trade in automated machinery accompanied this transition. Although components were imported or purchased from foreign-owned subsidiaries, the bulk of these items were still designed and installed by domestic vendors. The complexities of installation and the need for compatibility between components and machines were the major considerations which limited the opportunities for trade in automated products.

Third, the objectives of the designers and producers of automated machinery began to change. They sought to integrate the operations of a greater number of machines and robots by placing them all under the control of central computers. The goal, if realized, would mark a new phase in automation. However, it depends on the development of new technologies – fifth-generation computers, artificial intelligence, optical fibres and new material technology – none of which has yet been perfected. Even optimists expect that the creation of large, generalized systems cannot be realized until the next century. Critics contend that such a goal is fundamentally flawed unless factories are completely rebuilt. They argue that centralized systems will have a success rate of 20–30 per cent and will be too expensive to set up to save money.

Modern systems for factory automation now consist of a multitude of mechanical, electronic and software components as well as subsystems. Joint ventures are common, since very few companies have the capabilities to supply all these components. Unlike forms of collaboration in other fields of manufacturing, however, these agreements are very limited in duration. They are usually arrangements between manufacturers of various components who band together when installing a particular system. The absence of stable and formal lines of co-operation between suppliers reflects the diverse and complex needs associated with each installation. The practice permits the user greater freedom in combining different types of components but he also has to pay a higher price for system integration. Because each supplier has to develop the interfaces for a large number of complementary machines, few economies of scale can be realized.

At least some suppliers have attempted to extend the areas of expertise which they can offer. One group consists of firms with a traditional speciality in electronics, electrical engineering, computer hardware or information technology. Either through acquisitions or in-house development, large companies, such as General Electric, Westinghouse, Siemens, NEC and IBM, have established subsidiaries or divisions which supply robots and various subsystems. A second group is composed of firms with an expertise in mechanical engineering. They include major producers of machine tools which also manufacture numerical controls, robots or materials-handling equipment. So far, none of the firms in the latter group have developed a mastery of the computer hardware or computerized subsystems to aid in the design and manufacturing phases or computer-controlled sensor equipment which would be necessary to manufacture a complete system.

A third group of firms – the major users of automated systems – now provide an important source for development and change. Because robots quickly found applications in the automobile industry, car-makers gained considerable experience in the design, installation and operation of these machines. GM alone is now reported to be spending almost $9 billion a year on automation (*The Economist*, 5 April 1986). However, with few exceptions, automobile firms have not attempted to develop any commercial expertise of their own, preferring to maintain licensing agreements with major suppliers of automated systems or components. These initiatives are usually welcomed by the major suppliers, most of which assume that a broad range of products and subsystems are needed to win sales. Customers presumably prefer to buy all their products from a single supplier to ensure a higher degree of integration. However, attempts to provide a broad range of automation products can stretch the technical capabilities and research budgets of even the largest firms. Thus, suppliers actively seek to fill gaps in their product lines by licensing products developed by users.

The experience of Fanuc illustrates some of the reasons why suppliers find such arrangements attractive. Having previously established itself as a leader in the field of numerical controls for machine tools, Fanuc began to produce industrial robots by marrying different types of expertise and drawing on other talents in related industries. GM Fanuc, a joint venture with General Motors, is now the largest robot supplier in the USA. The linkup provided an overseas marketing arm which Fanuc lacked, as well as direct entry to GM. Similar arrangements have been made with other large, robot-using firms in the UK and West Germany. Factories using these robots also require sophisticated computer software to connect the robots and other devices into a wider network. Because Fanuc still cannot supply this software, it relies on both GM and Fujitsu.

Today, the pragmatic influence of users provides an important impetus for interfirm collaboration and technology development. One of the most serious problems for this group is the lack of compatibility between components and subsystems, which means that factory automation is still confined to islands within the assembly process. A typical enterprise may now have automated as many as fifty independent functional areas, each with its own hardware, software and data. The result is that the user is hostage to a variety of specialized technologies – none of which are compatible.

Standard data links which would allow computers, process controllers, robots and other machines to communicate would permit a greater degree of integration and, therefore, improved efficiency. In response to this need, users have banded together in an attempt to impose a common set of requirements on manufacturers of the many components. A highly publicized example has been GM's advocacy of a manufacturing automation protocol (MAP). Beginning in 1980, GM used its influence and buying power with suppliers of the computer equipment to encourage the establishment of MAP as an industry standard. Represent- atives of more than 300 US companies (including vendors) joined the group during the next five years, while an even larger number of firms in Europe, Japan and elsewhere were members of auxiliary groups. Current prototypes of MAP can link equipment from more than twenty suppliers and encompass up to twelve different industry standards. These range from the physical specifications for the cables used in the system to the software for various common tasks.

As the idea has gained acceptance, the orientation of the vendors has changed. Many have begun to market their machines as MAP-compatible – in much the same way as producers of computer software boast of IBM-compatibility. Such claims, however, are optimistic in view of the problems yet to be solved. These include methods for communication between different computers and machines, the form which the information should take and the ability of such delicate machines to work in factory environments where noise, vibration and uneven light are common. An even more fundamental issue is that the requirements of users may be too varied to be served by a uniform set of standards. To be applicable, MAP and similar protocols may have to be developed for different levels of automation.

In industries where the design phase is lengthy and complex, the perfection of computer-aided design (CAD) is a high priority. Ideally, these subsystems should permit technicians to design, draft and analyze parts or assem- blages on a computer screen. Such abilities would eliminate the labour intensive task of drafting and avoid the need to produce expensive test versions of products and compon- ents. Subsystems for CAD have existed since the 1960s but specifications which the computer can supply still have to be extensively supplemented and then translated into a form that machine tools can use. Engineers must perform numerous calculations and write separate computer programmes to direct the machines to cut the part. These tasks are tedious and expensive in industries such as aerospace where more than ten years are normally required to design and build a new plane. In response, US aircraft builders have formed a consortium and will spend more than $25 million by 1990 to link computer designs to the machines that make the parts. By doing so, they hope to reduce the manufacturing cycle and to cut the cost of the machined parts.

Even greater potential is foreseen if CAD is combined with computer-aided manufacture (CAM). Ideally, on-screen designing and testing would generate a bank of computer instructions to manufacture a product or to make the tools, dies and molds used to produce it. Integration of the two subsystems would shorten the time between design and production and reduce the cost of introducing new models and customized products. The importance of this achievement is suggested by the fact that 60–70 per cent of the current costs of manufacturing are thought to have nothing to do with the physical tasks involved but depend on the planning, scheduling and control of equipment and operators. A complete merger of CAD and CAM would have to overcome serious obstacles which may eventually prove to be insurmountable. Nevertheless, major firms, some working as private groups and others relying on government funding, have succeeded in perfecting some of the elements of a joint system.

In conclusion, projects such as those described above offer only a few examples of the extensive involvement of both users and producers in the development of various components and subsystems. Implicit throughout the discussion is the suggestion that such contacts and alliances have played an invaluable role in the development of products and markets for automated systems. Nevertheless, while there is ample evidence to support this general impression, two qualifications should be noted. First, the types of alliances and collaborative agreements described here entail drawbacks as well as advantages. There is a risk that proprietary technology will be leaked, through a collaborator, to the innovator's major competitors. Projects can also be downgraded, or even abandoned, as other agreements are formed and become more important. Second, excessive reliance on such alliances can jeopardise a firm's long-term independence. Companies that began to specialize in making specific bits of an entire product while relying on partners to supply the remainder may find that they lose the option of producing the entire product. Finally, the role of government has not been mentioned in the foregoing discussion. Policy-makers in almost every Western country accord the development of factory automation systems a high priority. However, because the activities described here are still at such an early stage in their commercialization, the choice of a national champion – whether with regard to technologies or companies – would be very difficult. Government assistance is generous but of a 'catch-all' nature, being designed to provide incentives for new entrants through subsidies, loans, grants and similar means. As the industry matures and technologies become well established, the pressure for policy-makers to provide much more specific forms of assistance will grow. At that point, the behaviour of leading firms is likely to change. Efforts to establish a leading position by weaving a network of interfirm alliances and contacts may be matched, or even overshadowed, by attempts to influence the outcome of policy discussions.

Supplementary Reading

Much of the debate with regard to the policies of LDCs towards high technology multinationals, such as computer-makers, is represented by two opposing views, one based on the theory of dependency and the other which advocates a strategy of bargaining and negotiation. In the first instance, useful sources are Cardoso (1973), Emmanuel (1976), Hymer (1972) and Wilbur (1973). Important statements representing the alternative interpretation are Kindleberger (1969, pp. 147–59), Vernon (1975, pp. 151–83 and 1977, pp. 139–74), and Bergsten, Horst and Moran (1978, pp. 369–81).

Brock's (1975) study of the US computer industry details elements of several microeconomic strategies involving imitative tactics, innovational moves and predatory take-overs. Katz and Phillips (1982) stress the profound influence of government activities on the computer industry. Once technologies are widely diffused and a commercial market is established they find that government influence takes new forms. In the LDCs the conditions for development of an indigenous computer industry are analyzed by O'Connor (1985). Grieco (1982) uses India's experience with international computer firms as the basis for a case study of the negotiating process between the multinational and government of the LDC.

The nature of interfirm linkages discussed in this chapter depends, at least in part, on the precise form of automation. Kaplinsky, (1984) suggests a useful typology which distinguishes between types of automation in three spheres: design, manufacturing and co-ordination. The same author (Kaplinsky, 1982) has carried out a detailed study of computer-aided design. Sciberras and Payne (1985) have studied the impact of technical change on international patterns of competitiveness in the machine tool industry. The ECE (1985) has compiled a detailed inventory of acquisitions, mergers, sales agreements and joint ventures among producers of robots. The same organization has also published a study of the development of flexible manufacturing systems used in metalcutting operations (ECE, 1986).

Statistical Appendix

Throughout most of this book the concept of value added is used to measure manufacturing production. However, the definition of the term will vary depending on the country and the type of data being used. Value added is ideally measured within a national accounting framework where it refers to the contribution to GDP by establishments in a particular 'industry' or economic sector. Statistics on national accounts provide sector-wide totals for value added in agriculture, manufacturing, services, construction and other fields. These figures, reported in current and constant US dollars, serve as a means of examining broad patterns of structural change at both national and international levels.

Most of the data in the early chapters of this book were originally compiled from the national accounts of individual countries. Preference for this source was based on two considerations. First, country coverage from national accounts is usually greater than that contained in alternative sources. Second, differences in the national accounting practices of various countries are thought to be of less significance than alternative statistical sources.

In some instances, however, national accounts data could not be used. The results of national industrial inquiries reported in the United Nations' *Yearbook of Industrial Statistics*, Vol. 1 (annual) had to be used instead. These inquiries may employ either of two definitions of value added, one of which is the national accounting concept described above. Alternatively, a 'census' concept of value added is used where value added is defined as the gross value of output less the cost of materials, fuels and other supplies, subcontracting, repairs and maintenance and commission work done by others.

Aside from differences in the definition of value added, there are conceptual reasons why national accounts figures will not agree with those derived from census or survey exercises (see Prakash, 1974, p. 20). First, national accounts will usually cover all manufacturing establishments, while coverage by census or survey

307

will frequently exclude small-scale firms. Second, certain activities (for example, repairs, services and trading) may be excluded from the industrial census/survey but incorporated in national accounts. Third, census/survey methods frequently report value added on a 'domestic' basis, although figures taken from national accounts are sometimes compiled on a 'national' basis. For these reasons, national accounts data and figures derived from censuses and/or surveys were not mixed in the same table. The one exception was Table 2.2. For years prior to 1963, sufficient data at constant prices were not available from national accounts sources. Figures for earlier years were built up from several sources, including industrial censuses, and had to be compiled at current prices. Some of the problems of data comparability which arise in connection with these issues are discussed later in this Appendix.

Although international comparisons of MVA are largely based on national accounts, they still suffer from certain weaknesses. The most obvious is the fact that socialist countries employ a statistical framework for national estimates which is not directly comparable with that used in most Western countries and LDCs. Socialist countries have adopted the concept of net material product rather than GDP and no precise derivation of value added is therefore possible. An additional complication is the fact that data are not collected for the manufacturing sector itself but for industry, that is, manufacturing plus construction. Where data for both socialist and Western countries appear in United Nations sources used here, adjustments have been made to account for these conceptual differences. However, the need to undertake additional estimates also means that international comparability is further limited.

Industry Data – General Characteristics and Shortcomings

In several parts of this book – particularly Chapter 4 – the discussion concerns patterns of structural change among specific groups of industries within the manufacturing sector. Here, the most convenient source of empirical evidence is offered by the International Standard Industrial Classification (ISIC) which provides data for twenty-eight industries making up the manufacturing sector. The original data are compiled by national statistical offices and the results published annually by the United Nations in the *Yearbook of Indutrial Statistics*, Vol. 1. As noted above, countries may use either a national accounting concept or a census concept of value added. In addition, the use of this data source in international (or cross-country) studies introduces other problems of comparability and consistency which should be noted. Five types of weaknesses are summarized below.

First, countries are not consistent in their statistical coverage of the manufacturing sector. In carrying out industrial censuses or annual surveys, many countries exclude some portion of small-scale industry – usually defined in terms of the size of the firm's work force or its level of investment. This practice can result from the fact that small-scale enterprises are outside the legal authority of the government agency responsible for the census or survey. Alternatively, the cost of collecting data for both large and small establishments may be excessive and some LDCs are forced to ignore the latter firms. Whatever the reason, one result is that the definition of 'manufacturing' establishments varies widely among countries. The most common practice is to exclude all establishments with less than five employees. But many countries impose a higher limit, ignoring establishments with less than 10 employees, less than 20 employees or even less than 50 employees. The problem has a second dimension: a national office may alter the scope of its collection exercise, as defined by size of establishment, in different years. In years when an industrial census is carried out, small-scale establishments may be included but are omitted in non-census years when a survey, usually based on a reduced sample, is carried out.

Second, national statistical classifications do not always conform to the present version of the ISIC. Although the national office may make an effort to convert the data to the ISIC, discrepancies remain. Differences in classifications give rise to several problems, but the most frequent is the reporting of data for an aggregate, that is, a combination of two or more industries, where an 'industry' is defined to be equivalent to the three-digit level of the ISIC. The types of combination will vary both among countries and over time.

Third, there are major differences in the definitions of common measures. Value added may be expressed either in factor costs or producers' prices. The former concept omits all duties and taxes levied on products but includes subsidies, while the treatment of taxes and subsidies is reversed when the concept of producers' prices is used. Likewise, employment data may refer to the number of persons engaged, that is, the total number working for the establishment during the reference year, or the number of employees (persons engaged excluding working proprietors and unpaid workers). Either of the two types of inconsistency mentioned here will be significant for cross-country studies of specific industries. For example, the treatment of indirect taxes and subsidies will be particularly important in the case of industries such as beverages, tobacco, petroleum refining or steel. Inconsistencies in employment concepts (as well as derived indicators relating to productivity) are especially apparent in employment-related studies of textiles, clothing and other industries, where small-scale establishments and cottage industries are important. A tabulation of the variation in country practices during the period 1970–80 can be found in UNIDO (1985c). The results show that no preferred definition exists and reveal frequent instances where countries have switched from one definition to another.

Fourth, in years when a census is not conducted an annual survey is usually the source of industrial data. In a few cases, these surveys concern only selected manufacturing industries. For instance, Mexican data for employment and wages and salaries cover only 58 out of 225 industrial groups in the national classification, while the Indonesian figures systematically exclude information on petroleum manufacturing activities (United Nations, *Yearbook of Industrial Statistics*, Vol. 1, 1985, p. 408 and p. 273).

Fifth, the need to adjust for non-response is a problem encountered in any statistical survey or census. Although the majority of countries carry out such adjustments, this is not always the case. The failure to take account of non-response may be due to a lack of sufficient information, insufficient staff to carry out this task, or a number of other reasons. The extent to which this factor will distort the census or survey results varies, depending upon the industry in question and the type of data (output, employment, wages, etc.) being examined.

Differences in national statistical practices, concepts and definitions can clearly result in many types of data irregularities, meaning that problems of comparability and consistency are a major concern for international studies. Some of these weaknesses, however, can be eliminated or the magnitude of the distortion can be reduced. This has been done by UNIDO in the course of work to develop a data base of industrial statistics for international studies (see UNIDO, 1985d). For this reason, the data published by UNIDO have been the preferred source of industry-level statistics in this book.

It is difficult, if not impossible, to get a clear impression of the extent to which all factors affect the comparability of figures for two or more countries. Indirect evidence on at least two of these aspects has been assembled, however. Table A.1 shows for a sample of countries the relationship between MVA as reported in their national accounts and from industrial censuses or surveys. Discrepancies between the alternative estimates of value added can be attributed to differences in concepts and in national practices (for example, methods of valuation and definition of the manufacturing sector) which were noted above. The comparisons clearly demonstrate that the researcher will obtain significantly different results depending on the type of data used. Even in instances where industrial censuses have provided the main source of information for development of the national accounts estimates,

Table A.1 Comparison of MVA Estimates from National Accounts and Industrial Censuses/Surveys, Selected Countries (ratio of national accounts to industrial census/survey)

LDCs	1975	1980
Chile	48	93
Colombia	115	109
Indonesia[a]	232	248
Kenya	105	102
Mexico	…	99
Philippines	153	150
Tunisia	114	94
Western countries		
France	100	100
Italy	112	124
Japan	95	94
Sweden	91	85
USA	82	76
West Germany	92	100

Sources: United Nations, *National Accounts Statistics: Main Aggregates and Detailed Tables, 1982* (New York: United Nations, 1985); *Yearbook of Industrial Statistics*, Vol. 1, 1979 edition (New York, 1981); *Yearbook of Industrial Statistics*, Vol. 1, 1982 edition (New York, 1985).

[a] Industrial census/survey excludes petroleum refining (ISIC 353) and miscellaneous products of petroleum and coal (ISIC 354).

311

differences in the treatment of specific components can lead to surprisingly wide variations in results. However, closer inspection often reveals that the underlying data for the two sets of estimates are not so divergent as might be expected.

One example is the treatment of miscellaneous costs for services – financial services, interest costs, social security, social welfare payments and similar expenditures. The statisticians who compile the industrial censuses or national accounts may have access to all these figures, but one group may choose to include them in their estimates for value added while the other does not. In some LDCs, this component can be 6–7 per cent of GDP and to make a true comparison between MVA from a census and national accounts the researcher would have to adjust for any differences in treatment of these and other components. Many such instances can be identified from inspection of national data. In the USA, the industrial census considers only those costs of inputs directly related to the production process, as well as fuel, energy consumption and contract work. Unlike the practice in some other countries – and unlike the construction of the national accounts for the USA – information on the cost of most purchased services is not considered. As a result, estimates of value added from the US census can be expected to exceed the corresponding national accounts figures (US Department of Commerce, 1981, pp. 25–27). These are only two examples which could lead to divergent estimates of MVA. The implication is that a proper comparison of estimates from the two sources would require a careful reconciliation of the figures, taking account of differences in the treatment of various types of underlying data.

The failure to include small establishments in reported figures on each industry will not only lead to underestimates of employment and production but can also bias estimates of relative factor intensity and related measures. To gain some impression of this fact, a comparison was made between national accounts statistics – which usually incorporate the contribution of small-scale operations firms – and industrial census estimates – which are known to exclude these operations. The difference between the two sets of figures can be attributed to several factors, including statistical, conceptual and definitional considerations, among them the differing treatment of small-scale firms.

It was also necessary to obtain estimates of value added of small-scale industry in selected years. In some instances this information was available from sample surveys. In others, the industrial census itself provides information on the distribution of MVA by size of establishment. The coverage of such data does not always match with the excluded portion of the manufacturing sector (for example, sample surveys or censuses sometimes provide details for firms with 10 to 19 employees, while those with less than 10 employees are omitted). For lack of anything better, the available figures were treated as 'representative' of the output and productivity in the uncovered segment. Using such figures, the difference between total MVA from national accounts and indus-trial censuses was broken down into two components – the amount attributed to small-scale operations and 'other'. Table A.2 shows the variation in country coverage by size of establishment and provides a rough estimate of the proportion of total MVA that may

Table A.2 Coverage of Small-Scale Establishments in MVA in the Mid-1970s, Selected LDCs

Country	Year	Estimated share of MVA (percentage)	Size of establishments excluded (number of employees)
Bangladesh	1975	25.6	Less than 10
Colombia	1975	11.1	Less than 10
Ecuador	1974	28.9	Less than 7, with an annual production of less than 180,000 sucres
Ethiopia	1974	19.1	Less than 10
Honduras	1971	16.5	Less than 5
India	1974	20.7	Less than 10, using power, or less than 20 not using power
Indonesia	1975	37.8	Less than 5, using power, or less than 10 not using power
Iraq	1975	28.8	Less than 10
Kenya	1975	18.8	Less than 50
Philippines	1974	20.0	Less than 50
Swaziland	1973	44.4	Less than 10
Tunisia	1975	12.8	Less than 50
Turkey	1975	10.3	Less than 10
Tanzania	1974	23.4	Less than 10
Venezuela	1974	26.2	Less than 5

Sources: *Yearbook of National Accounts Statistics, 1976, Vol. 1* (United Nations publication, Sales No. 77. XVII. 2, Vol. 1) and *Yearbook of Industrial Statistics*, 1976 Edition, Vol. 1 (United Nations publication, Sales No. 78. XVII. 3E).

be excluded from census or survey results due to omission of these firms.

Although the assumptions made are necessarily 'heroic', the results are still confidence shaking. Data based on census/survey results may underestimate the total MVA in some LDCs by 10–40 per cent. Whatever the discrepancies with regard to MVA, the user can be sure that related census/survey figures will underestimate employment and, perhaps, wages and salaries by an even larger margin. This is so because small-scale firms will be considerably more labour intensive than their larger counterparts.

In addition to the variations in the quality of national statistics, account must be taken of the fact that the time series for some countries are incomplete. Variations in country coverage will be greatest in most recent years, as some national offices lag behind in their reporting by 4–5 years. In any case, when figures representing averages for groups of countries are derived for a series of years, there is a need to ensure that the country sample remains constant, or that variations in the sample will have little effect on the estimates. A 'control' is needed in order to gauge the effects of year-to-year changes in the composition of the country sample. Relative to other years, tests showed that country coverage was most complete for 1975 and this year was used as a benchmark for judging the coverage of industrial statistics in other years (UNIDO, 1985d). In deriving group averages for years with poorer country coverage (1963 to 1980), the list of LDCs which reported in that year was first identified. Second, the share of these countries in the aggregate MVA of 'all' LDCs in 1975 was then calculated. When the resultant percentage was less than some predetermined value (for example, 90 per cent), country coverage in the particular year was regarded as incomplete.

Several of the statistical characteristics mentioned above can be of even greater consequence when the user requires a 'derived measure' or indicator rather than a straightforward estimate of magnitude. The difficulties encountered in the measurement of factor intensity (Chapter 6) are typical. They include the possibility of factor reversals, a lack of information regarding the elasticities of substitution between various factors, the choice of total or direct measures and the use of a stock or flow concept. These are only an abbreviated list of troublesome issues. Moreover, they cut across several fields, involving conceptual, theoretical and empirical problems.

Even when attention is focused on empirical issues alone, the difficulties faced by researchers are still daunting. First, the inability to identify a cluster of firms producing a similar, if not identical, product poses a serious dilemma for the researcher who wishes to compare estimates of an industry's factor intensities for different countries. The problem is less acute when the scope of study is limited to a single country (and, in this case, the use of national data sources would avoid several problems). However, many implications which might be derived from such estimates would be lost as the concept is most powerful when used in an international framework. The inability to take account of small-scale enterprises also emerges in this context. Small firms are of little significance in industries such as basic chemicals or chemical polymers and their omission would not seriously distort estimates of relative factor intensity. In contrast, these firms are of great importance in the production of textile fabrics and their omission will distort estimates of relative factor intensity.

Estimates of relative factor intensity can also be sensitive to the business cycle and this possibility means that comparisons of industry estimates for two points in time will not always be reliable. Excess capacity will emerge during the downswing in a business cycle but in countries where strict labour regulations are in force, the work force may be reduced by only a small proportion. This would mean that the share of wages in value added rises although production technologies are unchanged.

There are other statistical features that may be less important, but their cumulative effect on the estimates can still result in distortions. First, the influence of unionization and minimum wages will vary across countries for any given industry. Second, policies such as tariffs, quotas, measures to restrict entry into the industry or subsidies to foster the industry's expansion will further undermine the comparability of international estimates of relative factor intensity. Third, like value added, differences may arise in what is included in wages and salaries and affect the measurement of both the wage and non-wage shares in value added. This may be particularly true for the statistical treatment of supplementary benefits such as end-of-the-year bonuses. It would be difficult (if not impossible) to take account of all these aspects in constructing an international set of estimates for relative factor intensity. Because strict international comparability cannot be attained, it is often useful to supplement these studies by more detailed bilateral comparisons between key countries.

The discussion of structural change in Chapter 4 refers to various groupings of industry – light and heavy, consumer goods, intermediate goods and capital goods or early, middle and late industries. The distribution of MVA according to each of these groupings was shown in Table 4.2 and the arrangements of ISIC which were used to approximate each version are given in Table A.3.

Once the discussion turned to industrial processing of materials, more detailed sources of information were employed. Many of the characteristics of these data are similar to those already mentioned, but some of the implications should be noted. Data which were representative of microeconomic conditions were used in several instances: when referring to the cost structure in various fields of processing (Table 7.1), minimum economic plant size (Table 7.2) and investment requirements (Table 7.3). The figures, however, must be qualified.

In practice, the costs incurred in mineral extraction and processing are subject to a number of conditions. They are likely to vary widely, both over time and between countries, and the figures cited here should be regarded as rough indications or approximations. The investment required for mineral extraction will depend on the use of open-pit methods or underground mining, with the latter being much more expensive. Investment costs will also differ owing to infrastructure requirements or meteorological and terrain characteristics. Operating costs (for example, electric power, labour, finance charges and expenditures on maintenance) can vary by as much as 50 per cent, depending on the type of operation. And when minerals are of poor quality, large amounts of material must be removed for each tonne of mined ore and operating costs per tonne will rise accordingly.

Similar variations are encountered at later processing stages, such as smelting. The capital investment required per annual tonne of capacity, that is, specific investment, is contingent on the size of the plant, the quality of the mineral, the available infrastructure, the technology used and other factors. The components included in any estimate of investment costs can also differ. Figures may or may not include interest paid on borrowed capital during the construction period, the cost of disposal systems, training and start-up costs or working capital. In addition, the cost of construction will depend on the location, with construction in an LDC tending to be much more expensive than at a site in a Western country. For instance, a petrochemical plant built in the Middle East in 1979 cost roughly two-thirds more than one built in Western Europe (UNIDO, 1981a, p. 119). In LDCs with little local industry, much of the equipment and construction materials may have to be imported and this will raise costs. Construction time also tends to be longer in LDCs and personnel training is more expensive.

In the latter part of Chapter 7 the discussions of patterns of industrial processing utilizes international statistics on both production and trade. With regard to production trends, the main body of industrial data is available only in an aggregated form, that is, the three-digit level of the ISIC, which does not permit the user to arrange industries or products according to any ascending stage of processing. A smaller amount of data on commodity production (expressed in physical units) is compiled at a more detailed level and this source – the United Nations' *Yearbook of Industrial Statistics*, Vol. 2 – was used as a basis for examining production trends.

However, these data, too, are subject to certain weaknesses which should be noted. First, the coverage of countries sometimes varies, depending on the commodity or the year being considered. Where major producers are omitted, estimates of world production or its geographical distribution will obviously be distorted. To take one example, data on the production of cold-reduced steel hoop and strip includes only two LDCs, although other countries are certainly producing this item. And for other commodities (for example, zinc plates, sheets, strips or foil), major producers such as the USA are not reported. A related difficulty is that the national statistical classification of some countries does not always permit the reporting of data for each individual commodity. This eventuality emerges in the case of the USA, where production of steel castings is not reported separately but rather is lumped together with production of ingots. Finally, mention has been made elsewhere in this Appendix of the problem resulting from incomplete coverage of a country's manufacturing activities and the qualifications noted apply with equal force here.

With regard to estimates of trade by stage of processing (Tables 7.6 and 7.7), the general principles followed in developing this classification were outlined in Chapter 7. The trade of LDCs and Western countries was grouped into four product categories. The first of these was defined to include unprocessed goods which are exported and only later undergo some degree of industrial processing before they are ready for final consumption. A second category is those goods that are not processed before export but are ready for final use. All the items included in these two categories are supplied by primary sectors of the economy – agriculture, forestry, fishing, hunting or extractive industries. In addition, some items which are generally regarded as being at least partially processed are also included when nearly all their value is attributable to one of the primary sectors. Cotton, for example,

Table A.3 Industry Aggregations used to Measure Structural Change

ISIC	Light and heavy industries		Industries by end-use			Industries defined by income elasticities		
	Light	Heavy	Consumer non-durable	Industrial intermediate	Capital goods or consumer durables	Early industry	Middle industry	Late industry
311/2	×		×			×		
313	×		×			×		
314	×		×			×		
321	×		×			×		
322	×		×					×
323	×		×					×
324	×		×			×		×
331	×		×				×	
332	×		×				×	
341		×		×				×
342	×		×					×

351
352
353
354
355
356
361
362
369
371
372
381
382
383
384
385
390[a]

---

[a] Other manufactures (ISIC 390) is excluded from the definition of industries arranged by income elasticities.

undergoes a transformation when ginned, but most of the value of ginned cotton is the result of agricultural operations and the product is classified as unprocessed. Thus, the distinction between the two categories depends on the final user: goods used by industry comprise the first category while those consumed by households make up the second category. The third category is comprised of goods that are partly processed before they are exported and are processed further by industry in another country. The fourth category is those items which are processed by industry and are ready for final consumption by households before they are exported.

One weakness of this classification was mentioned in Chapter 7 and concerned the treatment of components used in the assembly of automobiles, electrical appliances, machine tools and so on. These were defined as finished goods, even though they are major inputs in the assembly of the final product. Another is the fact that various products (particularly food items) may be processed further by industry or, equally possible, they may be consumed by households in their existing form. Many food items can be placed in either category and the only way of distinguishing between processing stages is on an arbitrary, or conventional, basis. For example, food-grains which enter international trade are regarded as being for use in industry and therefore undergoing further processing, but fresh fruit and vegetables, even when traded internationally, are assumed to be ready for final consumption by households.

A more general shortcoming of the approach is that it fails to provide the user with a picture of trends in specific processing chains, that is, the series of successive stages of processing in which the output of one stage is the primary, or one of the primary, material inputs for the following stage. An example of such a chain is found in the case of oil-seeds where processing stages might include crushing, extracting and then refining before end-use. Such a resource-specific approach would be possible in certain cases but a more general application encounters several problems. One is that some processing chains 'explode'. The output of one or more processing stages becomes an input for several activities in the next phase and the identification of processing stages is obscured. A converse situation can also arise; at a given point in the processing chain inputs may be merged to produce a 'mixed' product such as tinplate or various chemical compounds. All these considerations have meant that a detailed rearrangement of trade statistics according to uniquely identified processing chains was not possible in most cases. The basis for development of the classification was United Nations (1970) which distinguishes between primary and processed goods destined for use either in households or industries and the reader will find a more complete description there.

With regard to measuring trade in manufactures, the 'infrastructure' for the collection of trade statistics in LDCs is more extensive than that available for other types of data. Because colonial administrations were particularly anxious to have information on their trade between the colony and the home market, the compilation of trade figures was begun long before other types of data were collected. Later, funds generated by tariffs came to be an important source of revenue for many of the poorer LDCs. More recently, the adoption of export-oriented strategies in many LDCs have focused attention on manufactured exports as a performance criterion. Trade statistics in Western countries have also come to be more relevant for policy-making purposes. The negotiation of voluntary export restraints, government decisions regarding the validity of industry appeals for protection and assessments of the extent to which imports have 'injured' a domestic industry are based on such data.

Despite these considerations, the accuracy of trade data can leave much to be desired. Most countries value imports on a cost-insurance-freight basis but several, including the USA, use other methods. Trade statistics are subject to intentional over- or under-invoicing, to avoid tariffs or other trade regulations. Traded items are sometimes incorrectly reported in other SITC categories and the composition of exports or imports is distorted as a result. Problems may arise in recording the trade flows of bordering countries, such as the USA and Canada, owing to the ease with which goods can be exchanged. These examples are only a few of the difficulties that may be encountered by users. Such issues, however, are not of direct relevance in studies of this type and more extensive discussion can be found elsewhere (e.g. Morgenstern, 1963; Yeats, 1978).

In the present study, the need to relate trade and production statistics gave rise to problems of another type, two of which are discussed here. One problem concerns the definition of manufactures. Exports of manufactures would ideally be expressed as that amount of value added (both direct and indirect) generated in the manufacturing sector to serve this purpose. However, it is seldom possible to estimate the portion of value added actually associated with manufactured exports. Instead, estimates of the value of manufactured exports are commonly built up from a process which first requires appropriate individual items to be identified and valued. However, the selection of these items introduces a degree of subjectivity and the researcher who wishes to measure the composition or growth of manufactured exports must choose from a number of alternative definitions. A survey of recent studies yield the following five versions:

(1) SITC 5 to 8 (United Nations, *Monthly Bulletin of Statistics*, March 1985, p. 21);
(2) SITC 5 to 9, excluding non-ferrous metals which is SITC 68 (World Bank, 1985, p. 235);
(3) SITC 5 to 8, less 'diamonds and gemstones' which is assumed to refer to SITC 667 (IMF, 1985, p. 198);
(4) SITC 5 to 8, excluding non-ferrous metals, SITC 68 (UNIDO, 1983, p. 190); and
(5) SITC 5 to 8, less SITC 67, iron and steel and SITC 68, non-ferrous metals (UNCTAD, 1984, Table 4.2).

These and other definitions are used by economists to measure export performance and change in various ways. Table A.4 provides a comparison of results for each of the five versions in terms of the estimated share of manufactures in total exports and rate of growth. The countries chosen for inclusion in the table are all major exporters of manufactures within their respective groups – the same list of countries as shown in Table 8.3. The results of the comparison provide some grounds for concern. Estimates of the share of manufactures in total exports reveal a fairly wide range. With the exceptions of Hong Kong, Pakistan and the USA the difference between the high and low estimate are at least 5 percentage points and for Singapore and Japan the range is 10 and 12.4 points, respectively. Variations in rates of growth were less widely dispersed. Estimated rates of growth in manufactured exports of India were between 9.1 and 17.4 per cent while those for Malaysia ranged from 15.9 to 22.9 per cent. Others, however, have observed surprisingly wide differences for some LDCs (Hill, 1985). In assessing the implications of the comparisons, the reader should note that evidence for only a few countries is considered. Inclusion of additional LDCs is almost certain to introduce even wider departures between respective estimates (see, e.g. Prakash, 1976). However, even the limited evidence presented here is sufficient to demonstrate the need for a more standardized approach to matters of statistical definition.

The analysis of the relationship between exports and manufacturing production illustrates another weakness of the available statistical definitions of manufactured exports. None of the five versions mentioned above constitute a bundle of goods which closely matches the list of products and processes included in production statistics for the manufacturing sector. The researcher is required to concord data based on two different, and largely incompatible, statistical systems. Previous writers (e.g. Keesing, 1979; Batchelor, Major and Morgan, 1980, Appendix C) have begun by adopting some definition of trade in manufactures specified in terms of the SITC and then selecting the relevant production data (derived from the ISIC) to approximate their definition. That approach suffers from two drawbacks. First, the range of domestic manufacturing activities associated with any measure of trade in manufactures is more limited than the concept of manufacturing employed in national accounts or industrial censuses. And, because the composition of output in the manufacturing sector varies widely among countries and over time, international comparisons of export/output ratios may be distorted. Second, production data are reported in a more aggregated form than trade statistics. Thus, it is difficult to arrange the former set of information to suit any predetermined definition expressed in terms of the SITC.

The export/output ratios used in Chapter 8 were compiled in a different manner. The traditional definition of the manufacturing sector (ISIC 300) was adopted as a starting point and the corresponding exports were then specified in terms of the SITC, rev. 1. For the reasons described above, this procedure led to the inclusion of certain industries ignored by researchers who choose to base their analysis on a definition of trade in manufactures. The industries in question depend mainly on the agricultural or mining sectors for their inputs and consist primarily of processing activities. Although value added per unit of output is relatively low in such industries, their contribution to export earnings and total manufacturing output is significant. For instance, if processing industries are regarded as those producing food, beverages, tobacco, petroleum and non-ferrous metals, their combined share in the MVA of all LDCs was 31 per cent in 1981, while the corresponding figure for Western countries was 15 per cent (UNIDO, 1985a, p. 12). Inclusion of these industries gave rise to a definition of trade in manufactures which is wider in scope than other, more commonly used, measures. Table A.5 shows the trade categories which make up the SITC equivalent of ISIC 300, along with an indication of remaining discrepancies.

Table A.4 Level and Growth of Manufactured Exports

	Share of manufactures in total exports, 1982					Growth rate of manufactured exports, 1975–82				
	A	B	C	D	E	A	B	C	D	E
LDCs										
Brazil	38.8	38.6	39.5	38.3	33.3	19.7	19.8	18.9	19.7	18.7
Hong Kong[c]	96.6	96.3	97.0	96.3	96.2	12.5	12.6	12.6	12.5	12.5
India[a] [f]	58.7	51.3	58.6	58.4	56.1	10.9	9.1	13.6	13.5	17.4
Malaysia[c]	28.3	28.2	23.1	22.8	22.7	15.9	15.9	22.5	22.9	22.9
Pakistan[d]	57.9	57.8	59.3	57.9	57.4	11.5	11.5	11.6	11.5	11.4
Singapore[c]	50.1	50.0	56.9	48.5	46.9	23.4	23.4	25.6	22.9	22.8
Korea, Republic of[b] [e]	91.5	91.5	91.0	90.9	83.4	18.7	18.7	18.6	18.6	18.1
Thailand	31.7	28.7	27.7	26.3	26.0	25.8	25.7	26.4	28.0	28.1

Western countries										
France	75.7	75.6	74.3	73.9	67.8	8.4	8.4	8.3	8.3	8.7
Italy	83.8	83.8	83.5	83.0	77.7	11.3	11.3	11.3	11.3	11.7
Japan	96.8	96.8	96.8	95.9	84.6	14.1	14.1	14.1	14.2	15.6
UK	67.5	65.7	67.8	65.1	62.8	8.7	9.1	8.8	8.6	8.7
USA	68.1	67.9	69.7	66.9	65.9	10.2	10.2	10.2	10.3	10.6
West Germany	87.1	86.8	86.9	85.0	79.4	9.8	9.7	9.7	9.7	10.3

Sources: United Nations, Commodity Trade Statistics, Series D, various issues; United Nations, Yearbook of International Trade Statistics, various issues; UNCTAD (1984).

a 1979.
b 1983.
c All growth rates are for the period 1976–82.
d All growth rates are for the period 1974–82.
e All growth rates are for the period 1976–83.
f All growth rates are for the period 1976–79.

Note: Definitions of trade in manufactures are as follows: A: SITC 5 to 8; B: SITC 5 to 8, less 667; C: SITC 5 to 9, less 68; D: SITC 5 to 8, less 68; E: SITC 5 to 8, less 67 and 68.

Table A.5 Approximate Concordance of SITC, rev. 1
with ISIC 300

Description of traded product (SITC, rev. 1)	Comments/discrepancies
Dried, salted or smoked meat (012)	
Meat preparations and meat in airtight containers (013)	
Milk and cream (022)	SITC includes fresh products outside ISIC 300. Trade in these items is assumed to be negligible.
Butter (023)	
Cheese and curd (024)	
Fish preparations and fish in airtight containers (032)	Certain SITC items (e.g. caviar, molluscs, etc.), which are processed on factory vessels, are not included in the ISIC.
Glazed or polished rice (0422)	
Meal and flour of wheat or meslin (046)	
Meal and flour of cereals (047)	
Preparations of cereal, flour and starch of fruits and vegetables (048)	
Preserved fruit and preparations (053)	
Preserved or prepared vegetables (055)	
Sugar and honey (061)	SITC includes items processed on farms.
Sugar confectionery and other preparations (062)	
Coffee extracts, essences and concentrates (0713)	SITC includes additional items processed on farms.
Cocoa powder, butter and paste (0722/3)	
Chocolate and related preparations (073)	
Tea and mate (074)	SITC includes additional items outside manufacturing.
Feeding stuff for animals (081)	SITC includes fresh feed and wastes which are not thought to be widely traded.
Margarine and shortening (091)	

326

Table A.5 (continued)

Description of traded product (SITC, rev. 1)	Comments/discrepancies
Other food preparations (099)	SITC includes minor items (e.g. soups and broths) which are not widely traded.
Non-alcoholic beverages (111)	
Alcoholic beverages (112)	
Tobacco manufactures (122)	
Flour and meal from oil-seeds, nuts and kernels (2219)	
Synthetic rubber (2312)	
Reclaimed rubber (2313)	
Wood, shaped or worked (243) items.	SITC includes certain agricultural items.
Pulp and waste paper (251)	
Wool shoddy, tops and other animal hair (2626–8)	
Cotton (263)	SITC includes raw cotton.
Synthetic and regenerated fibres (266)	
Petroleum products (332)	SITC includes natural gasoline.
Animal oils and fats (411)	SITC includes some agricultural items.
Vegetable oils and fats (421/2)	
Processed animal and vegetable oils (431)	SITC includes minor agricultural items.
Chemicals (5)	
Manufactures classified by material (6), less pearls and semi-precious stones (667)	Minor items from agriculture are included.
Machinery and transport equipment (7)	
Miscellaneous manufactures (8), less cinematographic film (863) and works of art (896).	

Source: Adapted from United Nations, *Classification of Commodities by Industrial Origin* (United Nations: New York), 1971.

Note: In addition to the discrepancies noted in the Table, other SITC categories which were not incorporated in the definition also contain items shown within ISIC 300. These trade categories were excluded because the bulk of the items are not traded.

Once a suitable matchup between the trade and production classifications was determined, a decision was required with regard to the concept of valuation to be used. In the case of production data, the usual practice is to express all figures on a net (value-added) basis and this concept has been used elsewhere in the book. However, trade statistics are compiled in terms of the gross value of the products, that is, the value of shipments, meaning that the cost of materials and services used in production and transport of the goods is also included. Because of this fact, the gross value of production data was used when estimating the share of exports in manufacturing production.

While this step means that the two sets of data are expressed according to concepts which are approximately comparable, difficulties can arise from the extensive exchange of intermediate products (inputs) between establishments in the same industry. These intra-industry sales, which are the result of specialization within industries, mean that production data stated in gross terms will contain an element of double counting once aggregate figures for the entire manufacturing sector are obtained. As a result of double counting, the share of exports in gross output will be underestimated. A related aspect is the fact that an increasing proportion of international trade consists of intermediate products. Thus the exports of an industry may include some portion of foreign value added, that is, the intermediate foreign input used to produce the exported product. Similarly, final products which are imported from abroad may contain domestically produced (and previously exported) inputs. For example, automobile components produced in Austria are exported to West Germany and then repurchased in the Austrian market where the German car is imported. The existence of international trade of this type will lead to an overestimate of the export share in gross output.

Finally, complete time series for the period 1970–80 were not always available for all countries shown in Tables 8.5 and 8.6 and estimates had to be made for some years. Complete information on MVA was available only from national accounts and referred to value added (not gross output). Moreover, these data are not necessarily compatible with existing figures for MVA or gross output, which are derived from industrial censuses or surveys and reported in the *Yearbook of Industrial Statistics*. The procedure followed was to calculate the ratio of value added reported by the two different sources (national accounts and censuses) for all available years in the period 1970–80. An unweighted average of these figures was then applied to MVA from national accounts to estimate census MVA for the missing years. Once the ratio between census MVA and gross output, both expressed at census levels, was obtained, a similar procedure was used to arrive at an estimate of gross output.

With regard to trade data, sufficient information to determine manufactured exports according to the ISIC equivalent were not available in a few instances. Estimates were made by first calculating the share of manufactures in total exports (SITC 0 to 9) in adjacent years (for example, 1971 or 1979). This share was then applied to the available figure for total exports in the year required. Whenever possible, re-exports were deducted from the trade data. Information was not available in the case of Singapore, a country where re-exports figure prominently. The share of re-exports in total exports for Hong Kong was therefore used as an estimate.

Bibliography

Abernathy, W. (1978), *The Productivity Dilemma: Roadblock to Innovation in the Automobile Industry* (Baltimore, Md: John Hopkins University Press).

Abernathy, W., Clark, K. and Kantrow, A. (1983), *Industrial Renaissance, Producing A Competitive Future for America* (New York: Basic Books).

Acs, Z. (1984), *The Changing Structure of the U.S. Economy: Lessons from the Steel Industry* (New York: Praeger).

Adams, F. (1983), 'Criteria for U.S. industrial policy strategies', in F. Adams and L. Klein, (eds), *Industrial Policies for Growth and Competitiveness* (Lexington, Mass.: D C Heath), pp. 393–420.

Aho, C. and Bayard, T. (1982), 'The 1980s: twilight of the open trading system?', *The World Economy*, vol. 5, no. 4, pp. 379–406.

AISI (1978), *The Economic Implications of Foreign Steel Pricing Practices* (Washington, DC: AISI).

AISI (1980), *Steel at the Crossroads: the American Steel Industry in the 1980s* (Washington, DC: AISI).

Altshuler, A., Anderson, M., Jones, D., Roos, D. and Womack, J. (1984), *The Future of the Automobile: The Report of MIT's International Automobile Programme* (Cambridge, Mass.: MIT Press).

Amsalem, M. (1984), 'Bauxite, copper and oil: bargaining power and the economies of natural resources', *Columbia Journal of World Business*, vol. 19, no. 1, pp. 19–25.

Arad, R. and Hirsch, S. (1981), 'Determination of trade flows and the choice of trade partners: reconciling the Heckscher-Ohlin and the Burenstein Linder models of international trade', *Weltwirtschaftliches Archiv*, vol. 117, no. 2, pp. 276–97.

Ariff, M. and Hill, H. (1985), *Export-Oriented Industrialisation: The ASEAN Experience* (London: George Allen & Unwin).

Arndt, H. (1985), 'The origins of structuralism', *World Development*, vol. 13, no. 2, pp. 151–59.

Bacon, T. and Eltis, W. (1976), *Britain's Economic Problem: Too Few Producers* (London: Macmillan).

Balassa, B. (1965), 'Trade liberalisation and "revealed" comparative advantage', *Manchester School of Economic and Social Studies*, vol. 33, no. 2, pp. 99–123.

330

Balassa, B. (1977), ' "Revealed" comparative advantage revisited: an analysis of relative export shares of the industrial countries, 1953–1971', *Manchester School of Economic and Social Studies*, vol. 45, no. 4, pp. 327–44.

Balassa, B. (1978a), 'The new protectionism and the international economy', *Journal of World Trade Law*, vol. 12, no. 5, pp. 409–36.

Balassa, B. (1978b), 'Exports and economic growth: further evidence', *Journal of Development Economics*, vol. 5, no. 2, pp. 181–89.

Balassa, B. (1978c), 'Export incentives and export performance in developing countries: a comparative analysis', *Weltwirtschaftliches Archiv*, vol. 114, no. 1, pp. 24–51.

Balassa, B. (1979a), 'The changing pattern of comparative advantage in manufactured goods', *Review of Economics and Statistics*, vol. 61, no. 2, pp. 259–66.

Balassa, B. (1979b), 'A "stages approach" to comparative advantage' in I. Adelman (ed), *Economic Growth and Resources*, vol. 4 (London: Macmillan), pp. 121–56.

Balassa, B. (1980), 'Structural change in trade in manufactured goods between industrial and developing countries' (Washington, DC: World Bank. Staff Working Paper no. 396).

Balassa, B. (1983), 'Industrial prospects and policies in the developed countries', in F. Machlup, G. Fels and H. Müller-Groeling (eds) *Reflections on a Troubled Economy* (London: Macmillan for the Trade Policy Research Centre), pp. 257–78.

Baldwin, R. (1970), *Nontariff Distortion of International Trade* (Washington, DC: Brookings Institution).

Baldwin, R. (1971), 'Determinants of the commodity structure of U.S. trade', *American Economic Review*, vol. 61, no. 1, pp. 126–46.

Ballance, R. (1985), *Shrinking Demand in an Ageing Industry: The Case of Steel* (Laxenburg, Austria: International Institute for Applied Systems Analysis).

Ballance, R., Ansari, J. and Singer, H. (1982), *The International Economy and Industrial Development* (Brighton: Harvester Press).

Ballance, R. and Sinclair, S. (1983), *Collapse and Survival: Industry Strategies in a Changing World* (London: George Allen & Unwin).

Ballance, R. and Sinclair, S. (1984), 'Re-industrialising America: policy makers and interest groups', *The World Economy*, vol. 7, no. 2, pp. 197–214.

Barnett, D. and Schorsch, L. (1983), *Steel: Upheaval in a Basic Industry* (Cambridge, Mass.: Ballinger).

Batchelor, R., Major, R. and Morgan, A. (1980), *Industrialization and the Basis for Trade* (Cambridge: Cambridge University Press for the National Institute of Economic and Social Research).

Bergsten, F., Horst, T. and Moran, T. (1978), *American Multinationals and American Interests* (Washington, DC: Brookings Institution).

Berndt, E. and Christensen, L. (1973), 'Testing for the existence of a consistent aggregate index of labor inputs', *American Economic Review*, vol. 64, no. 3, pp. 391–404.

Bhagwati, J. (1984), 'Splintering and disembodiment of services and developing nations', *The World Economy*, vol. 7, no. 2, pp. 133–43.

Bhalla, A. (1975), 'The concept and measurement of labour intensity', in A. Bhalla (ed.), *Technology and Employment in Industry: A Case Study Approach* (Geneva: International Labour Office), pp. 11–33.

Blackaby, F. (ed.) (1978), *De-industrialisation* (London: Heinemann).

Bluestone, B. and Harrison, B. (1982), *The Deindustrialization of America* (New York: Basic Books).

Bowden, R. (1983), 'The conceptual basis of empirical studies of trade in manufactured commodities: a constructive critique', *The Manchester School of Economic and Social Studies*, vol. 51, no. 3, pp. 209–34.

Bowen, H. (1983), 'Changes in the international distribution of resources and their impact on U.S. comparative advantage', *Review of Economics and Statistics*, vol. 65, no. 3, pp. 402–14.

Branson, W. and Junz, H. (1971), 'Trends in U.S. trade and comparative advantage', *Brookings Papers on Economic Activity*, no. 2, pp. 285–338.

Braun, E. and Macdonald, S. (1982), *Revolution in Miniature* (Cambridge: Cambridge University Press).

Bressand, A. (1983), 'Mastering the "world economy" ', *Foreign Affairs*, Spring 1983, pp. 745–72.

Brock, G. (1975), *The US Computer Industry: A Study of Market Power* (Cambridge, Mass.: Ballinger).

Brock, W. and Magee, S. (1978), 'The economics of special interest politics: the case of the tariff', *American Economic Review*, vol. 68, no. 2, pp. 246–50.

Brown, C. and Sheriff, T. (1978), 'De-industrialisation: a background paper' in F. Blackaby, op. cit., pp. 233–62.

Cable, V. and Clarke, J. (1981), *British Electronics and Competition with Newly Industrialising Countries* (London: Overseas Development Institute).

Cable, V. and Clarke, J. (1982), 'The Asian electronics industry looks to the future', *Institute of Development Studies Bulletin*, vol. 13, no. 2, pp. 24–34.

Cardoso, H. (1973), 'Associated-dependent development: theoretical and practical implications', in A. Stepan (ed) *Authoritarian Brazil: Origins, Politics, and Future* (New Haven, Conn.: Yale University Press), pp. 142–76.

Caves, R. (1980), 'Industrial organization, corporate strategy and structure', *Journal of Economic Literature*, vol. 18, no. 1, p. 64–92.

Chenery, H. (1960), 'Patterns of industrial growth', *American*

Economic Review, vol. 50, no. 4, pp. 624–54.

Chenery, H. (1977), 'Transitional growth and world industrialization' in B. Ohlin, P. Hesselborn and P. Wijkman (eds) *The International Allocation of Economic Activity* (London: Macmillan), pp. 457–90.

Chenery, H. (1979), *Structural Change and Development Policy* (Oxford: Oxford University Press for the World Bank).

Chenery, H. and Taylor, L. (1968), 'Development patterns: among countries and over time', *Review of Economics and Statistics*, vol. 50, no. 4, pp. 391–415.

Chenery, H. and Syrquin, M. (1975), *Patterns of Development 1950–1970* (Oxford: Oxford University Press for the World Bank).

Choi, K. (1983), *Theories of Comparative Economic Growth* (Ames, Iowa: Iowa State University Press).

Choi, Y-P., Chung, H. and Marian, N. (1985), *The Multi-fibre Arrangement in Theory and Practice* (London: Frances Pinter).

Clark, C. (1940), *The Conditions of Economic Progress* (London: Macmillan).

Cline, W. (1982), *"Reciprocity": A New Approach to World Trade Policy* (Washington, DC: Institute for International Economies).

Cooper, R. (1973), 'Trade policy is foreign policy', in R. Cooper (ed) *A Reordered World* (Washington, DC: Potomac Associates), pp. 46–64.

Cooper, R. (1985), 'Economic interdependence and coordination of economic policies', in R. Jones and P. Kenen (eds), *Handbook of International Economics*, Vol. 2 (Amsterdam: North-Holland) pp. 1196–234.

Corbo, V. and Meller, P. (1982), 'The substitution of labor, skill and capital: its implications for trade and employment', in A. Krueger, op. cit., pp. 193–213.

Corden, W. (1971), *The Theory of Protection* (Oxford: Clarendon Press).

Corden, W. (1974), *Trade Policy and Economic Welfare* (Oxford: Clarendon Press).

Corden, W. (1984), 'Booming sector and Dutch disease economics: survey and consolidation,' *Oxford Economic Papers*, vol. 36, no. 3, pp. 359–80.

Deardorff, A. (1984), 'Testing trade theories and predicting trade flows', in R. Jones and P. Kenen (eds) *Handbook of International Economics*, Vol. 1 (Amsterdam: North-Holland), pp. 467–517.

Denison, E. (1963), *Accounting for United States Economic Growth, 1929–1969*, (Washington DC: Brookings Institution).

Destler, I. (1980), *Making Foreign Economic Policy* (Washington, DC: Brooking Institution).

Donges, J. and Riedel, J. (1977), 'The expansion of manufactured exports in developing countries: an empirical assessment of supply and demand issues', *Weltwirtschaftliches Archiv*, vol. 113, no. 1, pp. 58–87.

333

Dosi, G. (1981), *Technical Change and Survival: Europe's Semiconductor Industry* (Brighton: Sussex European Research Centre).

Driscoll, R. and Behrman, J. (1984), *National Industrial Policies* (Cambridge, Mass.: Oelgeschlager, Gunn and Hain).

Duijn, J. van (1980), 'Another look at industry growth patterns' (College of Commerce, University of Illinois at Urbana-Champaign, Faculty Working Paper no. 667).

Duijn, J. van (1983), *The Long Wave in Economic Life* (London: George Allen & Unwin).

ECE (1974), *Annual Review of the Chemical Industry* (Geneva: United Nations).

ECE (1981), *Annual Review of the Chemical Industry* (Geneva: United Nations).

ECE (1982), *Market Trends for Chemical Products 1975–1980 and Prospects to 1990* (Geneva: United Nations).

ECE (1985), *Production and Use of Industrial Robots* (New York: United Nations).

ECE (1986), *Recent Trends in Flexible Manufacturing* (New York: United Nations).

Emery, R. (1967), 'The relation of exports and economic growth', *Kyklos*, vol. 20, no., 2, pp. 470–86.

Emmanuel, A. (1976), 'The multinational corporations and the inequality of development', *International Social Science Journal*, vol. 28, no. 4, pp. 760–64.

Erzan, R. (1983), *Turkey's Comparative Advantage, Production and Trade Patterns in Manufactures* (Institute for International Economic Studies, University of Stockholm, Monograph, Series, no. 14).

ESCAP (1983), *Transnational Corporations and the Distribution of Gains in the Bauxite/Aluminium Industry of Malaysia* (Bangkok: ESCAP).

Falvey, R. (1981), 'Commercial policy and intra-industry trade', *Journal of International Economics*, vol. 11, no. 4, pp. 495–511.

Fattah, Z. (1979), 'Development and structural change in the Iraqi economy and manufacturing industry: 1960–1970', *World Development*, vol. 7, no. 8/9, pp. 813–24.

Finger, M. (1975), 'A new view of the product cycle theory', *Weltwirtschaftliches Archiv*, vol. 111, no. 1, pp. 79–99.

Finger, M. and Yates, A. (1976), 'Effective protection by transportation costs and tariffs: a comparison of magnitudes', *Quarterly Journal of Economics*, vol. 40, no. 1, pp. 169–76.

Finger, M., Hall, H. and Nelson, D. (1982), 'The political economy of administered protection', *American Economic Review*, vol. 72, no. 3, pp. 452–66.

Fisher, A. (1939), 'Production, primary, secondary and tertiary', *Economic Record*, vol. 15, no. 1, pp. 24–38.

Flaherty, M. (1984), 'Field research on the link between technological innovation and growth: evidence from the international semiconductor industry', *American Economic Review*, vol. 74, no. 2, pp. 67–72.

Flammang, R. (1979), 'Economic growth and economic development: counterparts or competitors?', *Economic Development and Cultural Change*, vol. 28, no. 1, pp. 47–61.

Flanders, J. (1969), 'Agriculture versus industry in development policy: the planner's dilemma re-examined', *Journal of Development Studies*, vol. 5, no., 3, pp. 171–89.

Fong, C., Lim, K., Cheong, K. and Lin, T. (1981), *Comparative Advantage of Iron and Steel, Petro-chemical and Plastic Products Industries in Malaysia* (Tokyo: Institute of Developing Economies).

Forsyth, P. and Nicholas, S. (1983), 'The decline of Spanish industry and the price of revolution: a neoclassical analysis', *Journal of European Economic History*, vol. 12, no. 4, pp. 601–609.

Frank, I. (1961), *The European Common Market: An Analysis of Commercial Policy* (New York: Praeger).

Freeman, C. (1982), *The Economics of Industrial Innovation*, second edition, (Cambridge, Mass.: MIT Press).

Freeman, C., Clark, J. and Soete, L., (1982), *Unemployment and Technical Innovation: A Study of Long Waves of Economic Development* (London: Frances Pinter).

Frey, B. and Schneider, F. (1984), 'International political economy: a rising field', *Economia Internazionale*, vol. 37, no. 3–4, pp. 308–47.

Galbraith, K., (1967), *The New Industrial State* (Boston, Mass.: Houghton Mifflin).

Garnaut, R. and Clunies Ross, A. (1983), *Taxation of Mineral Rents* (London: Oxford University Press).

✓ GATT (1984), *Textiles and Clothing in the World Economy* (Geneva: GATT).

Geroski, P. and Jacquemin, A. (1985), 'Industrial change, barriers to mobility, and European industrial policy', *Economic Policy*, no. 1, pp. 170–218.

Giersch, H. (ed.) (1982), *Emerging Technologies: Consequences for Economic Growth, Structural Change, and Employment* (Tübingen: J.C.B. Mohr).

Giersch, H. and Wolter, F. (1983), 'Towards an explanation of the productivity slowdown: an acceleration-deceleration hypothesis', *Economic Journal*, vol. 98, no. 369, pp. 35–55.

Greenaway, D. (ed.) (1985), *Current Issues in International Trade* (London: Macmillan).

Greenaway, D. and Hindley, B. (1985), *What Britain Pays for Voluntary Export Restraints* (London: Trade Policy Research Centre).

Gregory, P. and Griffin, J. (1974), 'Secular and cross-section industrialization patterns: some further evidence on the Kuznets-Chenery controversy', *Review of Economics and Statistics*, vol. 56, no. 3, pp. 360–68.

Grieco, J. (1982), 'Between dependency and autonomy: India's experience with the international computer industry', *International Organization*, vol. 36, no. 3, pp. 609–32.

Grossman, G. (1981), 'The theory of domestic content protection and content preference', *Quarterly Journal of Economics*, vol. 96, no. 4, pp. 583–603.

Grunwald, J. and Flamm, K. (1985), *The Global Factory, Foreign Assembly in International Trade* (Washington, DC: Brookings Institution).

Guisinger, S. (1977), 'Patterns of industrial growth in Pakistan', *Pakistan Development Review*, vol. 17, no. 1, pp. 8–27.

Gupta, K. (1971), 'Development patterns: an interregional study', *Quarterly Journal of Economics*, vol. 85, no. 4, pp. 644–66.

Hadley, E. (1983), 'The secret of Japan's success', *Challenge*, vol. 26, no. 2, pp. 4–10.

Hamberg, D. (1966), *R and D: Essays in the Economics of Research and Development* (New York: Random House).

Hamilton, C. and Svensson, L. (1983), 'Should direct or total factor intensities be used in tests of the factor proportion hypothesis?', *Weltwirtschaftliches Archiv*, vol. 119, no. 3, pp. 453–63.

Hamilton, C. and Svensson, L. (1984), 'Do countries' factor endowments correspond to the factor contents in their bilateral trade flows?', *Scandinavian Journal of Economics*, vol. 86, no. 1, pp. 84–97.

Hansen, A. (1939), 'Economic progress and declining population growth', *American Economic Review*, vol. 29, no. 1, pp. 1–15.

✓ Hazewindus, N. (1982), *The U.S. Microelectronics Industry* (New York: Pergamon Press).

Helleiner, G. (1973), 'Manufactured exports from less-developed countries and multinational firms', *Economic Journal*, vol. 83, no. 329, pp. 21–47.

Hill, T. (1977), 'On goods and services', *Review of Income and Wealth*, vol. 23, no. 4, pp. 315–38.

Hill, H. (1985), 'LDC manufactured exports: do definitions matter?' (Canberra: Australian National University), mimeo.

Hirsch, S. (1967), *Location of Industry and International Competitiveness* (Oxford: Clarendon Press).

Hirsch, S. (1974), 'Capital or technology? confronting the neo-factor propositions and neo-technology accounts of international trade', *Weltwirtschaftliches Archiv*, vol. 110, no. 4, pp. 535–63.

Hirschman, A. (1968), 'The political economy of import-substituting industrialization in Latin America', *Quarterly Journal of Economics*, vol. 82, no. 1, pp. 1–32.

Hirschman, A. (1981), *Essays in Trespassing* (London: Cambridge University Press).

Hoffman, W. (1958), *The Growth of Industrial Economies* (Manchester: Manchester University Press).

Hoffman, S. (1977), 'An American social science: international relations', *Daedalus*, vol. 106, no. 3, pp. 41–60.

Hoover, C. (1946), 'The future of the German economy', *American Economic Review*, vol. 36, no. 2, pp. 642–49.

Hymer, S. (1972), 'The multinational corporation and the law of uneven development', in J. Bhagwati (ed.), *Economics and World Order: From the 1970s to the 1980s* (New York: Free Press).

IDE (1980), *The Electronics Industry in Japan* (Tokyo: IDE).

IISI (1982), *Indirect Trade in Steel – 1962 to 1979* (Brussels: IISI).

IISI (1985), 'Chairman's address to the nineteenth annual meeting and conference', (Brussels: IISI, IISI/E/1903/0).

ILO (annual), *ILO Yearbook* (Geneva: ILO).

IMF (1985), *World Economic Outlook* (Washington, DC: IMF).

Interfutures (1979), *Facing the Future: Mastering the Probable and Managing the Unpredictable* (Paris: OECD).

Jameson, K. (1975), 'Development patterns and regional imbalance in Brazil, *Review of Economics and Statistics*, vol. 57, no. 5, pp. 361–4.

Jameson, K. (1982), 'A critical examination of "The Patterns of Development" ', *Journal of Development Studies*, vol. 18, no. 4, pp. 431–46.

Johnson, H. (1966) 'Factor market distortions and the shape of the transformation curve', *Econometrica*, vol. 34, no. 4, pp. 686–98.

Johnson, H. (1975), *Technology and Economic Interdependence* (London: Macmillan).

Jones, D. (1981), *Maturity and Crisis in the European Car Industry: Structural Change and Public Policy* (Brighton: Sussex European Research Centre).

Jones, D. and Womack, J. (1985), 'Developing countries and the future of the automobile industry', *World Development*, vol. 13, no. 3, pp. 393–407.

Jones, K. (1979), 'Forgetfulness of things past: Europe and the steel cartel', *The World Economy*, vol. 2, no. 2, pp. 139–54.

Jones, K. (1984), 'The political economy of voluntary export restraint agreements', *Kyklos*, no. 1, vol. 37, pp. 82–101.

Jones, K. (1985), *Impasse and Crisis in Steel Trade Policy* (London: Trade Policy Research Centre).

Jones, K. (1986), 'Trade in steel: another turn in the protectionist spiral', *The World Economy*, vol. 8, no. 4, pp. 393–408.

Kaldor, N. (1966), *Causes of the Slow Rate of Economic Growth of the United Kingdom*, (Cambridge: Cambridge University Press).

Kaplinsky, R. (1982), *Computer Aided Design: Electronics, Comparative Advantage and Development* (London: Frances Pinter).

Kaplinsky, R. (1984), *Automation* (London: Longman).

Katz, B. and Phillips, A. (1982), 'Government, technological opportunities and the emergence of the computer industry', In H. Giersch (ed.), op. cit., pp. 419–69.

Kawahito, K. (1981), 'Japanese steel in the American market: conflict and causes', *The World Economy*, vol. 4, no. 3, pp. 229–50.

Keesing, D. (1966), 'Labor skills and comparative advantage', *American Economic Review, papers and proceedings*, vol. 56, no. 2, pp. 249–58.

Keesing, D. (1971), 'Different countries' labor skill coefficients and the skill intensity of international trade flows', *Journal of International Economics*, vol. 1, no. 4, pp. 443–52.

Keesing, D. (1979), *World Trade and Output of Manufactures: Structural Trends and Developing Countries' Exports*, Washington, DC, World Bank (Staff Working Paper no. 316).

Keesing, D. and Wolf, M. (1980), *Textile Quotas against Developing Countries* (London: Trade Policy Research Centre).

Kemp, T. (1978), *Historical Patterns of Industrialization* (London: Longman).

Kenen, P. (1965), 'Nature, capital and trade', *Journal of Political Economy*, vol. 73, no. 4, pp. 437–70.

Kenen, P. (1970), 'Labor skills and the structure of trade in manufactures', in P. Kenen and R. Lawrence (eds), *The Open Economy* (New York: Columbia University Press), pp. 3–18.

Keohane, R. (1984), *After Hegemony: Cooperation and Discord in the World Political Economy* (Princeton, NJ: Princeton University Press).

Keohane, R. and Nye, J. (1977), *Power and Interdependence: World Politics in Transition* (Boston, Mass.: Little, Brown).

Killick, T. (1976), 'The possibilities of development planning', *Oxford Economic Papers*, vol. 28, no. 2, pp. 161–84.

Killick, T. (1980), 'Trends in development economics and their relevance to Africa', *The Journal of Modern African Studies*, vol. 18, no. 3, pp. 367–86.

Killick, T. (1983), 'Development planning in Africa: experiences, weaknesses and prescriptions', *Development Policy Review*, vol. 1, no. 1, pp. 47–76.

Kilpatrick, P. and Lawson, T. (1980), 'On the nature of industrial decline in the UK', *Cambridge Journal of Economics*, vol. 4, no. 1, pp. 85–102.

Kindleberger, C. (1969), *American Business Abroad: Six Lectures on Direct Investment* (New Haven, Conn.: Yale University Press).

Kindleberger, C. (1973), *The World in Depression, 1919–1939* (London: Allen Lane).

Kindleberger, C. (1978), 'The aging economy', *Weltwirtschaftliches Archiv*, vol. 114, no. 3, pp. 407–21.

Kirkpatrick, C., Lee, N. and Nixson, F. (1984), *Industrial Structure and Policy in Less Developed Countries* (London: George Allen & Unwin).

Kotler, P., Fahey, L. and Jatusripitak, S. (1985), *The New Competition* (Englewood Cliffs, NJ: Prentice Hall).

338

Krause, L. (1968), *European Economic Integration and the United States* (Washington, DC: Brookings Institution).

Krause, L. (1982), *U.S. Economic Policy Towards the Association of Southeast Asian Nations: Meeting the Japanese Challenge* (Washington DC: Brookings Institution).

Krauss, M. (1979), *The New Protectionism, The Welfare State and International Trade* (Oxford: Blackwell).

Kravis, I. (1956), 'Wages and foreign trade', *Review of Economics and Statistics*, vol. 38, no. 1, pp. 14–30.

Kravis, I. (1970), 'Trade as a handmaiden of growth: similarities between the nineteenth and twentieth centuries', *Economic Journal*, vol. 80, no. 320, pp. 850–72.

Kronish, R. and Mericle, K. (1984), *The Political Economy of the Latin American Motor Industry* (Cambridge, Mass.: MIT Press).

Krueger, A. (ed.) (1982), *Trade and Employment in Developing Countries, Vol. 2, Factor Supply and Substitution* (Chicago: University of Chicago Press for National Bureau of Economic Research).

Krugman, P. (1982), 'Technology Gaps, Technology Transfers and the Changing Character of US Trade' (Cambridge, Mass.: National Bureau of Economic Research) mimeo.

Krugman, P. (1983), 'Targeted industrial policies: theory and evidence', in *Federal Reserve Bank of Kansas City*, pp. 123–55.

Krugman, P. (1984), 'The U.S. response to foreign industrial targeting', *Brookings Papers on Economic Activity*, pp. 77–131.

Kuznets, S. (1930), *Secular Movements in Production and Prices – Their Nature and their Bearing upon Cyclical Fluctuations* (Boston, Mass.: Houghton Mifflin).

Kuznets, S. (1965), *Economic Growth and Structure: Selected Essays* (New York: W.W. Norton).

Kuznets, S. (1966), *Modern Economic Growth: Rate, Structure and Spread* (New Haven, Conn. and London: Yale University Press).

Kuznets, S. (1967), 'Quantitative aspects of the economic growth of nations. Level and structure of foreign trade: long term trends', *Economic Development and Cultural Change*, vol. 15, no. 2, part 2, pp. 1–140.

Kuznets, S. (1971), *Economic Growth of Nations* (Cambridge, Mass.: Harvard University Press).

Lary, H. (1968), *Imports of Manufactures from Less Developed Countries* (New York: Columbia University Press).

Lawrence, C. and Lawrence, R. (1985), 'Manufacturing wage dispersion: an end game interpretation', in W. Brainard and G. Perry (eds), *Brookings Papers on Economic Activity*, vol. 1, pp. 47–116.

Lawrence, R. (1984), *Can America Compete?* (Washington, DC: Brookings Institution).

Leveson, L. and Wheeler, J. (ed.) (1980), *Western Economies in Transition* (Boulder, Colo: Westview Press).

Lewis, A. (1980), 'The slowing down of the engine of growth', *American Economic Review*, vol. 70, no. 4, pp. 555–64.

Lewis, A. (1981), 'The rate and growth of world trade, 1830–1973', in S. Grassman and E. Lundberg (eds) *The World Economic Order: Past and Prospects*, (London: Macmillan Press).

Lindbeck, A. (1981), 'Industrial policy as an issue in the economic environment', *The World Economy*, vol. 4, no. 4, pp. 391–406.

Linder, S. (1961), *An Essay on Trade and Transformation* (New York: John Wiley and Sons).

Little, I. (1982), *Economic Development: Theory, Policy and International Relations* (New York: Basic Books).

Machlup, F. (1958), 'Structure and structural change: weaselwords and jargon', *Zeitschrift für Nationalökonomie*, Band 18, pp. 280–98.

Maddison, A. (1979), 'Per capita output in the long run', *Kyklos*, vol. 32, no. 1/2, pp. 412–29.

Maddison, A. (1980), 'Western economic performance in the 1970s: a perspective and assessment', *Banca Nazionale del Lavoro Quarterly Review*, vol. 134, September, pp. 247–89.

Maddock, R. and McLean, I. (1984), 'Supply side shocks: the case of Australian Gold', *Journal of Economic History*, vol. 44, no. 4, pp. 1047–67.

Magaziner, I. and Reich, R. (1982), *Minding America's Business: The Decline and Rise of the American Economy* (New York: Harcourt Brace Jovanovich).

Magee, S. (1980), *International Trade* (Reading, Mass.: Addison-Wesley).

Maizels, A. (1970), *Growth and Trade*, (Cambridge: Cambridge University Press).

Majumdar, B. (1979), 'Innovations and international trade: an industry study of dynamic comparative advantage', *Kyklos*, vol. 32, no. 3, pp. 559–70.

Maxcy, G. (1981), *The Multinational Motor Industry* (London: Croom Helm).

Melman, S. (1983), *Profits without Production* (New York: Alfred A. Knopf).

Michaely, M. (1983), 'Trade in a changed world economy', *World Development*, vol. 11, no. 5, pp. 397–403.

Michalski, W. (1978), 'Wishful thinking and reality in the concept of vertical integration in developing countries in metal production', *Resources Policy*, vol. 4, no. 3, pp. 205–209.

Mikesell, R. (1975), *Foreign Investment in Copper Mining* (Baltimore, Md: Johns Hopkins University Press).

Moore, W. (1975), *International Trade Policy in Transition* (Lexington, Mass.: D.C. Heath and Company).

Morawetz, D. (1976), 'Elasticities of substitution in industry: what do we learn from econometric estimates?', *World Development*, 1976, vol. 4, no. 1, pp. 11–15.

Morawetz, D. (1977), *Twenty-five Years of Economic Development 1950–1975* (Baltimore, Md: Johns Hopkins University Press for the World Bank).

Morgenstern, O. (1963), *On the Accuracy of Economic Observations* (Princeton, NJ: Princeton University Press).

Mueller, D. (ed.) (1983), *The Political Economy of Growth* (New Haven, Conn.: Yale University Press).

Mueller, H. and Van der Ven, H. (1982), 'Perils in the Brussels-Washington Steel Pact', *The World Economy*, vol. 5, no. 3, pp. 259–78.

Murray, T., Schmidt, W. and Walter, I. (1978), 'Alternative forms of protection against market disruption', *Kyklos*, vol. 31, no. 4, pp. 624–37.

Murrell, P. (1982), 'The comparative structure of growth in the major developed capitalist nations', *Southern Economic Journal*, vol. 48, no. 4, pp. 985–95.

Norton, R. (1986), 'Industrial policy and American renewal', *Journal of Economic Literature*, vol. 24, no. 1, pp. 1–40.

O'Connor, D. (1985), 'The computer industry in the third world: policy options and constraints', *World Development*, vol. 13, no. 3, pp. 311–32.

Odaka, K. (ed.) (1983), *The Motor Vehicle Industry in Asia: A study of Ancillary Firm Development* (Singapore: Singapore University Press).

OECD (1977), *The Iron and Steel Industry in 1975* (Paris: OECD).

OECD (1984), *Industrial Structure Statistics, 1982* (Paris: OECD).

OECD (1986), *National Accounts, Vol. 1, 1960–84* (Paris: OECD).

OECD (annual), *Labour Force Statistics* (Paris: OECD).

Ohlin, G. (1978), 'Subsidies and other industrial aids', *International Trade and Industrial Policies*, S. Warnecke (ed.) (London: Macmillan), pp. 21–34.

Ohmae, K. (1985), *Triad Power: The Coming Shape of Global Competition* (New York: Macmillan).

Olechowski, A. and Sampson, G. (1980), 'Current trade restrictions in the EEC, the United States and Japan', *Journal of World Trade Law*, vol. 14, no. 3, pp. 220–31.

Olson, M. (1965), *The Logic of Collective Action* (Cambridge, Mass.: Harvard University Press).

Olson, M. (1982a), 'Stagflation and the political economy of the decline in productivity', *American Economic Review, Papers and Proceedings*, vol. 72, no. 2, pp. 143–48.

Olson, M. (1982b), *The Rise and Decline of Nations* (New Haven, Conn.: Yale University Press).

Olson, M. (1983), 'The south will fall again: the south as leader and laggard in economic growth' *Southern Economic Journal*, vol. 49, no. 4, pp. 917–32.

Oster, S. (1982), 'Intraindustry structure and the case of strategic change', *Review of Economics and Statistics*, vol. 64, no. 3, pp. 376–83.

Ozawa, T. (1980), 'Japan's new resource diplomacy: government-backed group investment', *Journal of World Trade Law*, vol. 14, no. 1, pp. 3–13.

Page, S. (1982), *The Management of International Trade*, Discussion Paper no. 29 (London: National Institute of Economic and Social Research).

Pasinetti, L. (1981), *Structural Change and Economic Growth: A Theoretical Essay on the Dynamics of the Wealth of Nations* (Cambridge: Cambridge University Press).

Peck, M. and Wilson, R. (1982), 'Innovation, imitation and comparative advantage: the performance of Japanese color television set producers in the U.S. market', in H. Giersch (ed.) op. cit., pp. 195–218.

Pelzman, J. (1983), 'Economic costs of tariffs and quotas on textile and apparel products imported into the United States: a survey of the literature and implications for policies', *Weltwirtschaftliches Archiv*, vol. 119, no. 3, pp. 523–42.

Pinchot, G. (1984), *Intrapreneuring* (New York: Harper and Row).

Pinder, J., Hosomi, T. and Diebold, A. (1979), *Industrial Policy and the International Economy* (New York: Trilateral Commission).

Plessz, N. (1981), 'Western Europe' in C. Saunders (ed.) *The Political Economy of New and Old Industrial Countries* (London: Butterworth and Company), pp. 217–39.

Pollard, S. (1981), *Peaceful Conquest: The Industrialization of Europe 1760–1970* (Oxford: Oxford University Press).

Pomfret, R. (1985), 'Discrimination in international trade: extent, motivation and implications', *Economica Internazionale*, vol. 38, no. 1, pp. 49–65.

Porter, M. (1979), 'The structure within industries and companies' performance', *Review of Economics and Statistics*, vol. 61, no. 2, pp. 214–28.

Porter, M. (1985), *Competitive Advantage* (New York: Free Press).

Posner, M. (1961), 'International trade and technical change', *Oxford Economic Papers*, vol. 13, no. 4, pp. 323–41.

Prakash, V. (1974), *Statistical Indicators of Industrial Development: A Critique of the Basic Data*, Washington, DC, World Bank (Staff Working Paper no. 189).

Prakash, V. (1976), *Measuring Industrial Exports: A Comparative Study of Variations Arising from Differences of Definition*, Washington, DC, World Bank (Staff Working Paper no. 225).

Prebisch, R. (1950), *The Economic Development of Latin America and its Principal Problems* (Lake Success, NY: United Nations).

Pugel, T., Kimura, Y. and Hawkins, R. (1982), 'Semiconductors and Computers: Emerging International Competitive Battle-grounds' (New York University), mimeo.

Pugel, T. and Walter, I. (1985), 'U.S. corporate interests and the political economy of trade policy', *Review of Economics and Statistics*, vol. 67, no. 3, pp. 465–73.

Rangarajan, L. (1984), 'The politics of international trade', in S. Strange (ed.), *Paths to International Political Economy* (London: George Allen & Unwin), pp. 126–63.

Ranis, G. (1984), 'Typology in development theory: retrospective and prospects', in M. Syrquin, L. Taylor and L. Westphal (eds), *Economic Structure and Performance* (Orlando, Fla: Academic Press), pp. 23–44.

Ray, E. and Marvel, H. (1984), 'The pattern of protection in the industrialized world', *Review of Economics and Statistics*, vol. 66, no. 3, pp. 452–58.

Reich, R. (1982), 'Making industrial policy', *Foreign Affairs*, Spring, pp. 852–81.

Reich, R. (1983), *The Next American Frontier* (New York: Times Books).

Reynolds, C. and Mamalakis, M. (1965), *Essays on the Chilean Economy* (Homewood, Ill.: Richard D. Irwin).

Riedel, J. (1984), 'Trade as the engine of growth in developing countries, revisited', *Economic Journal*, vol. 94, no. 373, pp. 56–73.

Scherer, F. (1965), 'Firm size, market structure, opportunity and the output of patented inventions', *American Economic Review*, vol. 55, no. 5, pp. 1097–125.

Schmitz, H. (1984), Industrialization strategies in less developed countries: some lessons of historical experience', *Journal of Development Studies*, vol. 21, no. 1, pp. 1–21.

Sciberras, E. and Payne, B. (1985), *Technical Change and International Competitiveness: The Machine Tool Industry* (London: Longman).

Servan-Schreiber, J.J. (1969), *The American Challenge* (Harmondsworth: Penguin).

Shepherd, G. (1981), *Textile-industry Adjustment in Developed Countries* (London: Trade Policy Research Centre).

Singh, A. (1977), 'UK industry and the world economy: a case of de-industrialisation?', *Cambridge Journal of Economics*, vol. 1, no. 2, pp. 113–36.

Soete, L. (1979), 'Firm size and inventive activity: the evidence reconsidered', *European Economic Review*, vol. 12, no. 4, pp. 319–40.

Solow, R. (1957), 'Technical change and the aggregate production function', *Review of Economics and Statistics*, vol. 39, no. 3, pp. 312–20.

Stewart, F. (1977), *Technology and Underdevelopment* (London: Macmillan).

Strange, S. (1982), 'Cave hic dragones: a critique of regime analysis', *International Organization*, vol. 36, no. 2, pp. 478–96.

Strange, S. (1985), 'Protectionism and world politics' *Industrial*

343

Organization, vol. 36, no. 2, pp. 233–59.

Stuckey, J. (1983), *Vertical Integration and Joint Ventures in the Aluminium Industry* (Cambridge, Mass.: Harvard University Press).

Sutcliffe, R. (1971), *Industry and Underdevelopment* (London: Addison-Wesley).

Taniura, T. (1981), *Comparative Advantage of Iron and Steel Industries in Asia* (Tokyo: Institute of Developing Economies).

Tilton, J. (1971), *International Diffusion of Technology: The Case of Semiconductors* (Washington, DC: Brookings Institution).

Toyne, B., Arpan, J., Ricks, D., Shimp, T. and Barnett, A. (1984), *The Global Textile Industry* (London: George Allen & Unwin).

Tuong, H. and Yeats, A. (1980), 'On factor proportions as a guide to the future composition of developing country exports', *Journal of Development Economics*, vol. 7, no. 4, pp. 521–39.

Turner, L. (1978), *Oil Companies in the International System* (London: George Allen & Unwin).

Turner, L. (1982a), 'Consumer electronics: the colour television industry', in L. Turner and N. McMullen (eds), op. cit., pp. 48–68.

Turner, L. (1982b), 'Petrochemicals' in L. Turner and N. McMullen (eds) op. cit., pp. 118–29.

Turner, L. and McMullen, N. (1982), *The Newly Industrializing Countries: Trade and Adjustment* (London: George Allen & Unwin).

Tyers, R. and Phillips, P. (1984), *Australia, ASEAN and Pacific Basin Merchandise Trade: Factor Composition and Performance in the 1970s*, ASEAN-Australia Economic Papers, no. 13 (Canberra: ASEAN-Australia Joint Research Project).

United Nations (1963a), *The Growth of World Industry, 1938–1961* (New York: United Nations).

United Nations (1963b), *A Study of Industrial Growth* (New York: United Nations).

United Nations (1970), *External Trade Statistics: Draft Classification by Broad Economic Categories*, E/CN.3/408 (New York: United Nations).

United Nations (annual), *Yearbook of Industrial Statistics, general industrial statistics*, Vol. 1 (New York: United Nations).

United Nations (annual), *Yearbook of Industrial Statistics, commodity production*, Vol. 2 (New York: United Nations).

United Nations (annual), *Yearbook of National Accounts Statistics*, (New York: United Nations).

United Nations (monthly), *Monthly Bulletin of Statistics* (New York: United Nations).

UNCTAD (1976), 'The dimensions of the required restructuring of world manufacturing output and trade in order to reach the Lima target' (Geneva: UNCTAD, TD/185/Suppl. 1).

UNCTAD (1979), *The Structure and Behaviour of Enterprises in the*

Chemical Industry and Their Effects on the Trade and Development of Developing Countries (Geneva: UNCTAD, ST/MD/23).

UNCTAD (1983), *Protectionism and Structural Adjustment: An overview* (Geneva: UNCTAD).

UNCTAD (1984), *Handbook of International Trade and Development Statistics, 1984 Supplement* (New York: United Nations).

UNCTC (1975), 'Transnational corporations and the processing of raw materials: impact on developing countries' (New York: United Nations, ID/B/209).

UNCTC (1981), *Transnational Corporations in the Bauxite/Aluminium Industry* (New York: United Nations).

UNIDO (1974), *Industrial Development Survey* (New York: United Nations).

UNIDO (1979a), *World Industry Since 1960: Progress and Prospects* (New York: United Nations).

UNIDO (1979)b, *Mineral Processing in Developing Countries* (New York: United Nations).

UNIDO (1980), *Picture for 1985 of the World Iron and Steel Industry* (Vienna: UNIDO, UNIDO/ICIS.161).

UNIDO (1981a), *World Industry in 1980* (New York: United Nations).

UNIDO (1981b), *Industrial Processing of Natural Resources* (New York: United Nations).

UNIDO (1981c), *Restructuring World Industry in a Period of Crisis – The Role of Innovation* (Vienna: UNIDO, UNIDO/IS. 285).

UNIDO (1981d), *Second World-Wide Study of the Petrochemical Industry: Process of Restructuring* (Vienna: UNIDO, UNIDO/IO/WG.336/3).

UNIDO (1982), *Changing Patterns of Trade in World Industry: An Empirical Study on Revealed Comparative Advantage* (New York: United Nations).

UNIDO (1983), *Industry in a Changing World* (New York: United Nations).

UNIDO (1985a), *A Statistical Review of the World Industrial Situation, 1984* (Vienna: UNIDO, UNIDO/IS.506).

UNIDO (1985b), *Industry in the 1980s: Structural Change and Interdependence* (New York: United Nations).

UNIDO (1985c), *Handbook of Industrial Statistics, 1984* (New York: United Nations).

UNIDO (1985d), *Industrial Statistics for Research Purposes* (Vienna: UNIDO, UNIDO/IS.558).

UNIDO (1986a), *World Industry: A Statistical Review, 1985* (Vienna: UNIDO, UNIDO/IS.590).

UNIDO (1986b), *Structural Change and Comparative Advantage* (Vienna: UNIDO, UNIDO/IS.625).

UNIDO (1986c), *International Comparative Advantage in Manufacturing* (Vienna: UNIDO).

US Department of Commerce (1981), *1977 Census of Manufactures, General Summary* (Washington, DC: Bureau of the Census).

Velasco, E., Almario, E., See, K., and Verdejo, P. (1981), *Comparative Advantage of Electronics and Wood-Processing Industries in the Philippines* (Tokyo: Institute of Developing Economies).

Vernon, R. (ed.) (1970), *The Technology Factor in International Trade* (New York: Columbia University Press).

Vernon, R. (1975), 'The power of multinational enterprises in developing countries', in C. Madden (ed.) *The Case for the Multinational Corporation* (New York: Praeger).

Vernon, R. (1977), *Storm Over the Multinationals: The Real Issues* (Cambridge, Mass.: Harvard University Press).

Vernon, R. (1979), 'The product cycle hypothesis in a new international environment', *Oxford Bulletin of Economics and Statistics*, vol. 41, no. 4, pp. 255–67.

Vernon, R. (1981), 'International economic relations in transition', *The World Economy*, vol. 4, no. 1, pp. 17–27.

Verreydt, E. and Waelbroeck, J. (1980), *European Community Protection Against Manufactured Imports from Developing Countries: A Case Study in the Political Economy of Protection*, Washington, DC, World Bank (Staff Working Paper no. 432).

Waeher, H. (1968), 'Wage rates, labor skills and United States foreign trade', in P. Kenen and R. Lawrence (eds) *The Open Economy* (New York: Columbia University Press), pp. 19–39.

Walter, I. and Jones, K. (1980), 'Industrial adjustment to competitive shocks: a tale of three industries', paper submitted to the International Symposium on Industrial Policies for the 1980s, Madrid 5–9 May.

Weeks, J. (1985), *The Economies of Central America* (New York: Holmes and Meier).

Wetter, T. (1985), 'Trade policy developments in the steel sector', *Journal of World Trade Law*, vol. 19, no. 5, pp. 485–96.

Wijnbergen, S. van (1984), 'The Dutch disease: a disease after all?', *Economic Journal*, vol. 94, no. 373, pp. 41–55.

Wilbur, C. (1973), *The Political Economy of Development and Underdevelopment* (New York: Random House).

Williams, M. (1984), 'The structure of production in the United States textile industry: the post-war period', *Weltwirtschaftliches Archiv*, vol. 120, no. 4, pp. 155–64.

Wilson,, R., Ashton, P. and Egan, P. (1980), *Innovation, Competition and Government Policy in the Semiconductor Industry* (Lexington, Mass.: Lexington Books).

World Bank (1985), *World Development Report*, 1985 (Washington, DC, Oxford University Press).

Yamazawa, I. (1980), 'Increasing imports and structural adjustment of the Japanese textile industry', *The Developing Economies*, vol. 18, no. 4, pp. 441–61.

Yeats, A. (1978), 'On the accuracy of partner country trade statistics', *Oxford Bulletin of Economics and Statistics*, vol. 40, no. 4, pp. 341–62.

Yeats, A. (1980), 'Tariff valuation, transport costs and the establishment of trade preferences among developing countries', *World Development*, vol. 8, no. 2, pp. 129–36.

Yeats, A. (1985), 'On the appropriate interpretation of the revealed comparative advantage index: implications of a methodology based on industry sector analysis', *Weltwirtschaftliches Archiv*, vol. 121, no. 1, pp. 61–73.

Journals and Newspapers

Far Eastern Economic Review (Hong Kong)
Financial Times (London)
Fortune (New York)
International Business Week (New York)
Iron and Steel Engineer (Pittsburgh)
Iron and Steel International (Guildford, Surrey)
The Economist (London)
Wall Street Journal (New York)

Author Index

348

Subject Index

Siemens 301
Sierra Leone 75
Singapore 2, 34, 75, 106, 135, 143,
    190, 194, 196, 198, 249, 251, 252,
    289
small-scale industry 310, 312–14
South Africa 232, 291, 322, 324
Southeast Asian Log Producers'
    Association (Sealpa) 242–3
South Korea 34, 55, 57, 74, 104, 106,
    122, 135, 138, 140, 143, 145, 148,
    149, 179, 190, 195, 196, 198, 221,
    228, 232, 235, 236, 240, 242, 249,
    252, 256, 261, 262, 280, 289, 291,
    324
Spain 122, 233
Sperry-Rand 273
Sri Lanka 75
Standard International Trade
    Classification (SITC) 186, 321–7
state ownership 2–3
    automobiles 224
    copper refining 171
    mining 171–3
    petrochemicals 226
    shipbuilding 227–8
    steel 217–18, 266
steel 25, 29, 91, 98, 102, 106, 116–18,
    158–9, 163, 165, 177, 215–22,
    230–6, 241, 264–7
    capacity reduction 218
    charcoal ironmaking 160–1
    demand 216
    dumping 230–1, 233, 235
    energy costs 160–1
    government subsidies 217–18, 235
    investment 29, 219
    material inputs 171, 216
    mini-mills 166, 218
    rolling mills 168
    special steels 96, 121–2, 265
    voluntary export restraints 230,
        236
    wage negotiations 220
structural change 12–16
    and causation 13–16
    and growth 77–9
    criticisms 68–9
    'typical' patterns 70–6
    universal determinants and group
        factors 64–8
    see also industrial structure
sub-contracting 84, 100–4, 226

supercomputers 281–3
    industry standards 268
    component supplies 286
Swaziland 313
Sweden 10, 50, 73, 116, 117, 118,
    134, 149, 197, 199, 266, 311
Switzerland 50
Syria 75, 76

Taiwan 106, 221, 228, 235, 240, 242,
    249, 251, 252, 256, 261, 289, 291
Taiwanese Fertilizer Company 173
Tanzania 313
tariffs on manufactures 47, 60, 66,
    209–10, 248
technological progress 113–14, 125–6
    and de-industrialization 81–2
    fast imitators 27–8
    internationalization of markets 5
Texas Instruments 260, 288
textiles 90, 98, 101–2, 121, 152–3
    spinning and weaving of fabrics
        101, 133–9
Thailand 75, 104, 190, 196, 198, 256,
    324
Thomson 239
Thorn 239
tin 143, 165–7, 169, 178
tobacco 90, 98
Tokyo Round 30
Toshiba 268
Toyota 226
trade restraints 118, 152–3, 202–8,
    229–43
    automobiles 141, 240–1
    consumer electronics 236–40
    semiconductors 255–6
    steel 230–6
    wood products 242–3
        see also tariffs, voluntary export
        restraints and orderly
        marketing agreements
transport 91, 98, 103
    see also automobiles
transport costs
    industrial processing 161–2
trigger price mechanism (TPM) 231,
    234
Trinidad and Tobago 75
Tunisia 75, 135, 143, 311, 313
Turkey 57, 135, 143, 197, 199, 313

Union of Soviet Socialist Republics 40